PRAISE FOR THE PRIVATE TUTOR SAT PREP COURSE SERIES:

Amy Lucas brings more than a decade of tutoring experience at the highest levels of the tutoring/test prep industry to this production. Starting with math vocabulary and then offering a discussion of the range of SAT problems from algebra to geometry to functions, this series offers the student the broadest coverage of the SAT math section. VERDICT: Highly recommended for students facing the SATs.

Library Journal, Math section review

In stark contrast to the "teacher in front of a chalk board"… the presentation is personal, conversational, relaxed, and effective.

Peggy Dominy, Liaison Librarian, Drexel University, Philadelphia, PA

I was really impressed! It gave me insight of an easier way to look at a problem… one of the best study skills books I've come across.

Amneris González, Instructional Support Svcs., Secondary Math, LAUSD

Library collections serving high school students as well as homeschoolers seeking instruction, practice, and basic standardized test-taking tips for the Math SAT will find this series an essential purchase.

School Library Journal, Starred review, Math section

Lucas divides the test into four categories—test numbers and operations, geometry and measurements, algebra and functions, and statistics and probability—and further breaks these categories into understandable chapters so that the complexity of both the subject and the test is reduced. Ten chapters provide step-by-step instructions and simplify concepts by utilizing illustrated sample problems as well as comprehensive drills at the end of each lecture.

Linda M. Teel, East Carolina University, Greenville, NC

I like the informal approach that the author uses to get on the student's level about the topics. Identifying each example and exercise with its relative difficulty also gives students a better sense ⟨ ⟩ ⟨expect on the exam... well done; the portions where Amy gives her e⟩ ⟨ ⟩s are well thought out and produced…

David Hammett, Math De⟩ ⟨ ⟩chool, Los Angeles

The three different techniques for reading based on ability is an amazing idea. I have never seen it addressed this way and it is so important. The sample readings were excellent... the one on video games was particularly good... the answer explanations are great and are key to a student's success. If they can understand their error it will help immensely.

Kevin Murchie, teacher, James A. Garfield Senior High School, Los Angeles, CA

The tutorial on the essay section covers the important points in a clear and concise manner… the technique she employs will produce results… it works.

Nick Garrison, private tutor, Greenwich, CT

This set of two DVDs and a workbook walks the viewer through the writing component of the SAT and offers advice on how to approach the test. Narrator and tutor Amy Lucas is attractive and vivacious… her delivery makes the videos easy to watch.

Rosemary Arneson, Univ. of Mary Washington Lib., Fredericksburg, VA

Lucas clearly states that she is coaching viewers on test-taking strategies, not teaching them general rules of grammar. Her examples are lucid and the suggestions consistent with those offered by other standardized test guides… VERDICT: Watching these DVDs and completing the workbook will not make the viewer a great writer, but the processes will help a student gain confidence in the writing skills required by the SAT.

Library Journal, Writing section review

…she has an expressive style that should hold the attention of students. All incorrect responses are explained clearly. There are easy-to-follow tips for writing the essay as well as sample essays that received high and low scores.

Ellen Frank, School Library Media Specialist, Jamaica High School, NY

Students looking for a comprehensive review of the Writing portion of the SAT will find this program very helpful, especially since they can select specific areas in which they need improvement.

School Library Journal, Writing section review

Your Complete SAT Critical Reading
Prep Course with Amy Lucas

©2012 Private Tutor

SAT® is a registered trademark of the College Entrance Examination Board. Neither The College Board nor The Educational Testing Service (ETS) was involved in the production and do not endorse this product.

For additional test prep coaching, contact Amy at www.testpreptutor4you.com.

Written by Amy Lucas
Layout and design by Kathy Cotter

All inquiries should be addressed to:
Private Tutor
15124 Ventura Blvd., Suite 206
Sherman Oaks, CA 91403
tel: 818.508.1296 • fax: 818.508.9076
info@PrivateTutorSAT.com

More SAT tutorial books and DVDs are available at www.PrivateTutorSAT.com.

PRINTED IN THE UNITED STATES OF AMERICA
9 8 7 6 5 4 3 2 1

Table of Contents

Introduction

Hi, I'm Amy Lucas and I'm going to be walking you through the SAT Critical Reading section, which is made up of multiple-choice questions that test your vocabulary and reading comprehension skills. I have included a vocabulary lesson, which features 6 lists, each with approximately 215 of the most popular SAT vocab words along with their definitions, an extensive reading comprehension section that covers three different techniques tailored to your specific reading needs, and 10 reading passages with which to practice and perfect your newly developed skills.

I'm going to be honest straight off the bat. The Critical Reading portion of the SAT can be the most difficult to improve. Students tend to show less point increase in their Critical Reading scores than they do on their Math and Writing scores. The good news? There are no formulas tested and no tricky math puzzles to solve or grammar rules to master. The maybe not-so-great news? The Reading section tests a muscle you have either been flexing with pride throughout your school career, or barely working out. It takes time to build muscle, but I can give you solid techniques to use and show you some tricks and shortcuts. With diligent practice and effort I am sure we can raise that Critical Reading score. If the Reading portion is your weakest link, work on your vocabulary and increase the number of Sentence Completions you answer correctly. Maximize your strengths!

So who are the Mensa geniuses behind the SAT? The SAT is owned by the College Board, but administered by the Educational Testing Service. I'm going to refer to the test makers as ETS. Many SAT experts will tell you that ETS is evil and out to get you. If that motivates you – use it! I personally think ETS could get a heck of a lot trickier. Either way, I'm here to help you master the game.

STRUCTURE

The Critical Reading portion of the SAT is made up of 67 multiple-choice questions divided into 19 Sentence Completion questions and 48 Reading Comprehension questions. The first Critical Reading section can fall anywhere between sections 2 and 7 of the SAT (it usually shows up in sections 2 through 4). You will be hit with two 25-minute sections and one 20-minute section.

EXPERIMENTAL SECTION

You might end up with with three 25-minute or two 20-minute Critical Reading sections on the SAT. If that is the case, one of the extra reading sections is the experimental section. Keep in mind that one of those sections is not going to affect your score. Leave it up to ETS to make you do an extra 20/25-minute Math, Writing, or Critical Reading section that doesn't count towards your score and makes the test a good 3 hours and 45 minutes long. ETS is using you as a guinea pig to test out future SAT questions. The experimental section does not affect your score in any way.

There is no way to know if you're on an experimental section. This means, treat every section as if it counts, and don't let any section rattle you. Think of it this way: If you bomb the first test of the semester, it doesn't mean you can't get great scores on the other tests and still get an A in the class.

CONTENT

Sentence Completions

Every Critical Reading section starts you off with 5, 6, or 8 Sentence Completion questions. It's your job to fill in the blank (or blanks) with the correct word (or words). Sentence Completion questions test your ability to understand the sentence and your knowledge of vocabulary. Below is a typical Sentence Completion question. Don't worry about working through the problem; you'll have a shot at that later. The examples are here in the Intro to familiarize you with the format.

6. The mass production of microprocessors -------
the burgeoning computer industry by making
home computers commercially ------- .

    (A) galvanized . . implausible
    (B) cheapened . . inexpensive
    (C) reformed . . excessive
    (D) altered . . unattainable
    (E) energized . . tenable

Reading Comprehension

The 48 Reading Comprehension questions will be divided between short and long reading passages. Some of these passages will be linked together as compare/contrast passages. Short passages are approximately 100 to 250 words in length and have anywhere from 2 to 4 questions, and long passages are approximately 400 to 850 words in length and contain 6 to 13 questions. Here's what a sample Reading Comprehension Short Passage with questions looks like:

Passage 1

Because the soul is progressive, it never quite repeats itself, but in every act attempts the production of a new and fairer whole. Thus in our fine arts, not imitation
Line but creation is the aim. In landscapes the painter should
5 give the suggestion of a fairer creation than we know. The details, the prose of nature he should omit and give us only the spirit and splendor. He will give the gloom of gloom and the sunshine of sunshine. In a portrait he must inscribe the character and not the features, and must
10 esteem the man who sits to him as himself only an imperfect picture or likeness of the aspiring original within.

(For source reference, see endnote ª)

9. The reference to "prose of nature" in line 6 serves to suggest that

(A) effective art is more of a realistic rendition than an imaginative interpretation
(B) art dictates to the artist the best means of its portrayal
(C) effective art requires identifying with the viewers' viewpoints
(D) artists need to create not pragmatically, but poetically
(E) nature is such that its spirit is more important than its composition

10. The last sentence of the passage suggests that the author feels a portrait should

(A) portray the subject as he is, rather than as he would like to be depicted
(B) reveal both the imperfections and virtues of its subject
(C) capture the essence of its subject at the expense of less than perfect details
(D) enhance its subject's merits and downplay its flaws
(E) represent the subject's character in the abstract, minimizing specific features

PROCESS OF ELIMINATION

Process of Elimination comes in handy on any standardized test. Often, the right answer choice is hidden among some very tempting wrong answers. The key is learning to spot and eliminate these wrong answers in order to increase your odds of choosing correctly. Every elimination increases your odds!

Guessing and Pacing

On multiple-choice questions you get 1/4 of a point off for each wrong answer. Do not be afraid to leave answers blank! You don't get penalized for blank answers, so take advantage! The reading tends to bog students down and, for some, the sections are difficult to complete in the allotted time. No sweat: YOU DO NOT HAVE TO ANSWER ALL THE QUESTIONS! Slow yourself down and get the questions you do answer right, rather than racing through a reading section and getting several wrong. For instance, to score a 600 on the Critical Reading portion you only need to do 22 out of 25 problems on the 25-minute sections, and 16 out of 19 problems on the 20-minute section. So, SLOW DOWN!

If you are on a Sentence Completion question, and you know NONE of the words in the answer choices, then leave it blank.

If you are on a Reading Comprehension question, and you can't even figure out what the question is asking, OR you reread the section of the passage the question is targeting and you have no idea what the author is saying, then walk away from the question.

Statistically, if you can eliminate one answer choice, it behooves you to take a guess. But if you've already reached your goal and answered your 22 questions, then I wouldn't even bother. If you can eliminate more than one, however, I would take the gamble and guess.

> **Vocab Alert:**
> *behooves*
> *means*
> *benefits*

ORDER OF DIFFICULTY

The Sentence Completion sections are arranged in order of difficulty. So if you are on a 5-question Sentence Completion section, problems 1 and 2 are easy, 3 and 4 are medium, and 5 is difficult.

On a 6-question section, 1 and 2 are easy, 3 and 4 are medium, and 5 and 6 are difficult.

On an 8-question section, 1-3 are easy, 4-6 are medium, and 7-8 are difficult.

FYI: The difficult Sentence Completion questions aren't difficult to comprehend, ETS just hits you with a lot of hard vocab words. If you know your vocab, you can get EVERY Sentence Completion question right.

The Reading Comprehension questions are NOT arranged in order of difficulty, so feel free to skip around and do the easy questions first.

HOW TO USE THIS BOOK

This is a technique-based book. I encourage you to work through the whole book and all the lessons. The only flexibility you have is with the three Reading Comprehension Techniques I teach. When you learn which of the three techniques works best for you, just concentrate on that one.

Don't be confused by the question numbers on the practice passages. I've designed the numbers to mimic those found on actual SAT sections, which will typically be numbered #7 - #13 for the long passages, and #6 - #9 for the short passages.

Since vocabulary is the key to a successful Critical Reading score, let's start with strengthening your mastery of words.

Chapter 1
Vocabulary

Life might be simpler if the English language didn't contain so many words, but it certainly wouldn't be as colorful. When you have a copious vocabulary, expression is easy and an improved Critical Reading score is even easier!

Favorite SAT vocab word!
Meaning:
plentiful

Vocabulary comes into play on both the Sentence Completion and the Reading Comprehension questions. While vocabulary is not to be studied at the expense of imperative practice and application of techniques, it is still an important component of SAT preparation. A solid vocabulary will help you move through the questions more quickly and with more surety, leaving you time to tackle more labyrinthine reading comprehension questions.

necessary

complex

Ideally, the average student should learn 800-1000 new words. Will the words you learn be on the SAT? You are bound to see some, and your score will be significantly boosted even if you only encounter a handful.

The vocabulary lists in this book contain the most frequently tested words on the SAT. ETS just doesn't get that creative and keeps its aggregation of words pretty contained. ETS will probably throw in a couple of weird, wacky words you have never heard of before, but you can count on ETS to use their favorites.

accumulation

Your Vocabulary Diet

- Start by memorizing the words in this book, including the roots, prefixes, and suffixes given.

- Every time you hear or read a word you do not know, look the definition up and add the word to your list.

- Organize your vocabulary into three categories:
  Rockin' - I am never going to forget these words.
  Rollin' - I know these words now but may forget them in a week.
  Sinkin' - I can't seem to memorize these words or I haven't learned them yet.

- Your goal is to get all the words into the *Rockin'* pile before test day!

6

Extra Tips

- Keep your words on a ring so you can take them with you and study during downtime.

- Carry a small dictionary with you at all times so you can easily find definitions. Better yet, download a dictionary app for your cell phone!

- Use the Internet as a resource. I can't live without Dictionary.com and Thesaurus.com.

- Check out *freerice.com* for extra vocabulary practice and donate rice through the United Nations World Food Programme with every correct answer!

Tackling Vocabulary on the SAT

- Slow down. Students often misread words, or they think they know the meaning of a word when they actually don't. Here are some common traps:

    Pristine – think it means *spotless*? It actually means *uncorrupted*, or *unchanged from the original*.

    What about *peruse*? Doesn't it mean to *quickly browse* something? No! It means to *read over something in detail*!

- Don't be too aggressive. While you want to eliminate answer choices, you don't want to get rid of words whose definitions are a bit unclear. Weigh it against the other answer choice words before crossing it off altogether.

- If ETS features an easy word in the answer choices, such as *fabric*, consider its secondary definition, which means *the framework/structure* (the fabric of life). Don't worry about the more difficult vocab words; ETS will stick with the primary definition; for example, *impoverish* will mean *to make poor*.

- If you come across a word whose meaning eludes you, think of where you've heard it before. Stick the word in a sentence or a familiar phrase to try to ascertain the meaning. For example, if you see the word *prodigal*, you might think *Prodigal Son*, and if you know the parable you can find your way to the definition (*wasteful*).

    figure out

- Be careful of words that have similar spellings; they are easily confused. For instance, *chafe* means *to rub against and make sore*. *Chaff* means *to tease lightheartedly*.

Methods of Memorization

Flashcards

This old school memorization technique is still my favorite. You can transfer the words in this book onto 3 x 5 flashcards, or you can purchase a vocabulary app for your smartphone on our website:

www.privatetutorsat.com

But remember, writing the word and definition helps you memorize!

> *Break your study sessions into 20-minute chunks*

Start with 5 words. Read through your stack of 5 several times, and then try repeating the definition of each word before flipping the card over to read the definition on the back. Once you've mastered those 5, put them aside and pick up 5 more. Repeat the process, and when you feel solid, put the two stacks together, mix up the words, and go through the stack of ten.

> *Keep it manageable and aim to learn 30 new words a day*

Review your words everyday and utilize your ***rockin', rollin',*** and ***sinkin'*** categories.

Flashcard game:
Remember that Memory Match game you played when you were a kid? Some students find it helpful to separate the words and definitions onto two different cards. Using about 40 words at a time, mix all the words and definitions up and then lay the cards face down in neat rows. Turn over two cards to see if you have a matching word and definition. If so, remove them from the pile, if not, flip them back over, and pick another two cards, all the while trying to match a word with its definition. Not only will you have to memorize the definitions, you'll also have to remember where they are hiding!

Mnemonic Devices

Imagination:
Add some imagination to the mix. Word association is one of the most effective memory aids. To help me remember the word *irascible* (crabby), I think of my friend Tasha in the morning when she doesn't have a cup of coffee.

Use a word or phrase to help you remember tricky words. For example, the way I remember the word *insular* (narrow-minded, isolated) is by remembering this sentence: *Insular people live insulated lives.*

Other mnemonic devices include rhyming lyrics and phrases. Get creative and make up a rhyming poem or song with several new vocabulary words!

Record Yourself

Record yourself saying the words with a pause before the definitions. Listen to the mp3 when you are working out, commuting, or falling to sleep at night. Osmosis works wonders!

Vocab Lists

The following vocab lists are designed to be studied over 6 weeks. I have separated almost 1300 words into lists made up of about 215 words per week. That's about 31 words a day! If you have more prep time, then trim the lists down and make the memorization easier for yourself.

I didn't include EVERY definition of each of the words. I only list the definitions ETS is most likely to test. For some of the words I list more than one definition, and others I keep simple with one definition. If the word is an easy word, I've only included the more unfamiliar definition(s).

I have also included a master alphabetical list of all the vocab words in this book for your reference. That way if you are adding words you encounter throughout your day to your vocab stacks, you can check to see if I have already included them in the lists.

I intentionally did not include the parts of speech for any of these words. It is just one more thing to memorize and it is not necessary to know a word's part of speech in order to memorize the gist of a word's meaning. I don't need to know that *abate* is a **verb** that means *to lessen*; I only need to know that it **means** *to lessen*. And if I were to see *abate* in another form, such as *abatement*, it isn't important that I know it's now being used as a **noun**; I only need to know that it has something to do with *lessening*. I am not saying that understanding parts of speech is not important; I am only saying that it is not imperative to implementing vocabulary effectively on the Critical Reading portions of the SAT. And when given the task of memorizing more than 1000 new words, it is best to simplify.

Also take time for the list of root words that follows the vocab lists. If you know your roots, you can effectively analyze an unknown vocab word and take a better educated guess. For instance, let's say you stumble over the word *loquacious*. If you know the meaning of the root *loq* (*speaks*) you will have a better idea of whether to pick or eliminate *loquacious* depending on the question. *Loquacious* means *talkative*!

Remember, vocab knowledge is powerful and impressive and will not only ensure success on the SAT, but will also carry you through to success in all aspects of your life.

Vocabulary List 1

Abase – to lower in rank or esteem; to degrade

Abash – to embarrass

Abate – to lessen, to decline

Acrid – bitter, sour

Acrimonious – spiteful, bitter, nasty

Acumen – mental sharpness, common sense, intuition

Agrarian – having to do with the land, farming

Alacrity – cheerfulness, promptness

Allege – to assert, to claim with no proof

Amorphous – lacking shape, formless

Anachronistic – no longer in use or out of place in time, incongruous

Analogy – a comparison, a similarity

Appreciate – to increase in worth

Apprehensive – anxious, afraid

Approbation – praise, admiration

Ascetic – self-denying, like a hermit

Assiduous – hard-working, active

Assimilate – to take in, to learn, or to adjust

Assuage – to relieve the pain, to calm

Astute – perceptive, brainy

Banal – dull, tasteless

Beget – to create, to reproduce

Benefactor – a supporter, a philanthropist

Bolster – to help, to support

Cacophony – a harsh unpleasant noise

Cadence – rhythm, pitch

Catholic – all-embracing, broad-minded

Censure – to criticize severely, to blame

Chagrin – displeasure, frustration

Chronic – never-ending, accustomed

Circumlocution – indirect speech, a euphemism

Coalesce – to blend, or to unite

Compelling – forcing to act

Compendium – a summary

Complacent – contented, confident, comfortable

Consummate – ultimate, perfect

Construe – to interpret, to define

Contrived – invented, labored

Convivial – cheerful, festive

Covet – to crave, to long for

Credible – believable

Cryptic – mysterious, incomprehensible

Daunt – to frighten, to bully

Debacle – catastrophe, devastation

Debase – to disgrace, to shame

Debauchery – excess, depravity, lewdness

Debilitate – to cripple, to weaken

Disaffected – alienated, discontented

Discern – to figure out, to foresee

Disparage – to criticize, to slander

Disparate – at odds, unlike

Dissipate – to disappear, to waste

Dormant – inactive, unconscious

Ebullient – enthusiastic, bouncy

Eccentric – unusual, odd

Eclectic – wide-ranging, diverse

Effrontery – boldness, arrogance

Effusion – an outpouring, wordiness

Egalitarian – equal, unbiased

Exacting – demanding, picky

Exalt – to promote, to praise

Exuberant – enthusiastic, lively

Exult – to jump for joy

Fabrication – a lie, something made up

Faction – a group who shares a belief, or a disagreement within a group

Fervor – passion, earnestness

Foment – to provoke, to arouse

Futile – hopeless, in vain

Gaffe – a goof, a blunder

Guile – cunning, trickery

Hackneyed – corny, played-out

Hedonism – indulgence in pleasure

Hyperbole – exaggeration

Icily – coldly, frigidly

Illusory – fake, deceptive

Imbibe – to drink heavily

Imbroglio – a misunderstanding, an argument

Imbrue – to soak

Immaculate – pure, spotless

Immaterial – insignificant, not essential

Imminent – happening soon, impending

Immutable – unchangeable, inflexible

Impalpable – intangible, imperceptible

Impartial – unbiased, fair

Impecunious – poor

Inchoate – beginning, preliminary

Incoherent – disconnected, confused

Incongruous – out of place, contradictory

Inhume – to bury

Insidious – dishonest, sneaky

Insinuate – to hint at, to imply

Interim – temporary, or a break

Interminable – endless

Intermittent – occasional, irregular

Influx – a flowing in

Inundate – to overwhelm, to flood

Invoke – to call on for assistance

Irascible – irritable

Jaded – done it all, wearied

Kinetic – energetic, animated

Labyrinth – a maze, a complication

Laconic – brief, to the point

Levity – silliness, frivolity

Linchpin – the anchor, the foundation

Lucid – obvious, clear

Machination – a ploy, a conspiracy

Maelstrom – chaos, confusion

Magnanimous – bighearted, giving

Medley – an assortment, a mixture

Melancholy – depressed

Mire – a swamp, or to slow down

Mirth – amusement, fun

Monolithic – huge

Monotonous – tedious, unchanging

Mundane – ordinary, dull

Myriad – multiple, infinite

Nadir – the lowest point

Nebulous – unclear, shapeless

Negligent – careless, sloppy

Novel – innovative, original

Nuance – a slight difference

Obdurate – stubborn, relentless

Obfuscate – to confuse, or to lose consciousness

Opulent – luxurious, wealthy

Ostracism – banishment, rejection

Palette – an oval board a painter mixes paints on, or a range of colors

Palliate – to relieve, to lessen

Pallid – pale, weak

Pander – to cater to, to serve

Panoramic – far-reaching, all-embracing

Paradigm – a prototype, ideal

Paradox – a contradiction, a puzzle

Paragon – a perfect example, the best

Partisan – someone who is devoted to a cause, biased

Pedantic – academic, formal

Penultimate – next to the last

Phlegmatic – unemotional, aloof

Pillage – to destroy, to ransack

Pinnacle – the top, the high point

Polarized – contradictory, opposed

Precipitous – abrupt, falling sharply

Preclude – to restrain, to make impossible

Precocious – advanced for one's age, mature

Procure – to obtain, to acquire

Profane – immoral, indecent

Profess – to confess, to declare

Prodigal – wasteful

Prodigious – huge, extraordinary

Prodigy – a child genius

Prowess – expertise, skill

Proximity – closeness

Pungency – bitterness

Punitive – punishing, vindictive

Purported – asserted, suggested

Quagmire – a dilemma, a difficulty

Quaint – old-fashioned, picturesque

Rail – to criticize severely, to rant

Rambunctious – energetic, loud

Ramification – a consequence, a branching out

Rapacious – predatory, savage

Recrimination – an accusation

Rectitude – honesty, integrity

Redolent – scented, or remindful of

Relinquish – to give up, to hand over

Remedial – healing, corrective, instructional

Remiss – thoughtless, neglectful

Repertory – a collection, a supply

Replenish – to replace, to renew

Reprimand – to blame, to lecture

Reprisal – retaliation, repayment

Resolute – determined, courageous

Resolve – a decision, an objective

Ruse – a trick, a ploy

Sacrilege – irreverence, sin

Sacrosanct – sacred, holy

Sagacious – smart, wise

Scintillate – to sparkle, to twinkle

Scourge – a plague, a curse

Scrupulous – careful, conscientious

Semaphore – to indicate, to give a sign to

Seminal – influential, important

Somber – serious, sad

Somnolent – sleepy

Spawn – offspring

Static – stationary or unchanging

Staunch – loyal, or to hold back

Steadfast – loyal, committed

Stoic – dispassionate, calm

Stringent – severe, inflexible

Sullen – sad, brooding

Superfluous – extra, not necessary

Supple – flexible, agile

Synthesis – a mixture, a combination

Tacit – unspoken, implied

Taciturn – silent, reserved

Tactile – tangible, concrete

Temerity – recklessness, boldness

Temper – to calm, to make reasonable

Temperate – moderate, calm

Toady – a flatterer, a kiss-butt

Tractable – obedient, polite

Transcend – to rise above, to go beyond

Transgress – to misbehave, to sin

Tribulation – misfortune, suffering

Turgid – bloated or pompous, pretentious

Turpitude – corruption, evil

Ubiquitous – everywhere, omnipresent

Unflagging – persistent, untiring

Vacuous – unintelligent, dim

Verbose – wordy

Vilify – to speak badly of, to criticize

Voracious – hungry, insatiable

Wallow – to luxuriate in, or to move about clumsily

Wistful – thoughtful, reflective

Yoke – repression, burden

Zealous – enthusiastic, passionate

Vocabulary List 2

Abdicate – to give up a right, position or power

Aberration – abnormal, different from the norm

Abhor – to hate

Acute – sharp, intense, clever

Adamant – determined, stubborn

Adhere – to stick to, to conform to the rules

Affectation – pretended behavior used to impress

Agenda – a list of things to do

Aggregate – a collection of separate parts

Altruism – unselfish concern, generosity

Amalgam – a mixture

Amoral – not concerned with moral standards

Amorous – loving, affectionate

Antiquated – outdated

Antithesis – the exact opposite

Archaic – old, ancient

Articulate – well-spoken

Artifice – deception, a hoax

Autonomous – independent

Avarice – greed

Bane – cause of unhappiness, a burden, curse

Beleaguer – to harass, to annoy

Belie – to disprove, to deceive

Bemused – confused, stunned

Blasphemy – heresy, cussing

Bucolic – rural, rustic

Callow – immature, untrained

Candor – honesty, justice

Caustic – burning, sarcastic

Cerebral – analytical, intelligent

Charlatan – a con artist

Chastise – to scold, to punish

Choleric – irritable, quick-tempered

Chronicle – a report, a narrative

Circuitous – circular, indirect

Circumscribe – to confine, to be on the edge

Clemency – forgiveness, compassion

Complement – a counterpart, the finishing touch

Consecrate – to honor as sacred

Contingent – likely to happen

Contrite – sorrowful, apologetic

Corroborate – to support, to substantiate

Credulous – naïve, over-trusting

Definitive – clear-cut, final

Defunct – extinct, not functioning

Degenerate – corrupt, decayed

Deleterious – harmful, destructive

Delineate – to describe, to sketch out

Delude – to fool, to trick

Deluge – a flood, or to overwhelm

Demagogue – a political rabble-rouser, a troublemaker

Demure – reserved, proper

Denizen – a resident, a native

Dictum – a saying, a proverb

Docile – easy-going, submissive

Egregious – extremely bad, intolerable

Elliptical – oval-shaped, curved

Eloquent – articulate, expressive

Elusive – difficult to grasp, mysterious

Embellish – to decorate, to enhance

Empathetic – understanding, compassionate, feeling

Enormity – atrocity, evil, or enormousness

Entreat – to plead with

Exacerbate – to make worse, to annoy

Extraneous – unnecessary, irrelevant

Extrapolate – to assume, to deduce

Farcical – slapstick, funny

Fatalist – one who believes everything is determined by fate and cannot be changed

Fecund – fertile, abundant

Felicity – bliss, joy

Flaunt – to show off

Fortuitous – lucky, unforeseen

Gauche – tacky, clumsy

Genre – a classification, a brand

Gravity – seriousness

Harbinger – an omen, a sign

Hegemony – authority, leadership

Hierarchy – chain of command

Homily – a sermon, a doctrine

Iconoclast – a non-conformist, a rebel

Idiosyncrasy – a quirk, an eccentricity

Illegible – unreadable

Impel – to provoke, to incite

Impertinence – bold disrespect

Imperturbable – calm, self-possessed

Impervious – unable to be penetrated, sealed

Impetuous – rash, impulsive, forceful

Implausible – not believable, doubtful

Implement – to make possible, to bring about

Impregnable – indestructible, unyielding

Improvident – reckless, uneconomical

Impugn – to criticize, to cast doubt on

Impunity – exemption from guilt

Impute – to attribute, to ascribe, to blame

Inadvertent – accidental

Inaugurate – to begin, to ordain

Incipient – initial, beginning

Incisive – intelligent, keen

Indomitable – unbeatable, ruthless

Infallible – error-free, unquestionable

Infamous – having a bad-reputation

Inscrutable – mysterious, unexplainable

Invigorate – to stimulate, to excite

Invincible – unconquerable, indestructible

Ire – wrath

Jocular – amusing, playful

Knave – a rascal, a scoundrel

Languish – to become dull, to suffer

Larceny – theft, burglary

Lethargy – laziness, disinterest

Limpid – obvious, clear

Lithe – flexible, graceful

Lugubrious – sad, gloomy

Malleable – flexible, easygoing

Mandate – an order, or an authorization

Manifest – clear; to exhibit, to reveal

Manifesto – a public announcement

Matriculate – to enroll, to enlist

Mediocre – average, humdrum

Metamorphosis – transformation, rebirth

Meticulous – detailed, thorough

Minuscule – teeny, undersized

Misanthropic – antisocial, solitary

Morass – a confusing situation

Mores – established customs

Nefarious – wicked, perverse

Neologism – a new word, slang

Nihilism – anarchy, rejection of established law

Noisome – offensive, harmful

Nonchalance – casualness, indifference

Nurture – to care for, or upbringing

Obscure – difficult to understand, lacking fame; to conceal

Obsolete – no longer used, dated

Onerous – difficult, grueling

Opaque – impossible to see through or understand, nontransparent

Orthodox – customary, traditional, accepted

Pacify – to calm, make peaceful

Painstaking – careful, thorough

Patriarch – male head, the chief

Paucity – scarcity, a lack

Peccadillo – a bad habit, an indiscretion

Pedagogical – instructional

Penurious – cheap, stingy

Perfunctory – careless, indifferent, superficial

Peripatetic – constantly wandering

Periphery – the outskirts, edge

Pert – lively, bold

Pertinent – relevant, on target

Pervade – to penetrate, to encumber

Pious – devout, religious

Pithy – to the point and meaningful in expression

Potable – safe to drink

Potentate – monarch, royalty

Precedent – an example, a model

Precept – a rule, a tenet

Precipice – a cliff, a sheer drop

Presumptuous – ready to presume, unreasonably bold

Pretense – pretended behavior, artifice

Pretentious – conceited, snobby

Pristine – clean, pure

Privation – poverty, hardship

Proletariat – working class

Promulgate – to announce, to declare; to teach

Propitious – favorable, beneficial

Proponent – an advocate, a supporter

Protract – to drag on, to delay

Prurient – vulgar, erotic

Punctilious – careful, meticulous, finicky

Qualify – to modify; to restrict, to limit

Recapitulate – to recap, to summarize

Raucous – noisy, jarring

Raze – to demolish, to flatten

Reciprocal – give-and-take, exchanged

Reciprocate – return the compliment or favor

Reclusive – antisocial, isolated

Recommence – to restart, to resume

Recondite – difficult, esoteric, obscure

Redouble – to double in size, to strengthen

Redoubtable – dreadful, terrible

Refract – to bend

Repose – rest, quietude

Rustic – country, rural

Sallow – pale

Salutary – healthful, nourishing

Scrutinize – to inspect, to analyze

Scurrilous – insulting, scandalous

Scuttle – to scurry, to scamper

Secular – non-religious, earthly

Sedentary – inactive, sitting

Segregate – to separate, to keep apart

Sentient – conscious, alert

Serpentine – winding, twisting

Sinister – menacing, threatening

Sinuous – curving gracefully, winding

Sporadic – infrequent, once in a while

Strife – trouble, conflict

Subdue – to hold back, to calm down

Surreptitious – secret, underhanded

Surrogate – substitute, replacement

Taut – stretched tight, stiff

Temporal – earthly, non-spiritual; pertaining to time

Temporize – to stall for time

Thwart – to prevent, to frustrate

Tranquil – calm, peaceful

Transient – temporary, fleeting

Unctuous – oily, greasy, or insincere

Undermine – to weaken, to thwart

Utopia – an ideal place, Eden

Venal – unethical, bribable

Venerate – to idolize, to adore

Veracity – truth, sincerity

Vigilant – watchful, alert

Wanton – unjustifiable, immoral, headstrong

Willful – stubborn, unruly

Vocabulary List 3

Abject – hopeless, wretched

Abnegate – to give up, to renounce

Abortive – unsuccessful, hopeless

Admonish – to warn, to criticize strongly

Adroit – skilled

Adulation – excessive praise

Affinity – an attraction to something

Affluent – wealthy

Alleviate – to relieve, to make bearable

Allocate – to allot, to distribute for a purpose

Alloy – a combination, usually of two metals

Ambiguous – having more than one meaning

Amenable – cooperative, ready to agree

Amiable – friendly

Apartheid – racial segregation

Apathetic – not interested, showing no emotion

Arable – suitable for farming

Arbiter – a mediator, a judge

Augment – to increase, to improve

Auspicious – favorable, encouraging, fortunate

Bastion – a fortress

Benevolent – charitable, kind

Benign – kind, favorable

Bequest - something given in a will, an amount of money

Bombastic – big-talking, pompous

Cantankerous – bad-tempered, difficult

Capitulate – to give in, to accept

Charisma – charm, ability to enchant

Civil – civilized, courteous, relating to citizens

Clandestine – secret, undercover

Coerce – to force, to intimidate

Cogent – compelling, convincing, relevant

Cognitive – pertaining to mental processes

Coherent – clear, understandable

Collusion – a secret agreement, usually in the service of a fraud

Commensurate – adequate, proportionate

Condescend – to patronize, to talk down to

Condone – to excuse, to overlook, to give tacit approval to

Contentious – argumentative, causing controversy

Convoluted – complex, confusing

Culpable – deserving blame

Curative – healing, curing

Deprecate – to cut down to size, to belittle

Deride – to make fun of, to scorn

Despondent – depressed

Despot – a dictator

Desultory – random, chaotic

Detriment – disadvantage, liability

Dilatory – procrastinating, lax

Dilettante – an amateur; a lover of art

Dirge – a sad song, a hymn

Disperse – to distribute, to scatter

Disseminate – to scatter, to distribute

Duplicity – deception, cunning

Empirical – practical, based on observation

Emulate – to copy, to compete with

Encroach – to butt in, to trespass

Endemic – local, native

Enervate – to wear out, to weaken

Enfranchise – to set free, to give the rights of citizenship to

Epigram – a witty saying, a joke

Equanimity – levelheadedness, calm and cool

Equitable – fair, unbiased

Exhort – to warn, to advise urgently

Exonerate – to free from blame

Exorbitant – extravagant, excessive

Facetious – joking, not serious

Facile – easy, effortless

Fidelity – devotion, faithfulness

Finesse – adeptness, know-how

Flag – to decline

Forbear – to avoid, or to withhold

Gesticulate – to gesture, to signal

Gourmand – someone who likes to eat and drink, gourmet

Grandiose – extravagant, flamboyant

Heterogeneity – variety, an assortment

Hiatus – a pause, a break

Husbandry – farming; management of resources

Ignominious – disgraceful, shameful

Illusive – deceptive

Immerse – to soak, to saturate

Immigrate – to move into a new country from a foreign land

Inane – absurd, silly

Inapt – inappropriate or unsuitable, awkward

Inarticulate – speechless, stammering

Inborn – natural, innate

Incandescent – glowing, shining

Incantation – a chant, a spell

Incapacitate – to weaken, to damage

Incendiary – dangerous, subversive, inflammatory

Incense – to make angry

Incessant – constant, unrelenting

Inclination – a tendency

Incontrovertible – indisputable, certain

Incorrigible – wicked, hopeless, unable to be reformed

Increment – advancement, an increase

Indict – to accuse, to charge

Indifferent – uninterested, not caring

Indigenous – native

Indigent – poor

Indignant – furious, angry

Inept – unskilled, incompetent, clumsy

Inert – lifeless, not moving

Irk – to rub the wrong way, to aggravate

Jubilant – full of joy

Knell – the sound of a bell, a mournful sound

Lampoon – parody

Legacy – inheritance, birthright

Legerdemain – trickery, sleight of hand

Libel – a malicious lie, defamation

Licentious – unprincipled, uncontrolled

Lurid – gruesome, disgusting

Malediction – a curse, a condemnation

Malign – to speak ill of, to attack

Martyr – someone who sacrifices, a sufferer

Mawkish – emotional, gushy

Maxim – a saying, a motto

Meager – small, inadequate

Mediate – to negotiate, to reconcile

Mélange – a mixture, a hodgepodge

Mellifluous – pleasing to the ear, harmonic

Milieu – atmosphere, setting

Mortify – to humiliate

Motley – varied, multi-colored

Nascent – beginning, growing

Nondescript – dull, undistinguished, run-of-the-mill

Notorious – well-known for something bad, disreputable

Obstreperous – noisy, rambunctious

Occlusion – a barricade, blockade

Odoriferous – aromatic

Ominous – doomed, dismal

Oscillate – to teeter-totter, to sway

Palpable – touchable, clear, obvious

Paltry – minor, worthless

Panacea – a cure, assistance

Pertinacious – determined, resolute, obstinate

Perturb – to disturb, to upset

Peruse – to examine in detail

Petulant – grouchy, irritable

Philanthropy – generosity, charity

Philistine – barbaric, improper

Pittance – a small amount, a trifle

Pivotal – important, vital

Placate – to soothe, to calm

Placebo – a pill or medicine whose benefit is imagined

Poignant – painful, heartbreaking

Posthumous – after-death, postmortem

Postulate – to speculate, to guess

Precursor – something that comes before another, a forerunner

Predilection – an inclination, a preference

Preeminent – the most important, supreme

Premise – hypothesis, thesis

Preponderance – dominance, majority

Proficient – skilled, accomplished

Profligate – corrupt

Proliferate – to increase rapidly, to multiply in number

Prolific – productive, highly fruitful

Protean – versatile, able to assume different forms

Provident – thrifty, showing forethought

Qualitative – pertaining to the quality of something versus the quantity

Quandary – a dilemma, a bind

Rapport – a bond, compatibility

Recalcitrant – disobedient, hard to manage

Recant – to take back something said, to renounce

Reconcile – to make peace

Refurbish – to spruce up, to rejuvenate

Refute – to discredit, to contradict

Reiterate – to repeat, to recheck

Relish – to enjoy immensely

Remonstrate – to challenge, to combat

Remuneration – payment

Renaissance – rebirth, renewal

Renovate – to fix up

Reparation – compensation, settlement

Repartee – banter, retort

Reprieve – a delay of punishment, temporary relief

Reproach – to criticize, to shame

Rousing – stimulating, exciting

Sanguine – confident, optimistic; reddish

Sardonic – sarcastic, mocking

Sensory – pertaining to the senses

Sensual – arousing, erotic

Servile – obedient, submissive

Sibilant – hissing, characterized by a hissing sound

Singular – remarkable, outstanding, unique

Slovenly – messy, careless

Sobriety – soberness, moderation

Sophomoric – immature, unsophisticated

Soporific – causing sleep, hypnotic

Sordid – dirty, distasteful

Sovereign – a ruler or independent

Stricture – a restriction, a criticism

Strident – loud, harsh

Succulent – juicy, moist

Succumb – to give in, to surrender

Surfeit – excess, a surplus

Surmise – to guess, to deduce

Teem – to be plentiful, full

Terse – abrupt, brief

Theology – the study of religion

Tome – a large book

Torrid – very hot or passionate, sexy

Trepidation – fear, anxiety

Truculent – hostile, defiant

Truncate – to shorten, to abbreviate

Uniform – consistent, identical

Unpalatable – distasteful, inedible

Variegated – multicolored

Verisimilitude – authenticity, genuineness

Vernacular – dialect, lingo

Vicarious – experienced as if one were taking part in the emotions or experience of another

Virulent – powerful, venomous

Voluminous – huge

Wary – cautious, distrustful

Wheedle – to persuade with flattery

Zenith – a high point, a peak

Vocabulary List 4

Abridge – to shorten

Absolute – unlimited, unrestricted

Absolve – to free from responsibility or blame

Adulterate – to alter, often for profit, or to contaminate

Adverse – unfavorable, opposing

Amenity – an advantage, comfort

Amnesty – a pardon from the government

Anarchy – lawlessness, disorder

Anecdote – an interesting or amusing story

Anguish – excruciating pain

Angularity – the quality of being angular

Animosity – unfriendliness, resentment

Aphorism – saying or proverb

Apocalypse – mass destruction, the end of the world

Apocryphal – questionable, fictitious

Apotheosis – glorification, the perfect example

Appease – to calm, to satisfy

Ardent – passionate, enthusiastic

Arduous – difficult, burdensome

Arid – dry

Belittle – to put down, to humiliate

Belligerent – argumentative, combative

Beset – to attack, to cause or become hurt

Blatant – obvious, showy

Blithe – cheerful, carefree

Burgeon – to blossom, to thrive

Callous – insensitive, unsympathetic, hardened

Catalyst – an agitator, a stimulus

Categorical – certain, clear-cut

Circumspect – cautious, alert, well-considered

Circumvent – to bypass, to avoid by deception, to mislead

Colloquial – informal, particular to an area

Complicity – conspiracy, partnership in wrongdoing

Comprehensive – inclusive, covering everything

Comprise – to consist of

Conciliatory – peaceable, apologetic

Concise – brief, to the point

Concord – harmony, agreement

Conducive – favorable to, useful

Conflagration – a large fire

Confluence – a coming together, a meeting

Congenial – friendly

Covenant – a pact, a promise

Culinary – appetizing, related to cooking

Debunk – to disprove, to ridicule

Decadent – corrupt, self-indulgent

Denounce – to attack, to blame

Depravity – corruption, evil

Destitute – bankrupt, lacking

Dexterous – skilled, masterly

Dialectical – logical, rational

Didactic – academic, instructive

Diffident – reluctant, bashful

Digress – to get sidetracked

Diligent – hard-working, careful

Doctrinaire – opinionated, dogmatic without regard for practicality

Egocentric – conceited, selfish

Egoism – self-centeredness, conceit

Equivocal – uncertain, vague

Eradicate – to destroy, to wipe out

Erratic – unpredictable, oddball

Espouse – to approve, to advocate

Ethereal – airy, celestial, heavenly, delicate

Euphemism – a nice way to say something

Evanescent – short-lived, fleeting

Expatriate – an exile, an outcast

Expedient – appropriate, advisable

Fastidious – very careful, particular, hard to please, critical

Fauna – the animal kingdom

Flagrant – flashy, noticeable, not modest

Flippant – sassy, disrespectful

Foible – a character flaw, a quirk

Frugal – thrifty, penny-pinching

Garrulous – talkative

Grandiloquent – pretentious, big talking

Heresy – opinion that goes against accepted (religious) doctrine, nonconformity

Histrionic – melodramatic, theatrical

Holistic – total, whole

Icon – an image, representation

Imperative – necessary, crucial

Imperious – bossy, commanding

Impious – irreverent, not religious

Indiscernible – hidden, vague

Indiscriminate – aimless, having no goal

Induct – to initiate into an organization

Indulgent – lenient, going along with

Inebriate – to intoxicate

Ineffable – beyond words, inexpressible

Inexorable – merciless, dead set on

Inexpedient – unadvisable

Inexplicable – unable to be explained

Infatuate – foolishly in love

Infer – to deduce, to assume

Infinitesimal – miniature, negligible

Inflammable – flammable, combustible

Infringe – to trespass, to interrupt

Infuse – to introduce, to impart

Ingenious – original, clever

Ingenuous – honest, innocent

Ingratiate – to flatter, to charm

Inherent – characteristic, hereditary

Invective – verbal abuse

Inveterate – habitual

Irate – angry

Judicious – wise, discerning

Kudos – praise, credit

Latent – concealed, undeveloped

Laud – to praise, to admire

Lenient – easygoing, tolerant

Libertarian – an advocate of liberty and free-will

Lilt – a song or a rhythm

Malignant – deadly, destructive

Malinger – to pretend illness to avoid work, etc

Mar – to disfigure, to damage

Marshal – to guide, to assemble

Mentor – counselor, a guide

Mercenary – a person who fights for money

Meritorious – honorable, deserving

Microcosm – a little world, a miniature example of a larger world/universe

Modicum – a small amount

Mollify – to soothe, to calm

Munificent – generous

Narcissism – egotism, self-love

Neophyte – a beginner

Novice – a beginner

Obstinate – stubborn

Obtuse – dumb, not sharp

Omnipotent – all-powerful

Omnipresent – everywhere, universal

Ossified – fossilized, hardened

Paramount – the main, dominant

Pariah – a social outcast

Parity – balance, equality

Penitent – regretful, shamed

Pensive – deep in thought, solemn

Perpetual – constant

Perpetuate – to maintain, to preserve

Placid – calm, peaceful

Plaintive – pathetic, sad

Plaudit – applause, acclaim

Plausible – believable, likely

Plenitude – plenty, an abundance

Ponderous – humongous, dull

Portent – an omen, a premonition

Pragmatic – sensible, logical

Precarious – dangerous, doubtful

Precipitate – to speed up, to bring about

Prepossess – to influence, to prejudice favorably

Prerogative – choice, right

Presage – a prediction, or to forecast

Propagate – to reproduce, to grow

Propensity – an inclination, a bias

Provincial – small-town, unsophisticated

Provisional – conditional or temporary

Puerile – childish

Pugnacious – aggressive, argumentative

Quell – to defeat or to calm

Querulous – complaining, grouchy

Rapture – ecstasy

Rash – daring, hasty

Recessive – passive, inactive

Redundant – repetitious

Regurgitate – to vomit

Relegate – to hand over, to entrust, to place in an inferior position

Relentless – unstoppable, determined

Renounce – to give something up, to deny

Replete – well-stocked, full

Reprehensible – deserving rebuke, shameful

Repudiate – to reject

Repugnant – disgusting

Ribald – vulgar, foul-mouthed

Rigorous – hard, strict

Rogue – a cheater, a con artist

Sate – to satisfy, to fill

Satiated – satisfied

Scarce – limited, insufficient

Scathing – scornful, wounding, searing

Sequester – to isolate, to close off

Serendipity – chance, destiny

Spate – a fast flow, rush, or outpouring

Speculative – theoretical, pertaining to speculation as opposed to fact

Spontaneity – impulsiveness, spur of the moment

Squalor – filth, poverty

Squander – to spend, to throw away

Stagnation – inactivity, sluggishness

Staid – serious, unadventurous

Stigmatize – to brand, to mark in disgrace

Subjugate – to conquer, to enslave

Subordinate – inferior, secondary

Substantiate – to validate, to prove

Tentative – hesitant, uncertain

Tenuous – weak, shaky

Terrestrial – earthly, mundane

Therapeutic – healing, beneficial

Torpid – lazy, slow

Torpor – lethargy, inactivity

Transmute – to change, to transform

Treacle – an antidote, a sweet liquid, sweetness

Tryst – a rendezvous, a meeting between lovers

Unalloyed – genuine, authentic

Unconscionable – immoral

Usurp – to seize, to take over

Vacillate – to waver, to think twice

Validate – to confirm, to certify

Vehement – passionate, violent

Verdant – green, fertile

Viable – possible, practical

Vicissitude – a change, a reversal

Vignette – a sketch, a scenario

Viscous – sticky, syrupy

Vituperative – insulting, malicious

Volatile – unstable, explosive

Watershed – a turning point

Wax – to become fuller, to swell

Whimsical – playful, quirky, given to sudden changes in behavior or preference

Zephyr – a gentle wind

Vocabulary List 5

Abstinent – self-denying, restraining behavior

Abstract – conceptual, theoretical, difficult to understand

Abstruse – hard to understand

Address – to speak to

Agnostic – a person who is uncertain if God exists

Aloof – reserved, withdrawn

Ambivalence – simultaneous conflicting feelings

Ameliorate – to improve

Anomaly – something that is not typical

Antecedent – something that went before

Antipathy – strong dislike

Appropriate – to set apart for some use, to steal

Aptitude – ability, inclination

Arbitrary – random, whimsical

Arboreal – pertaining to, resembling, or inhabiting trees

Arcane – mysterious, understood by few, secret

Ascend – to go up

Ascertain – to make certain

Avuncular – relating to an uncle

Awry – off course, crooked

Axiom – a self-evident truth

Beneficial – advantageous, for the best

Bereaved – deprived, saddened

Bourgeois – middle-class, commonplace

Brevity – shortness, to the point

Bureaucracy – administration, government

Cajole – to flatter, to influence

Capricious – fickle, flaky, whimsical

Catharsis – a release, a purging

Celibacy – chastity, purity

Chicanery – deception, trickery

Chimera – a dream, a fantasy

Clique – a group of friends, an association

Cognizant – aware, conscious

Connoisseur – an authority, a fan

Conspicuous – obvious, easily seen

Contiguous – neighboring, touching

Conventional – normal, unoriginal

Copious – abundant, plentiful

Cordial – friendly, sociable

Cosmopolitan – cultured, worldly

Countenance – appearance, expression

Cursory – hasty, sloppy

Cynic – a nonbeliever, a skeptic

Decimate – to destroy, to kill off

Decorous – appropriate, suitable

Deduce – to figure out, to assume

Derivative – a by-product, borrowed

Derogatory – offensive, critical

Desiccate – to dry up, to wither

Discreet – cautious, careful

Discrete – individual, unconnected

Discriminate – to differentiate, to identify

Dogmatic – opinionated, bullheaded

Dubious – doubtful

Elicit – to draw out, to bring about

Engender – to provoke, to produce

Enigma – a mystery

Epitome – the perfect example

Erudite – scholarly, well-educated

Esoteric – hard to understand, mysterious

Exasperate – to aggravate, to anger

Exhaustive – thorough, complete

Exigency – an emergency, a dilemma

Existential – relating to existence, based on experience

Fatuous – idiotic, absurd

Fetter – to tie-up, to restrict

Figurative – symbolic, metaphorical

Forego – to relinquish, to do without

Founder – to fail, to sink

Frank – honest, tell it like it is

Genteel – sophisticated, aristocratic

Gratuitous – free of charge, or unjustified

Hermetic – waterproof, completely sealed

Homogeneous – the same

Hubris – excessive pride

Impassive – emotionless, cool

Impeccable – flawless, perfect

Impotent – powerless

Impoverish – to make poor

Imprudent – careless, reckless

Impudence – arrogance, boldness

Inimical – hostile, harmful

Iniquity – an injustice

Innovative – creative, original

Innuendo – suggestion, insinuation (often disparaging)

Inordinate – excessive, unreasonable

Inquisitive – curious

Insatiable – unable to be satisfied

Insentient – lifeless, or inanimate

Insolence – disrespectful, impolite

Instigate – to provoke

Insular – narrow-minded, bigoted, isolated

Intangible – unable to be touched

Integral – essential, necessary

Intelligible – comprehensible

Intemperance – drunkenness

Intercede – to mediate, to intervene

Iridescent – rainbow-colored

Irrevocable – unchangeable, unable to be revoked

Itinerant – roaming, nomadic

Juxtapose – to set side-by-side, to compare

Lament – to mourn, to cry

Lavish – splendid, abundant

Lionize – to celebrate a person, to lavish attention

Litigate – to press charges, to bring into court

Loathe – to hate

Malevolent – wicked, sinister

Malfeasance – misbehavior, dishonesty

Manifold – abundant, diverse

Martial – aggressive, combative, warlike

Miser – a Scrooge, cheapskate

Missive – written communication

Mitigate – to soothe, to help

Moderate – middle-of-the-road

Modulate – harmonize, balance

Mutable – changeable, fickle

Myopia – narrow-mindedness, short-sightedness

Negate – nullify, deny

Nocturnal – active during the night

Noxious – harmful, foul

Oblivion – unconsciousness, nothingness

Obsequious – fawning, flattering

Oration – a speech, a sermon

Ornate – glitzy, elaborately adorned

Patent – crystal clear, or a copyright on an invention

Paternal – fatherly, protective

Patrician – upper-class, royal

Patronage – advocacy, assistance

Patronize – to treat like a child, to condescend, or to support a cause

Peremptory – overbearing, dictatorial

Perennial – enduring, continual

Perfidy – betrayal, corruption

Permeate – to spread throughout, to infuse

Pernicious – damaging, dangerous

Plethora – excess, a surplus

Pliable – flexible, adaptable

Prescience – prediction, foresight

Prescribe – to command, to guide

Prevail – to succeed

Prevaricate – to exaggerate, to misrepresent

Primeval – ancient, primitive

Probity – equality, honesty

Proclivity – an inclination, a tendency

Profound – thoughtful, enlightened

Profundity – wisdom, experience

Profuse – excessive, plentiful

Putative – commonly believed, hypothetical

Putrid – contaminated, stinking

Quiescent – at rest, inactive

Rebuke – to blame, to reprimand

Rebut – to argue against

Repulse – a rejection

Requisition – a demand, an appeal

Requite – to repay, or to take vengeance

Rescind – to back out of, to cancel

Reservoir – storage, a repository

Resilient – quick to recover

Resplendent – gorgeous, shining

Restitution – compensation

Reticent – shy, hesitant, silent

Retraction – a withdrawal of a previous statement, a disavowal of an opinion

Retroactive – effective or operative from a date, or for a period, in the past

Revel – a celebration, or to cut loose and celebrate

Rife – overflowing, plentiful

Robust – healthy, strong

Ruminate – to brainstorm, to contemplate

Salient – significant, noticeable

Sanctimonious – self-righteous, smug

Savant – an intellectual, a wise person

Serene – calm, peaceful

Sloth – laziness, inactivity

Solace – comfort, relief

Solvent – financially stable

Specious – false, inaccurate

Spurious – fake, counterfeit

Stipulate – to specify, to instruct

Stolid – unresponsive, emotionless

Stupefy – to amaze, to surprise

Stymie – to confuse

Sublime – inspirational, magnificent

Submissive – obedient, meek

Tangential – unrelated, beside the point

Tautological – repetitious, redundant

Tedious – dull, boring

Tempest – a thunderstorm, a hurricane

Tenet – a belief

Tirade – an outburst, a rant

Touchstone – criterion, a standard

Tout – to publicize, to flaunt

Travesty – a charade, a sham

Tremulous – trembling, timid

Trenchant – severe, biting

Unremitting – constant

Unscrupulous – unprincipled, lacking moral standards

Unwitting – unsuspecting, ignorant

Urbane – sophisticated, refined

Verbatim – word-for-word, exact

Vestige – a trace, a sign

Vex – to annoy, to trouble

Vigor – energy, vitality

Vindicate – to free from blame, to prove right

Vindictive – mean, unforgiving

Virtue – a good quality, an asset

Virtuoso – a genius, a prodigy

Visionary – a prophet, a creative thinker

Vitiate – to abolish, to undermine

Vitriolic – spiteful, hurtful

Vocation – a career

Volition – freewill

Warrant – to call for, to necessitate

Wily – scheming, sly

Winnow – to separate, to select

Vocabulary List 6

Abysmal – immeasurable, bottomless, profound, extremely hopeless

Accolade – strong praise, approval

Accost – to approach someone aggressively, to annoy

Acerbic – bitter, sharp, sour

Acquiesce – to agree with reluctance, to accept

Aesthetic – pertaining to beauty

Affable – friendly

Allusion – An indirect reference, a hint

Ambience – environment, atmosphere

Archetype – original example, model

Aristocracy – the privileged class, the nobility

Artful – cunning, shrewd

Atheist – someone who doesn't believe in the existence of God

Attrition – regret, gradually wearing down

Audacity – boldness, daring

Austere – stern, severe in manner

Autocratic – complete authority

Aversion – dislike, disgust

Avow – to declare, to admit truth

Belabor – to dwell on

Blight – a disease

Bovine – a cow, or cow-like

Broach – to propose, to bring up a topic

Burlesque – comic, or a bawdy show

Capitalism – economic structure of private ownership

Caricature – cartoonish representation of something

Castigate – to scold, to criticize

Chasm – a gap, a fissure

Cliché – an overused phrase

Concur – to agree, to acquiesce

Concurrent – simultaneous, uniting

Congenital – natural, innate

Congregate – to come together, to assemble

Conjecture – a guess, an assumption

Conjure – to cast a spell, to implore, to appeal to

Consensus – an agreement

Consonant – agreeing, appropriate

Corollary – an expected consequence, a deduction

Coup – an achievement, the overthrow of a government

Covert – secret, undercover

Criterion – a point of comparison, a benchmark

Culminate – to come to a head, to climax

Curtail – to cut short, to trim

Dearth – absence, scarcity

Defame – to bad-mouth, to slander

Deference – obedience, consideration

Disclose – to reveal, to confess

Disdain – dislike, scorn

Disinterested – not caring, uninvolved

Dissolution – separation, undoing, breaking into parts

Distend – to swell, to distort, to stretch

Distinguish – to tell the difference

Divulge – to admit, to blab

Domestic – having to do with the home and family

Edify – to educate, enlighten

Efface – to erase, to cancel

Emigrate – to move from a country

Eminent – important, famous

Expedite – to make something happen faster, to accelerate

Explicit – direct, clear, precise

Extol – to brag about

Extricate – to bail out, to free

Extrovert – an outgoing, sociable person

Fallacy – an error, a misconception

Flout – to insult, to disregard

Forsake – to abandon

Fraternal – brotherly, affiliated

Frenetic – frantic, manic

Furtive – sneaky, stealthy

Glut – a surplus

Gregarious – sociable, friendly

Hapless – unlucky, cursed

Heyday – high point, the pinnacle

Hypothetical – concocted, assumed

Idyllic – perfect, picturesque, pleasant

Illicit – illegal

Impede – to block, to obstruct

Imperial – majestic, regal

Imperil – to endanger, to jeopardize

Implicit – implied, hinted at

Impolitic – unwise, rash

Importune – to demand, to pester

Inconsequential – insignificant, insufficient

Indelible – unable to be erased, permanent

Indolent – lazy, inactive

Injunction – a court order

Innocuous – harmless

Insipid – tasteless

Insuperable – invincible, overwhelming

Insurgence – an uprising

Intractable – stubborn, unyielding

Intransigent – uncompromising, inflexible

Intrepid – fearless, bold

Intrinsic – basic, inborn

Introspective – thoughtful, contemplative

Inure – to make ready, to toughen, to familiarize

Invariable – unchangeable

Invidious – envious

Ironic – the opposite of one's intended meaning, sarcastic

Laceration – a cut, an injury

Largess – generosity, charity

Listless – without energy, drowsy

Loquacious – talkative

Luminous – bright, glowing

Magnate – a successful businessperson

Malaise – anxiety, sickness

Maudlin – overemotional

Maverick – a rebel, a free spirit

Mendacious – dishonest, untrue

Mendicant – a beggar

Mercurial – fluctuating, inconstant, flighty, lively

Moribund – dying

Morose – gloomy, negative

Multifarious – various, complicated

Multiplicity – an abundance, a collection

Naïveté – inexperience, gullibility

Nomadic – roaming, migratory

Nominal – theoretical, in name only, so-called

Oblique – slanting or indirect

Odious – hateful, awful

Officious – authoritative, self-important, meddlesome

Ostensible – alleged, purported, apparent

Ostentatious – showy, flamboyant

Parochial – narrow-minded, conservative

Parody – a satire, a spoof

Parsimonious – stingy, greedy

Pathology – the study of disease

Pathos – deep sadness, emotion

Pedestrian – dull, boring

Pejorative – negative, uncomplimentary

Pellucid – clear, simple

Penchant – an inclination, an affection

Perjury – lying under oath, dishonesty

Perplex – to confuse, to bewilder

Perquisite – a perk, a bonus

Perspicacious – aware, perceptive

Plasticity – flexibility, resilience

Platitude – an overused saying, a cliché

Plebeian – working class

Pluralistic – having multiple characteristics or parts

Polemic – argumentative

Pomposity – conceit, arrogance

Preempt – to take over, to usurp

Premeditated – planned, calculated

Proprietary – having exclusive ownership

Propriety – proper behavior, appropriateness

Prosaic – unimaginative, boring

Proscribe – to exclude, to forbid

Proselytize – to convert, to promote beliefs

Prospectus – the plan, a syllabus

Protagonist – the central character

Prudent – careful

Pundit – an expert

Quixotic – romantic, dreamy

Quotidian – ordinary, everyday

Rancid – rotten, foul

Rancor – bitterness, hostility

Repentant – sorry, apologetic

Repercussion – a consequence, a side effect

Reprobate – corrupt, a wicked person, or to disapprove

Reprove – to scold

Reputable – popular, respectable

Respite – a break, an intermission

Restive – restless, stubborn

Revere – to admire

Revoke – to take back, to cancel

Rhapsodize – to babble, to talk wildly

Rhetoric – a long speech or a style of speech

Risqué – improper, indecent

Rudimentary – basic, simplest

Ruffian – a criminal, a thug

Saccharine – sugary, sweet

Salve – to soothe, to comfort

Salvo – a barrage, bombardment, salute or applause

Sedition – troublemaking, treason

Sedulous – hard-working, determined

Slander – to insult

Solicitous – considerate or concerned

Soluble – dissolvable

Spurned – rejected, snubbed

Stark – bleak, bare

Stratum – a layer, a section

Strenuous – tiring, hard

Subversive – rebellious

Succinct – to the point, brief

Sumptuous – luxurious, extravagant

Supercilious – arrogant, snooty

Superficial – on the surface, exterior

Swarthy – dark-complexioned, tan

Sycophant – a flatterer, a brown-noser

Tangible – touchable, concrete

Tantamount – equal, the same as

Tenable – reasonable or safe

Tenacious – stubborn, persistent

Timorous – timid, nervous

Topography – scenery, geography

Tortuous – winding, convoluted

Trite – unoriginal, clichéd

Trivial – unimportant

Trove – an accumulation, a hoarding

Tumultuous – noisy, disorderly

Umbrage – offence, displeasure; shade

Uncanny – weird, strange

Undulate – to rise and fall, to move in a wavelike motion

Unstinting – generous, helpful

Utilitarian – useful, practical

Valor – courage, bravery

Vapid – lifeless, uninspiring

Veneer – a pretense, a superficial layer

Vivacious – lively, cheerful

Vociferous – loud and enthusiastic

Vulnerable – helpless, or open to

Wane – to decrease, to fade

Winsome – charming, attractive

Wizened – wrinkled, aged

Wrath – anger, fury

Alphabetical Vocabulary List

Abase – to lower in rank or esteem; to degrade

Abash – to embarrass

Abate – to lessen, to decline

Abdicate – to give up a right, position or power

Aberration – abnormal, different from the norm

Abhor – to hate

Abject – hopeless, wretched

Abnegate – to give up, to renounce

Abortive – unsuccessful, hopeless

Abridge – to shorten

Absolute – unlimited, unrestricted

Absolve – to free from responsibility or blame

Abstinent – self-denying, restraining behavior

Abstract – conceptual, theoretical, difficult to understand

Abstruse – hard to understand

Abysmal – immeasurable, bottomless, profound, extremely hopeless

Accolade – strong praise, approval

Accost – to approach someone aggressively, to annoy

Acerbic – bitter, sharp, sour

Acquiesce – to agree with reluctance, to accept

Acrid – bitter, sour

Acrimonious – spiteful, bitter, nasty

Acumen – mental sharpness, common sense, intuition

Acute – sharp, intense, clever

Adamant – determined, stubborn

Address – to speak to

Adhere – to stick to, to conform to the rules

Admonish – to warn, to criticize strongly

Adroit – skilled

Adulation – excessive praise

Adulterate – to alter, often for profit, or to contaminate

Adverse – unfavorable, opposing

Aesthetic – pertaining to beauty

Affable – friendly

Affectation – pretended behavior used to impress

Affinity – an attraction to something

Affluent – wealthy

Agenda – a list of things to do

Aggregate – a collection of separate parts

Agnostic – a person who is uncertain if God exists

Agrarian – having to do with the land, farming

Alacrity – cheerfulness, promptness

Allege – to assert, to claim with no proof

Alleviate – to relieve, to make bearable

Allocate – to allot, to distribute for a purpose

Alloy – a combination, usually of two metals

Allusion – An indirect reference, a hint

Aloof – reserved, withdrawn

Altruism – unselfish concern, generosity

Amalgam – a mixture

Ambience – environment, atmosphere

Ambiguous – having more than one meaning

Ambivalence – simultaneous conflicting feelings

Ameliorate – to improve

Amenable – cooperative, ready to agree

Amenity – an advantage, comfort

Amiable – friendly

Amnesty – a pardon from the government

Amoral – not concerned with moral standards

Amorous – loving, affectionate

Amorphous – lacking shape, formless

Anachronistic – no longer in use or out of place in time, incongruous

Analogy – a comparison, a similarity

Anarchy – lawlessness, disorder

Anecdote – an interesting or amusing story

Anguish – excruciating pain

Angularity – the quality of being angular

Animosity – unfriendliness, resentment

Anomaly – something that is not typical

Antecedent – something that went before

Antipathy – strong dislike

Antiquated – outdated

Antithesis – the exact opposite

Apartheid – racial segregation

Apathetic – not interested, showing no emotion

Aphorism – saying or proverb

Apocalypse – mass destruction, the end of the world

Apocryphal – questionable, fictitious

Apotheosis – glorification, the perfect example

Appease – to calm, to satisfy

Appreciate – to increase in worth

Apprehensive – anxious, afraid

Approbation – praise, admiration

Appropriate – to set apart for some use, to steal

Aptitude – ability, inclination

Arable – suitable for farming

Arbiter – a mediator, a judge

Arbitrary – random, whimsical

Arboreal – pertaining to, resembling, or inhabiting trees

Arcane – mysterious, understood by few, secret

Archaic – old, ancient

Archetype – original example, model

Ardent – passionate, enthusiastic

Arduous – difficult, burdensome

Arid – dry

Aristocracy – the privileged class, the nobility

Artful – cunning, shrewd

Articulate – well-spoken

Artifice – deception, a hoax

Ascend – to go up

Ascertain – to make certain

Ascetic – self-denying, like a hermit

Assiduous – hard-working, active

Assimilate – to take in, to learn, or to adjust

Assuage – to relieve the pain, to calm

Astute – perceptive, brainy

Atheist – someone who doesn't believe in the existence of God

Attrition – regret, gradually wearing down

Audacity – boldness, daring

Augment – to increase, to improve

Auspicious – favorable, encouraging, fortunate

Austere – stern, severe in manner

Autocratic – complete authority

Autonomous – independent

Avarice - greed

Aversion – dislike, disgust

Avow – to declare, to admit truth

Avuncular – relating to an uncle

Awry – off course, crooked

Axiom – a self-evident truth

Banal – dull, tasteless

Bane – cause of unhappiness, a burden, curse

Bastion – a fortress

Beget – to create, to reproduce

Belabor – to dwell on

Beleaguer – to harass, to annoy

Belie – to disprove, to deceive

Belittle – to put down, to humiliate

Belligerent – argumentative, combative

Bemused – confused, stunned

Benefactor – a supporter, a philanthropist

Beneficial – advantageous, for the best

Benevolent – charitable, kind

Benign – kind, favorable

Bequest – something given in a will, an amount of money

Bereaved – deprived, saddened

Beset – to attack, to cause or become hurt

Blasphemy – heresy, cussing

Blatant – obvious, showy

Blight – a disease

Blithe – cheerful, carefree

Bolster – to help, to support

Bombastic – big-talking, pompous

Bourgeois – middle-class, commonplace

Bovine – a cow, or cow-like

Brevity – shortness, to the point

Broach – to propose, to bring up a topic

Bucolic – rural, rustic

Bureaucracy – administration, government

Burgeon – to blossom, to thrive

Burlesque – comic, or a bawdy show

Cacophony – a harsh, unpleasant noise

Cadence – rhythm, pitch

Cajole – to flatter, to influence

Callous – insensitive, unsympathetic, hardened

Callow – immature, untrained

Candor – honesty, justice

Cantankerous – bad-tempered, difficult

Capitalism – economic structure of private ownership

Capitulate – to give in, to accept

Capricious – fickle, flaky, whimsical

Caricature – cartoonish representation of something

Castigate – to scold, to criticize

Catalyst – an agitator, a stimulus

Categorical – certain, clear-cut

Catharsis – a release, a purging

Catholic – all-embracing, broad-minded

Caustic – burning, sarcastic

Celibacy – chastity, purity

Censure – to criticize severely, to blame

Cerebral – analytical, intelligent

Chagrin – displeasure, frustration

Charisma – charm, ability to enchant

Charlatan – a con artist

Chasm – a gap, a fissure

Chastise – to scold, to punish

Chicanery – deception, trickery

Chimera – a dream, a fantasy

Choleric – irritable, quick-tempered

Chronic – never-ending, accustomed

Chronicle – a report, a narrative

Circuitous – circular, indirect

Circumlocution – indirect speech, a euphemism

Circumscribe – to confine, to be on the edge

Circumspect – cautious, alert, well-considered

Circumvent – to bypass, avoid by deception, mislead

Civil – civilized, courteous, relating to citizens

Clandestine – secret, undercover

Clemency – forgiveness, compassion

Cliché – an overused phrase

Clique – a group of friends, an association

Coalesce – to blend, or to unite

Coerce – to force, to intimidate

Cogent – compelling, convincing, relevant

Cognitive – pertaining to mental processes

Cognizant – aware, conscious

Coherent – clear, understandable

Colloquial – informal, particular to an area

Collusion – a secret agreement, usually in the service of a fraud

Commensurate – adequate, proportionate

Compelling – forcing to act

Compendium – a summary

Complacent – contented, confident, comfortable

Complement – a counterpart, the finishing touch

Complicity – conspiracy, partnership in wrongdoing

Comprehensive – inclusive, covering everything

Comprise – to consist of

Conciliatory – peaceable, apologetic

Concise – brief, to the point

Concord – harmony, agreement

Concur – to agree, to acquiesce

Concurrent – simultaneous, uniting

Condescend – to patronize, to talk down to

Condone – to excuse, to overlook, to give tacit approval to

Conducive – favorable to, useful

Conflagration – a large fire

Confluence – a coming together, a meeting

Congenial – friendly

Congenital – natural, innate

Congregate – to come together, to assemble

Conjecture – a guess, an assumption

Conjure – to cast a spell, to implore, to appeal to

Connoisseur – an authority, a fan

Consecrate – to honor as sacred

Consensus – an agreement

Consonant – agreeing, appropriate

Conspicuous – obvious, easily seen

Construe – to interpret, to define

Consummate – ultimate, perfect

Contentious – argumentative, causing controversy

Contiguous – neighboring, touching

Contingent – likely to happen

Contrite – sorrowful, apologetic

Contrived – invented, labored

Conventional – normal, unoriginal

Convivial – cheerful, festive

Convoluted – complex, confusing

Copious – abundant, plentiful

Cordial – friendly, sociable

Corollary – an expected consequence, a deduction

Corroborate – to support, to substantiate

Cosmopolitan – cultured, worldly

Countenance – appearance, expression

Coup – an achievement, the overthrow of a government

Covenant – a pact, a promise

Covert – secret, undercover

Covet – to crave, to long for

Credible – believable

Credulous – naïve, over-trusting

Criterion – a point of comparison, a benchmark

Cryptic – mysterious, incomprehensible

Culinary – appetizing, related to cooking

Culminate – to come to a head, to climax

Culpable – deserving blame

Curative – healing, curing

Cursory – hasty, sloppy

Curtail – to cut short, to trim

Cynic – a nonbeliever, a skeptic

Daunt – to frighten, to bully

Dearth – absence, scarcity

Debacle – catastrophe, devastation

Debase – to disgrace, to shame
Debauchery – excess, depravity, lewdness
Debilitate – to cripple, to weaken
Debunk – to disprove, to ridicule
Decadent – corrupt, self-indulgent
Decimate – to destroy, to kill off
Decorous – appropriate, suitable
Deduce – to figure out, to assume
Defame – to bad-mouth, to slander
Deference – obedience, consideration
Definitive – clear-cut, final
Defunct – extinct, not functioning
Degenerate – corrupt, decayed
Deleterious – harmful, destructive
Delineate – to describe, to sketch out
Delude – to fool, to trick
Deluge – a flood, or to overwhelm
Demagogue – a political rabble-rouser, a
    troublemaker
Demure – reserved, proper
Denizen – a resident, a native
Denounce – to attack, to blame
Depravity – corruption, evil
Deprecate – to cut down to size, to belittle
Deride – to make fun of, to scorn
Derivative – a by-product, borrowed
Derogatory – offensive, critical
Desiccate – to dry up, to wither
Despondent – depressed
Despot – a dictator
Destitute – bankrupt, lacking
Desultory – random, chaotic
Detriment – disadvantage, liability
Dexterous – skilled, masterly
Dialectical – logical, rational
Dictum – a saying, a proverb
Didactic – academic, instructive
Diffident – reluctant, bashful
Digress – to get sidetracked
Dilatory – procrastinating, lax
Dilettante – an amateur; a lover of art
Diligent – hard-working, careful
Dirge – a sad song, a hymn
Disaffected – alienated, discontented
Discern – to figure out, to foresee
Disclose – to reveal, to confess

Discreet – cautious, careful
Discrete – individual, unconnected
Discriminate – to differentiate, to identify
Disdain – dislike, scorn
Disinterested – not caring, uninvolved
Disparage – to criticize, to slander
Disparate – at odds, unlike
Disperse – to distribute, to scatter
Disseminate – to scatter, to distribute
Dissipate – to disappear, to waste
Dissolution – separation, undoing, breaking into
    parts
Distend – to swell, to distort, to stretch
Distinguish – to tell the difference
Divulge – to admit, to blab
Docile – easy-going, submissive
Doctrinaire – opinionated, dogmatic without
    regard for practicality
Dogmatic – opinionated, bullheaded
Domestic – having to do with the home and family
Dormant – inactive, unconscious
Dubious – doubtful
Duplicity – deception, cunning
Ebullient – enthusiastic, bouncy
Eccentric – unusual, odd
Eclectic – wide-ranging, diverse
Edify – to educate, enlighten
Efface – to erase, to cancel
Effrontery – boldness, arrogance
Effusion – an outpouring, wordiness
Egalitarian – equal, unbiased
Egocentric – conceited, selfish
Egoism – self-centeredness, conceit
Egregious – extremely bad, intolerable
Elicit – to draw out, to bring about
Elliptical – oval-shaped, curved
Eloquent – articulate, expressive
Elusive – difficult to grasp, mysterious
Embellish – to decorate, to enhance
Emigrate – to move from a country
Eminent – important, famous
Empathetic – understanding, compassionate, feeling
Empirical – practical, based on observation
Emulate – to copy, to compete with
Encroach – to butt in, to trespass
Endemic – local, native

Enervate – to wear out, to weaken

Enfranchise – to set free, to give the rights of citizenship to

Engender – to provoke, to produce

Enigma – a mystery

Enormity – atrocity, evil, or enormousness

Entreat – to plead with

Epigram – a witty saying, a joke

Epitome – the perfect example

Equanimity – levelheadedness, calm and cool

Equitable – fair, unbiased

Equivocal – uncertain, vague

Eradicate – to destroy, to wipe out

Erratic – unpredictable, oddball

Erudite – scholarly, well-educated

Esoteric – hard to understand, mysterious

Espouse – to approve, to advocate

Ethereal – airy, celestial, heavenly, delicate

Euphemism – a nice way to say something

Evanescent – short-lived, fleeting

Exacerbate – to make worse, to annoy

Exacting – demanding, picky

Exalt – to promote, to praise

Exasperate – to aggravate, to anger

Exhaustive – thorough, complete

Exhort – to warn, to advise urgently

Exigency – an emergency, a dilemma

Existential – relating to existence, based on experience

Exonerate – to free from blame

Exorbitant – extravagant, excessive

Expatriate – an exile, an outcast

Expedient – appropriate, advisable

Expedite – to make something happen faster, to accelerate

Explicit – direct, clear, precise

Extol – to brag about

Extraneous – unnecessary, irrelevant

Extrapolate – to assume, to deduce

Extricate – to bail out, to free

Extrovert – an outgoing, sociable person

Exuberant – enthusiastic, lively

Exult – to jump for joy

Fabrication – a lie, something made up

Facetious – joking, not serious

Facile – easy, effortless

Faction – a group who shares a belief, or a disagreement within a group

Fallacy – an error, a misconception

Farcical – slapstick, funny

Fastidious – very careful, particular, hard to please, critical

Fatalist – someone who believes everything is determined by fate and cannot be changed

Fatuous – idiotic, absurd

Fauna – the animal kingdom

Fecund – fertile, abundant

Felicity – bliss, joy

Fervor – passion, earnestness

Fetter – to tie-up, to restrict

Fidelity – devotion, faithfulness

Figurative – symbolic, metaphorical

Finesse – adeptness, know-how

Flag – to decline

Flagrant – flashy, noticeable, not modest

Flaunt – to show off

Flippant – sassy, disrespectful

Flout – to insult, to disregard

Foible – a character flaw, a quirk

Foment – to provoke, to arouse

Forbear – to avoid, or to withhold

Forego – to relinquish, to do without

Forsake – to abandon

Fortuitous – lucky, unforeseen

Founder – to fail, to sink

Frank – honest, tell it like it is

Fraternal – brotherly, affiliated

Frenetic – frantic, manic

Frugal – thrifty, penny-pinching

Furtive – sneaky, stealthy

Futile- hopeless, in vain

Gaffe – a goof, a blunder

Garrulous – talkative

Gauche – tacky, clumsy

Genre – a classification, a brand

Genteel – sophisticated, aristocratic

Gesticulate – to gesture, to signal

Glut – a surplus

Gourmand – someone who likes to eat and drink, gourmet

Grandiloquent – pretentious, big talking

Grandiose – extravagant, flamboyant

Gratuitous – free of charge, or unjustified
Gravity – seriousness
Gregarious – sociable, friendly
Guile – cunning, trickery
Hackneyed – corny, played-out
Hapless – unlucky, cursed
Harbinger – an omen, a sign
Hedonism – indulgence in pleasure
Hegemony – authority, leadership
Heresy – opinion that goes against accepted (religious) doctrine, nonconformity
Hermetic – waterproof, completely sealed
Heterogeneity – variety, an assortment
Heyday – high point, the pinnacle
Hiatus – a pause, a break
Hierarchy – chain of command
Histrionic – melodramatic, theatrical
Holistic – total, whole
Homily – a sermon, a doctrine
Homogeneous – the same
Hubris – excessive pride
Husbandry – farming; management of resources
Hyperbole - exaggeration
Hypothetical – concocted, assumed
Icily – coldly, frigidly
Icon – an image, representation
Iconoclast – a non-conformist, a rebel
Idiosyncrasy – a quirk, an eccentricity
Idyllic – perfect, picturesque, pleasant
Ignominious – disgraceful, shameful
Illegible – unreadable
Illicit – illegal
Illusive – deceptive
Illusory – fake, deceptive
Imbibe – to drink heavily
Imbroglio – a misunderstanding, an argument
Imbrue – to soak
Immaculate – pure, spotless
Immaterial – insignificant, not essential
Immerse – to soak, to saturate
Immigrate - to move into a new country from a foreign land
Imminent – happening soon, impending
Immutable – unchangeable, inflexible
Impalpable – intangible, imperceptible
Impartial – unbiased, fair

Impassive – emotionless, cool
Impeccable – flawless, perfect
Impecunious – poor
Impede – to block, to obstruct
Impel – to provoke, to incite
Imperative – necessary, crucial
Imperial – majestic, regal
Imperil – to endanger, to jeopardize
Imperious – bossy, commanding
Impertinence – bold disrespect
Imperturbable – calm, self-possessed
Impervious – unable to be penetrated, sealed
Impetuous – rash, impulsive, forceful
Impious – irreverent, not religious
Implausible – not believable, doubtful
Implement – to make possible, to bring about
Implicit – implied, hinted at
Impolitic – unwise, rash
Importune – to demand, to pester
Impotent – powerless
Impoverish – to make poor
Impregnable – indestructible, unyielding
Improvident – reckless, uneconomical
Imprudent – careless, reckless
Impudence – arrogance, boldness
Impugn – to criticize, to cast doubt on
Impunity – exemption from guilt
Impute – to attribute, to ascribe, to blame
Inadvertent – accidental
Inane – absurd, silly
Inapt – inappropriate or unsuitable, awkward
Inarticulate – speechless, stammering
Inaugurate – to begin, to ordain
Inborn – natural, innate
Incandescent – glowing, shining
Incantation – a chant, a spell
Incapacitate – to weaken, to damage
Incendiary – dangerous, subversive, inflammatory
Incense – to make angry
Incessant – constant, unrelenting
Inchoate – beginning, preliminary
Incipient – initial, beginning
Incisive – intelligent, keen
Inclination – a tendency
Incoherent – disconnected, confused
Incongruous – out of place, contradictory

Inconsequential – insignificant, insufficient

Incontrovertible – indisputable, certain

Incorrigible – wicked, hopeless, unable to be reformed

Increment – advancement, an increase

Indelible – unable to be erased, permanent

Indict – to accuse, to charge

Indifferent – uninterested, not caring

Indigenous – native

Indigent – poor

Indignant – furious, angry

Indiscernible – hidden, vague

Indiscriminate – aimless, having no goal

Indolent – lazy, inactive

Indomitable – unbeatable, ruthless

Induct – to initiate into an organization

Indulgent – lenient, going along with

Inebriate – to intoxicate

Ineffable – beyond words, inexpressible

Inept – unskilled, incompetent, clumsy

Inert – lifeless, not moving

Inexorable – merciless, dead set on

Inexpedient – unadvisable

Inexplicable – unable to be explained

Infallible – error-free, unquestionable

Infamous – having a bad-reputation

Infatuate – foolishly in love

Infer – to deduce, to assume

Infinitesimal – miniature, negligible

Inflammable – flammable, combustible

Influx – a flowing in

Infringe – to trespass, to interrupt

Infuse – to introduce, to impart

Ingenious – original, clever

Ingenuous – honest, innocent

Ingratiate – to flatter, to charm

Inherent – characteristic, hereditary

Inhume – to bury

Inimical – hostile, harmful

Iniquity – an injustice

Injunction – a court order

Innocuous – harmless

Innovative – creative, original

Innuendo – suggestion, insinuation (often disparaging)

Inordinate – excessive, unreasonable

Inquisitive – curious

Insatiable – unable to be satisfied

Inscrutable – mysterious, unexplainable

Insentient – lifeless, or inanimate

Insidious – dishonest, sneaky

Insinuate – to hint at, to imply

Insipid – tasteless

Insolence – disrespectful, impolite

Instigate – to provoke

Insular – narrow-minded, bigoted, isolated

Insuperable – invincible, overwhelming

Insurgence – an uprising

Intangible – unable to be touched

Integral – essential, necessary

Intelligible – comprehensible

Intemperance – drunkenness

Intercede – to mediate, to intervene

Interim – temporary, or a break

Interminable – endless

Intermittent – occasional, irregular

Intractable – stubborn, unyielding

Intransigent – uncompromising, inflexible

Intrepid – fearless, bold

Intrinsic – basic, inborn

Introspective – thoughtful, contemplative

Inundate – to overwhelm, to flood

Inure – to make ready, to toughen, to familiarize

Invariable – unchangeable

Invective – verbal abuse

Inveterate – habitual

Invidious – envious

Invigorate – to stimulate, to excite

Invincible – unconquerable, indestructible

Invoke – to call on for assistance

Irascible – irritable

Irate – angry

Ire – wrath

Iridescent – rainbow-colored

Irk – to rub the wrong way, to aggravate

Ironic – the opposite of one's intended meaning, sarcastic

Irrevocable – unchangeable, unable to be revoked

Itinerant – roaming, nomadic

Jaded – done it all, wearied

Jocular – amusing, playful

Jubilant – full of joy

Judicious – wise, discerning

Juxtapose – to set side-by-side, to compare

Kinetic – energetic, animated

Knave – a rascal, a scoundrel

Knell – the sound of a bell, a mournful sound

Kudos – praise, credit

Labyrinth – a maze, a complication

Laceration – a cut, an injury

Laconic – brief, to the point

Lament – to mourn, to cry

Lampoon – parody

Languish – to become dull, to suffer

Larceny – theft, burglary

Largess – generosity, charity

Latent – concealed, undeveloped

Laud – to praise, to admire

Lavish – splendid, abundant

Legacy – inheritance, birthright

Legerdemain – trickery, sleight of hand

Lenient – easygoing, tolerant

Lethargy – laziness, disinterest

Levity – silliness, frivolity

Libel – a malicious lie, defamation

Libertarian – an advocate of liberty and free-will

Licentious – unprincipled, uncontrolled

Lilt – a song or a rhythm

Limpid – obvious, clear

Linchpin – the anchor, the foundation

Lionize – to celebrate a person, to lavish attention

Listless – without energy, drowsy

Lithe – flexible, graceful

Litigate – to press charges, to bring into court

Loathe – to hate

Loquacious – talkative

Lucid – obvious, clear

Lugubrious – sad, gloomy

Luminous – bright, glowing

Lurid – gruesome, disgusting

Machination – a ploy, a conspiracy

Maelstrom – chaos, confusion

Magnanimous – bighearted, giving

Magnate – a successful businessperson

Malaise – anxiety, sickness

Malediction – a curse, a condemnation

Malevolent – wicked, sinister

Malfeasance – misbehavior, dishonesty

Malign – to speak ill of, to attack

Malignant – deadly, destructive

Malinger – to pretend illness to avoid work, etc.

Malleable – flexible, easygoing

Mandate – an order, or an authorization

Manifest – Clear; to exhibit, to reveal

Manifesto – a public announcement

Manifold – abundant, diverse

Mar – to disfigure, to damage

Marshal – to guide, to assemble

Martial – aggressive, combative, warlike

Martyr – someone who sacrifices, a sufferer

Matriculate – to enroll, to enlist

Maudlin – overemotional

Maverick – a rebel, a free spirit

Mawkish – emotional, gushy

Maxim – a saying, a motto

Meager – small, inadequate

Mediate – to negotiate, to reconcile

Mediocre – average, humdrum

Medley – an assortment, a mixture

Melancholy – depressed

Mélange – a mixture, a hodgepodge

Mellifluous – pleasing to the ear, harmonic

Mendacious – dishonest, untrue

Mendicant – a beggar

Mentor – counselor, a guide

Mercenary – a person who fights for money

Mercurial – fluctuating, inconstant, flighty, lively

Meritorious – honorable, deserving

Metamorphosis – transformation, rebirth

Meticulous – detailed, thorough

Microcosm – a little world, a miniature example of a larger world/universe

Milieu – atmosphere, setting

Minuscule – teeny, undersized

Mire – a swamp, or to slow down

Mirth – amusement, fun

Misanthropic – antisocial, solitary

Miser – a Scrooge, cheapskate

Missive – written communication

Mitigate – to soothe, to help

Moderate – middle-of-the-road

Modicum – a small amount

Modulate – harmonize, balance

Mollify – to soothe, to calm

Monolithic – huge
Monotonous – tedious, unchanging
Morass – a confusing situation
Mores – established customs
Moribund – dying
Morose – gloomy, negative
Mortify – to humiliate
Motley – varied, multi-colored
Multifarious – various, complicated
Multiplicity – an abundance, a collection
Mundane – ordinary, dull
Munificent – generous
Mutable – changeable, fickle
Myopia – narrow-mindedness, short-sightedness
Myriad – multiple, infinite
Nadir – the lowest point
Naïveté – inexperience, gullibility
Narcissism – egotism, self-love
Nascent – beginning, growing
Nebulous – unclear, shapeless
Nefarious – wicked, perverse
Negate – nullify, deny
Negligent – careless, sloppy
Neologism – a new word, slang
Neophyte – a beginner
Nihilism – anarchy, rejection of established law
Nocturnal – active during the night
Noisome – offensive, harmful
Nomadic – roaming, migratory
Nominal – theoretical, in name only, so-called
Nonchalance – casualness, indifference
Nondescript – dull, undistinguished,
    run-of-the-mill
Notorious – well-known for something bad,
    disreputable
Novel – innovative, original
Novice – a beginner
Noxious – harmful, foul
Nuance – a slight difference
Nurture – to care for, or upbringing
Obdurate – stubborn, relentless
Obfuscate – to confuse, or to lose consciousness
Oblique – slanting or indirect
Oblivion – unconsciousness, nothingness
Obscure – difficult to understand, lacking fame;
    to conceal

Obsequious – fawning, flattering
Obsolete – no longer used, dated
Obstinate - stubborn
Obstreperous – noisy, rambunctious
Obtuse – dumb, not sharp
Occlusion – a barricade, blockade
Odious – hateful, awful
Odoriferous – aromatic
Officious – authoritative, self-important, meddlesome
Ominous – doomed, dismal
Omnipotent – all-powerful
Omnipresent – everywhere, universal
Onerous – difficult, grueling
Opaque – impossible to see through or understand,
    nontransparent
Opulent – luxurious, wealthy
Oration – a speech, a sermon
Ornate – glitzy, elaborately adorned
Orthodox – customary, traditional, accepted
Oscillate – to teeter-totter, to sway
Ossified – fossilized, hardened
Ostensible – alleged, purported, apparent
Ostentatious – showy, flamboyant
Ostracism – banishment, rejection
Pacify – to calm, make peaceful
Painstaking – careful, thorough
Palette – an oval board a painter mixes paints on,
    or a range of colors
Palliate – to relieve, to lessen
Pallid – pale, weak
Palpable – touchable, clear, obvious
Paltry – minor, worthless
Panacea – a cure, assistance
Pander – to cater to, to serve
Panoramic – far-reaching, all-embracing
Paradigm – a prototype, ideal
Paradox – a contradiction, a puzzle
Paragon – a perfect example, the best
Paramount – the main, dominant
Pariah – a social outcast
Parity – balance, equality
Parochial – narrow-minded, conservative
Parody – a satire, a spoof
Parsimonious – stingy, greedy
Partisan – someone who is devoted to a cause, biased
Patent – crystal clear, or a copyright on an invention

Paternal – fatherly, protective

Pathology – the study of disease

Pathos – pity, compassion

Patriarch – male head, the chief

Patrician – upper-class, royal

Patronage – advocacy, assistance

Patronize – to treat like a child, to condescend, or
    to support a cause

Paucity – scarcity, a lack

Peccadillo – a bad habit, an indiscretion

Pedagogical – instructional

Pedantic – academic, formal

Pedestrian – dull, boring

Pejorative – negative, uncomplimentary

Pellucid – clear, simple

Penchant – an inclination, an affection

Penitent – regretful, shamed

Pensive – deep in thought, solemn

Penultimate – next to the last

Penurious – cheap. stingy

Peremptory – overbearing, dictatorial

Perennial – enduring, continual

Perfidy – betrayal, corruption

Perfunctory – careless, indifferent, superficial

Peripatetic – constantly wandering

Peripheral – outside, irrelevant

Periphery – the outskirts, edge

Perjury – lying under oath, dishonesty

Permeate – to spread throughout, to infuse

Pernicious – damaging, dangerous

Perpetual – constant

Perpetuate – to maintain, to preserve

Perplex – to confuse, to bewilder

Perquisite – a perk, a bonus

Perspicacious – aware, perceptive

Pert – lively, bold

Pertinacious – determined, resolute, obstinate

Pertinent – relevant, on target

Perturb – to disturb, to upset

Peruse – to examine in detail

Pervade – to penetrate, to encumber

Petulant – grouchy, irritable

Philanthropy – generosity, charity

Philistine – barbaric, improper

Phlegmatic – unemotional, aloof

Pillage – to destroy, to ransack

Pinnacle – the top, the high point

Pious – devout, religious

Pithy – to the point and meaningful in expression

Pittance – a small amount, a trifle

Pivotal – important, vital

Placate – to soothe, to calm

Placebo – a pill or medicine whose benefit is
    imagined

Placid – calm, peaceful

Plaintive – pathetic, sad

Plasticity – flexibility, resilience

Platitude – an overused saying, a cliché

Plaudit – applause, acclaim

Plausible – believable, likely

Plebeian – working class

Plenitude – plenty, an abundance

Plethora – excess, a surplus

Pliable – flexible, adaptable

Pluralistic – having multiple characteristics or parts

Poignant – painful, heartbreaking

Polarized – contradictory, opposed

Polemic – argumentative

Pomposity – conceit, arrogance

Ponderous – humongous, dull

Portent – an omen, a premonition

Posthumous – after-death, postmortem

Postulate – to speculate, to guess

Potable – safe to drink

Potentate– monarch, royalty

Pragmatic – sensible, logical

Precarious – dangerous, doubtful

Precedent – an example, a model

Precept – a rule, a tenet

Precipice – a cliff, a sheer drop

Precipitate – to speed up, to bring about

Precipitous – abrupt, falling sharply

Preclude – to restrain, to make impossible

Precocious – advanced for one's age, mature

Precursor – something that comes before another,
    a forerunner

Predilection – an inclination, a preference

Preeminent – the most important, supreme

Preempt – to take over, to usurp

Premeditated – planned, calculated

Premise – hypothesis, thesis

Preponderance – dominance, majority

Prepossess – to influence, to prejudice favorably

Prerogative – choice, right

Presage – a prediction, or to forecast

Prescience – prediction, foresight

Prescribe – to command, to guide

Presumptuous – ready to presume, unreasonably bold

Pretense – pretended behavior, artifice

Pretentious – conceited, snobby

Prevail – to succeed

Prevaricate – to exaggerate, to misrepresent

Primeval – ancient, primitive

Pristine – clean, pure

Privation – poverty, hardship

Probity – equality, honesty

Proclivity – an inclination, a tendency

Procure – to obtain, to acquire

Prodigal – wasteful

Prodigious – huge, extraordinary

Prodigy – a child genius

Profane – immoral, indecent

Profess – to confess, to declare

Proficient – skilled, accomplished

Profligate – corrupt

Profound – thoughtful, enlightened

Profundity – wisdom, experience

Profuse – excessive, plentiful

Proletariat – working class

Proliferate – to increase rapidly, to multiply in number

Prolific – productive, highly fruitful

Promulgate – to announce, to declare; to teach

Propagate – to reproduce, to grow

Propensity – an inclination, a bias

Propitious – favorable, beneficial

Proponent – an advocate, a supporter

Proprietary – having exclusive ownership

Propriety – proper behavior, appropriateness

Prosaic – unimaginative, boring

Proscribe – to exclude, to forbid

Proselytize – to convert, to promote beliefs

Prospectus – the plan, a syllabus

Protagonist – the central character

Protean – versatile, able to assume different forms

Protract – to drag on, to delay

Provident – thrifty, showing forethought

Provincial – small-town, unsophisticated

Provisional – conditional or temporary

Prowess – expertise, skill

Proximity – closeness

Prudent – careful

Prurient – vulgar, erotic

Puerile – childish

Pugnacious – aggressive, argumentative

Punctilious – careful, meticulous, finicky

Pundit – an expert

Pungency – bitterness

Punitive – punishing, vindictive

Purported – asserted, suggested

Putative – commonly believed, hypothetical

Putrid – contaminated, stinking

Quagmire – a dilemma, a difficulty

Quaint – old-fashioned, picturesque

Qualify – to modify; to restrict, to limit

Qualitative – pertaining to the quality of something versus the quantity

Quandary – a dilemma, a bind

Quell –to defeat or to calm

Querulous – complaining, grouchy

Quiescent – at rest, inactive

Quixotic – romantic, dreamy

Quotidian – ordinary, everyday

Rail – to criticize severely, to rant

Rambunctious – energetic, loud

Ramification – a consequence, a branching out

Rancid – rotten, foul

Rancor – bitterness, hostility

Rapacious – predatory, savage

Rapport – a bond, compatibility

Rapture – ecstasy

Rash – daring, hasty

Raucous – noisy, jarring

Raze – to demolish, to flatten

Rebuke – to blame, to reprimand

Rebut – to argue against

Recalcitrant – disobedient, hard to manage

Recant – to take back something said, to renounce

Recapitulate – to recap, to summarize

Recessive – passive, inactive

Reciprocal – give-and-take, exchanged

Reciprocate – return the compliment or favor

Reclusive – antisocial, isolated

Recommence – to restart, to resume

Reconcile – to make peace

Recondite – difficult, esoteric, obscure

Recrimination – an accusation

Rectitude - honesty, integrity

Redolent – scented, or remindful of

Redouble – to double in size, to strengthen

Redoubtable – dreadful, commanding respect, feared

Redundant – repetitious

Refract – to bend

Refurbish – to spruce up, to rejuvenate

Refute – to discredit, to contradict

Regurgitate – to vomit

Reiterate – to repeat, to recheck

Relegate – to hand over, to entrust, to place in an inferior position

Relentless – unstoppable, determined

Relinquish – to give up, to hand over

Relish – to enjoy immensely

Remedial – healing, corrective, instructional

Remiss – thoughtless, neglectful

Remonstrate – to challenge, to combat

Remuneration – payment

Renaissance – rebirth, renewal

Renounce – to give something up, to deny

Renovate – to fix up

Reparation – compensation, settlement

Repartee – banter, retort

Repentant – sorry, apologetic

Repercussion – a consequence, a side effect

Repertory – a collection, a supply

Replenish – to replace, to renew

Replete – well-stocked, full

Repose – rest, quietude

Reprehensible – deserving rebuke, shameful

Reprieve – a delay of punishment, temporary relief

Reprimand – to blame, to lecture

Reprisal – retaliation, repayment

Reproach – to criticize, to shame

Reprobate – corrupt, a wicked person, or to disapprove

Reprove – to scold

Repudiate – to reject

Repugnant – disgusting

Repulse – a rejection

Reputable – popular, respectable

Requisition – a demand, an appeal

Requite – to repay, or to take vengeance

Rescind – to back out of, to cancel

Reservoir – storage, a repository

Resilient – quick to recover

Resolute – determined, courageous

Resolve – a decision, an objective

Respite – a break, an intermission

Resplendent – gorgeous, shining

Restitution – compensation

Restive – restless, stubborn

Reticent – shy, hesitant, silent

Retraction – a withdrawal of a previous statement, a disavowal of an opinion

Retroactive – effective or operative from a date, or for a period, in the past

Revel – a celebration, or to cut loose and celebrate

Revere – to admire

Revoke – to take back, to cancel

Rhapsodize – to babble, to talk wildly

Ribald – vulgar, foul-mouthed

Rife – overflowing, plentiful

Rhetoric – a long speech or a style of speech

Rigorous – hard, strict

Risqué – improper, indecent

Robust – healthy, strong

Rogue – a cheater, a con artist

Rousing – stimulating, exciting

Rudimentary – basic, simplest

Ruffian – a criminal, a thug

Ruminate – to brainstorm, to contemplate

Ruse – a trick, a ploy

Rustic – country, rural

Saccharine – sugary, sweet

Sacrilege – irreverence, sin

Sacrosanct – sacred, holy

Sagacious – smart, wise

Salient – significant, noticeable

Sallow – pale

Salutary – healthful, nourishing

Salve – to soothe, to comfort

Salvo – a barrage, bombardment, salute or applause

Sanctimonious – self-righteous, smug

Sanguine – confident, optimistic; reddish

Sardonic – sarcastic, mocking

Sate – to satisfy, to fill

Satiated – satisfied

Savant – an intellectual, a wise person

Scarce – limited, insufficient

Scathing – scornful, wounding, searing

Scintillate – to sparkle, to twinkle

Scourge – a plague, a curse

Scrupulous – careful, conscientious

Scrutinize – to inspect, to analyze

Scurrilous – insulting, scandalous

Scuttle – to scurry, to scamper

Secular – non-religious, earthly

Sedentary – inactive, sitting

Sedition – troublemaking, treason

Sedulous – hard-working, determined

Segregate – to separate, to keep apart

Semaphore – to indicate, to give a sign to

Seminal – influential, important

Sensory – pertaining to the senses

Sensual – arousing, erotic

Sentient – conscious, alert

Sequester – to isolate, to close off

Serendipity – chance, destiny

Serene – calm, peaceful

Serpentine – winding, twisting

Servile – obedient, submissive

Sibilant – hissing, characterized by a hissing sound

Singular – remarkable, outstanding, unique

Sinister – menacing, threatening

Sinuous – curving gracefully, winding

Slander – to insult

Sloth – laziness, inactivity

Slovenly – messy, careless

Sobriety – soberness, moderation

Solace – comfort, relief

Solicitous – considerate or concerned

Soluble – dissolvable

Solvent – financially stable

Somber – serious, sad

Somnolent – sleepy

Sophomoric – immature, unsophisticated

Soporific – causing sleep, hypnotic

Sordid – dirty, distasteful

Sovereign – a ruler or independent

Spate – a fast flow, rush, or outpouring

Spawn – offspring

Specious – false, inaccurate

Speculative – theoretical, pertaining to speculation as opposed to fact

Spontaneity – impulsiveness, spur of the moment

Sporadic – infrequent, once in a while

Spurious – fake, counterfeit

Spurned – rejected, snubbed

Squalor – filth, poverty

Squander – to spend, to throw away

Stagnation – inactivity, sluggishness

Staid – serious, unadventurous

Stark – bleak, bare

Static – stationary or unchanging

Staunch – loyal, or to hold back

Steadfast – loyal, committed

Stigmatize – to brand, to mark in disgrace

Stipulate – to specify, to instruct

Stoic – dispassionate, calm

Stolid – unresponsive, emotionless

Stratum – a layer, a section

Strenuous – tiring, hard

Stricture – a restriction, a criticism

Strident – loud, harsh

Strife – trouble, conflict

Stringent – severe, inflexible

Stupefy – to amaze, to surprise

Stymie – to confuse

Subdue – to hold back, to calm down

Subjugate – to conquer, to enslave

Sublime – inspirational, magnificent

Submissive – obedient, meek

Subordinate – inferior, secondary

Substantiate – to validate, to prove

Subversive – rebellious

Succinct – to the point, brief

Succulent – juicy, moist

Succumb – to give in, to surrender

Sullen – sad, brooding

Sumptuous – luxurious, extravagant

Supercilious – arrogant, snooty

Supple – flexible, agile

Superficial – on the surface, exterior

Superfluous – extra, not necessary

Surfeit – excess, a surplus

Surmise – to guess, to deduce
Surreptitious – secret, underhanded
Surrogate – substitute, replacement
Swarthy – dark-complexioned, tan
Sycophant – a flatterer, a brown-noser
Synthesis – a mixture, a combination
Tacit – unspoken, implied
Taciturn – silent, reserved
Tactile – tangible, concrete
Tangential – unrelated, beside the point
Tangible – touchable, concrete
Tantamount – equal, the same as
Taut – stretched tight, stiff
Tautological – repetitious, redundant
Tedious – dull, boring
Teem – to be plentiful, full
Temerity – recklessness, boldness
Temper – to calm, to make reasonable
Temperate – moderate, calm
Tempest – a thunderstorm, a hurricane
Temporal – earthly, non-spiritual; pertaining to time
Temporize – to stall for time
Tenable – reasonable or safe
Tenacious – stubborn, persistent
Tenet – a belief
Tentative – hesitant, uncertain
Tenuous – weak, shaky
Terrestrial – earthly, mundane
Terse – abrupt, brief
Theology – the study of religion
Therapeutic – healing, beneficial
Thwart – to prevent, to frustrate
Timorous – timid, nervous
Tirade – an outburst, a rant
Toady – a flatterer, a kiss-butt
Tome – a large book
Topography – scenery, geography
Torpid – lazy, slow
Torpor – lethargy, inactivity
Torrid – very hot or passionate, sexy
Tortuous – winding, convoluted
Touchstone – criterion, a standard
Tout – to publicize, to flaunt
Tractable – obedient, polite
Tranquil – calm, peaceful
Transcend – to rise above, to go beyond

Transgress – to misbehave, to sin
Transient – temporary, fleeting
Transmute – to change, to transform
Travesty – a charade, a sham
Treacle – an antidote, a sweet liquid, sweetness
Tremulous – trembling, timid
Trenchant – severe, biting
Trepidation – fear, anxiety
Tribulation – misfortune, suffering
Trite – unoriginal, clichéd
Trivial – unimportant
Trove – an accumulation, a hoarding
Truculent – hostile, defiant
Truncate – to shorten, to abbreviate
Tryst – a rendezvous, a meeting between lovers
Tumultuous – noisy, disorderly
Turgid – bloated or pompous, pretentious
Turpitude – corruption, evil
Ubiquitous – everywhere, omnipresent
Umbrage – offence, displeasure; shade
Unalloyed – genuine, authentic
Uncanny – weird, strange
Unconscionable - immoral
Unctuous – oily, greasy, or insincere
Undermine – to weaken, to thwart
Undulate – to rise and fall, to move in a wavelike motion
Unflagging – persistent, untiring
Uniform – consistent, identical
Unpalatable – distasteful, inedible
Unremitting – constant
Unscrupulous – unprincipled, lacking moral standards
Unstinting – generous, helpful
Unwitting – unsuspecting, ignorant
Urbane – sophisticated, refined
Usurp – to seize, to take over
Utilitarian – useful, practical
Utopia – an ideal place, Eden
Vacillate – to waver, to think twice
Vacuous – unintelligent, dim
Validate – to confirm, to certify
Valor – courage, bravery
Vapid – lifeless, uninspiring
Variegated – multicolored
Vehement – passionate, violent

Venal – unethical, bribable

Veneer – a pretense, a superficial layer

Venerate – to idolize, to adore

Veracity – truth, sincerity

Verbatim – word-for-word, exact

Verbose – wordy

Verdant – green, fertile

Verisimilitude – authenticity, genuineness

Vernacular – dialect, lingo

Vestige – a trace, a sign

Vex – to annoy, to trouble

Viable – possible, practical

Vicarious – experienced as if one were taking part in the emotions or experience of another

Vicissitude – a change, a reversal

Vigilant – watchful, alert

Vignette – a sketch, a scenario

Vigor – energy, vitality

Vilify – to speak badly of, to criticize

Vindicate – to free from blame, to prove right

Vindictive – mean, unforgiving

Virtue – a good quality, an asset

Virtuoso – a genius, a prodigy

Virulent – powerful, venomous

Viscous – sticky, syrupy

Visionary – a prophet, a creative thinker

Vitiate – to abolish, to undermine

Vitriolic – spiteful, hurtful

Vituperative – insulting, malicious

Vivacious – lively, cheerful

Vocation – a career

Vociferous – loud and enthusiastic

Volatile – unstable, explosive

Volition – freewill

Voluminous – huge

Voracious – hungry, insatiable

Vulnerable – helpless, or open to

Wallow – to luxuriate in, or to move about clumsily

Wane – to decrease, to fade

Wanton – unjustifiable, immoral, headstrong

Warrant – to call for, to necessitate

Wary – cautious, distrustful

Watershed – a turning point

Wax – to become fuller, to swell

Wheedle – to persuade with flattery

Whimsical – playful, quirky, given to sudden changes in behavior or preference

Willful – stubborn, unruly

Wily – scheming, sly

Winnow – to separate, to select

Winsome – charming, attractive

Wistful – thoughtful, reflective

Wizened – wrinkled, aged

Wrath – anger, fury

Yoke – repression, burden

Zealous – enthusiastic, passionate

Zenith – a high point, a peak

Zephyr – a gentle wind

List of Root Words

Root	Meaning	Example
a/n	not, without	Anarchy – without government or law
a	on	Ashore – on the shore
ab/s, a	from, away, off	Abdicate – to give away the throne
ac, ad	to, toward, near	Advance - to move forward
acro	top, height, tip, beginning	Acrophobia – fear of height
act	do	Activate – to make active
aer/o	air	Aerodynamics – the study of the motion of air
agr/i/o	farming	Agrarian – relating to land
alg/o	pain	Fibromyalgia – a disease characterized by pain in the muscles and joint tissue
ambi, amphi	both, on both sides, around	Amphibian – live part of their lives in water and part on land or both land and water
ambul	walk, move	Ambulatory – capable of walking
ami/o	love	Amiable – friendly
andr/o	man, male	Androgynous – having both male and female characteristics
anim	life, spirit	Animated – full of life
ann/enn	year	Annual – once a year
ante	before, in front	Antecede – something that went before
anthrop/o	human	Misanthrope – someone who dislikes people
anti	against, opposite of	Antithesis – the exact opposite
apo, apho	away, off, separate	Aphonia – loss of voice

aqu/a	water	Aquarium – a tank that holds water and fish
arbor	tree	Arboreal – treelike
arch/i/e/o/ae	chief, most important, rule	Archetype – the model on which subsequent copies are based
archa/e, archi	primitive, ancient	Archaic – old, ancient
arthr/o	joint	Arthrectomy – surgery to remove a joint
art	skill	Artistry – artistic skill
astro, aster	star, stars, outer space	Astrology – the study of the effect of stars and outer space on humans
aud/i/io	hear	Auditory – relating to hearing
auto	self, same, one	Autonomous – self-governing, independent
avi/a	bird	Aviary – an enclosure for birds
bar/o	pressure, weight	Barometer – an instrument that measures pressure
bell/i	war	Belligerent – ready to fight
bene	good, well	Benign – favorable
bi/n	two, twice, once in every two	Bifocal – having two focuses
bibli/o	book	Bibliomaniac – a fanatic for books
bio	life, living matter	Biology – the science of life
capt, cept	take, hold	Capture – to take by force
cardi/o	heart	Cardiovascular – affecting the heart
carn/i	flesh, meat	Carnivore – an animal that eats meat
cata	down, against completely, intensive, according to	Catacomb – an underground cemetery

caust, caut	to burn	Caustic – capable of burning
cede, ceed, cess	go, yield	Succeed – to yield the desired result
ceive, cept	take	Intercept – to take from someone
celer	fast	Accelerate – to make the speed faster
cent/i	hundred, hundredth	Century – 100 years
centr/o/i	center	Concentric – having a common center
cerebr/o	brain	Cerebral – relating to the brain
cert	sure	Certainty – being absolutely sure
chrom/o, chromat/o, chros	color, pigment	Chromatics – pertaining to color
chron/o	time	Anachronistic – something or someone that is not in the correct time
chrys/o	gold, yellow	Chrysography – writing in ink made of powdered gold
cide, cise	cut, kill	Genocide – the systematic killing of a racial, cultural, or political group
circum, circle	around, about	Circumlocution – to talk around a subject
claim, clam	shout, speak out	Declamation – an emotional speech
clar	clear	Clarity – clearness in understanding
cline	lean	Recline – to lean back
clud, clus	close	Occlusion – a barricade, a blockade
co	with, together, joint	Coalesce – to come together
col	together, jointly	Collusion – a secret agreement between two people

com	together, common	Communal – used or shared by everyone in a group
cogn/i	know	Cognitive – concerning the mind
con	with, jointly	Contemporary – of the same time period
contra/o	against, opposite	Contradict – to argue against
corp/o	body	Corpse – a dead body
cosm/o	universe	Cosmopolitan – relating to the world
counter	opposite, contrary, opposing	Counterattack – an attack in response to an attack
cranio	skull	Cranium – the skull
cred	believe	Credible – believable
crypto	hidden, secret	Cryptic – a hidden meaning
cumul	mass, heap	Cumulare – to pile up
cycl	circle, ring	Cyclical – occurring in cycles
de	reduce, away, down, remove	Decrease – to reduce the amount
dec/a, deka	ten	Decagon – a polygon with 10 sides and 10 angles
deci	one tenth	Decimeter – 1/10 of a meter
dem/o	people	Epidemic – spreading from person to person
demi	half, less than	Demigod – a mythological figure that is half person, half god
dendr/o/i	tree	Dendrite – a branched figure that looks like a tree
dent, dont	tooth	Orthodontist – a doctor that straightens teeth
derm/a	skin	Epidermis – the outer layer of the skin
di/plo	two, twice	Dimorphism – two different forms of a species

di/s	apart, away, not, to the opposite	Digest – to break apart in the stomach
dia	through, between, apart, across	Diameter – a straight line that passes through the center of a circle
dict	speak	Dictum – an authoritative declaration
domin	master	Dominion – ultimate control
don/at	give	Donation – a free contribution
duc/t	lead	Conductor – a person who leads a symphony
du/o	two, twice	Duologue – a two-person conversation
dur	harden, to last, lasting	Durability – long-lasting, able to resist wear
dyn/a/am	power, energy, strength	Dynast – a powerful ruler
dys	abnormal, bad	Dysgraphia – inability to write
e-	out, away	Emigrant – a person who leaves his or her country
ego	self	Egoism – selfishness
endo	within, inside	Endoplasm – the inner part of a cell's cytoplasm
enn/i, anni	years	Anniversary – the date an event took place in a previous year.
en, in	inside, inwards	Enamored – in love with
ep/i	on, upon, over, among, at, after, to, outside	Epicenter – a point directly over the center of a disturbance.
equ/i	equal, equally	Equality – the quality of being equal
erg/o	work	Ergonomics – the study of workers and their environment
esth/aesth	feeling, sensation, beauty	Aesthetic – relating to a sense of beauty

ethno	race, people	Ethnocentrism – the belief that one's own ethnic group is superior
eu	good, well	Eulogy – a speech of praise
ex	from, out	Extend – to stretch out
extra, extro	outside, beyond	Extraterrestrial – beyond the Earth
fac/t	make, do	Factory – a place where people make goods
fer	bear, bring, carry	Fertilization – the step toward bearing offspring
fid	faith	Fidelity – faithfulness
flect	bend	Flection – the act of bending
flor/a, fleur	flower	Florist – a person who arranges and takes care of flowers
fore	in front of, previous, earlier	Foresight – to know what is going to happen before it happens
fract, frag	break	Fracture – to break
fug	flee, run away, escape	Fugitive – someone who has escaped
funct	perform, work	Functioning – capable of performing
fus	pour	Affusion – to pour water on another liquid
gastr/o	stomach	Gastritis – inflammation of the stomach
gen/o/e/ genesis	birth, production, formation, kind	Genetics – the study of heredity
geo	earth, soil, global	Geologist – someone who studies the earth's structure
ger	old age	Gerontonym – an old word
giga	a billion	Gigantic – huge
gon	angle	Polygon – a figure with 3 or more angles
gram	letter, written	Telegram – a message sent by telegraph

graph/y	writing, recording, written	Polygraph – an instrument that records fluctuations in the activities of the body
grat	pleasing	Grateful – thankful
gyn/o/e	woman, female	Gynephobia – fear of women
gress, grad/e/i	to step, to go	Regress – to go backward
helic/o	spiral, circular	Helix – a spiral
heli/o	sun	Heliotropic – growing toward the light of the sun
hemi	half, partial	Hemisphere – half of the earth
hem/o/a	blood	Hemophilia – a disease that results in excessive bleeding
hepa	liver	Hepatitis – inflammation of the liver
hept/a	seven	Heptagon – a polygon with 7 sides and 7 angles
herbi	grass, plant	Herbivore – an animal that eats plants
hetero	different, other	Heterosexual – a person who is attracted to the opposite sex
hex/a	six	Hexagon – a polygon with 6 sides and 6 angles
histo	tissue	Histogenesis – living tissue
homo, homeo	like, alike, same	Homosexual – a person who is attracted to the same sex
hydr/o	liquid, water	Hydrate – to add water to
hygr/o	moisture, humidity	Hygrometer – an instrument used to measure humidity
hyper	too much, over, excessive, beyond	Hypercritical – excessively critical
hyp/o	under	Hypoglycemic – having blood sugar under the normal measurements

icon/o	image	Iconic – characteristic of a symbolic or conventional image
idio	peculiar, personal, distinct	Idiosyncrasy – a peculiar quirk
ig, il, im, in, ir	not, without	Irrelevant – not relevant
imag	likeness	Imagery – a collection of visual likenesses
infra	beneath, below	Infrared – beneath the normal light spectrum
inter	between, among, jointly	Interpersonal – the relations between two people
intra, intro	within, inside	Intramural – only occurring within the limits of a particular community or association
iso	equal	Isosceles – a triangle with 2 equal sides
ject	throw	Reject – to refuse something
jud	law	Judicial – having to do with the courts of law
junct	join	Adjunct – something joined to something else but not an essential part of it
juven	young	Rejuvenate – to make more youthful
kilo	thousand	Kilograms – 1,000 grams
kine/t/mat	motion, division	Kinetics – study of the force of motion
lab	work	Laboratory – a place where scientists work
lact/o	milk	Lactate – to produce milk
later	side	Lateral – coming from the side
leuk/o, leuc/o	white, colorless	Leukocytes – white blood cells
lex	word, law, reading	Lexicon – a dictionary

liber	free	Liberty – freedom
lingu	language, tongue	Linguist – a person who studies languages
lip/o	fat	Lipomata – a harmless tumor made up of fatty tissue
lite, ite, lith/o	mineral, rock, fossil	Meteorite – a stone or metal object from outer space that strikes earth
loc	place	Location – a place
log/o	word, doctrine, discourse	Monologue – a solo speech
loqu, locu	speak	Loquacious – talkative
luc	light	Luciferous – bestowing light
lumin	light	Luminous – radiating light
lun/a/i	moon	Lunar – pertaining to the moon
macro	large, great	Macroaggregate – a large particle
magn/a/i	great, large	Magnanimous – extremely giving
mal/e	bad, ill, wrong	Malign – to speak badly of
man/i/u	hand	Manicure – cosmetic beautification of the hands
mand	to order	Mandate – an official order
mania	madness, insanity, excessive desire	Egomaniac – someone who has excessive love for himself
mar/i	sea	Marine – pertaining to the sea
mater, matr/i	mother	Matriarch – the female head of a household
max	greatest	Maximize – to increase to the greatest amount
medi	middle	Median – situated in the middle
mega	great, large, million	Megaphone – a device that magnifies the voice so it can be heard in a large auditorium or from far away

melan/o	black	Melancholy – sad, depressed, in a "black" mood
memor/i	remember	Memorandum – a note about something that needs to be remembered
meso	middle	Mesoamerica – Middle America
meta	change, after, beyond, between	Metamorphosis – a transformation
meter, metr/y	measure	Odometer – an instrument that measures distance
micro	very small, short, minute	Micromanage – to manage with extreme attention to small details
mid	middle	Midpoint – the point in the middle
migr	move	Migrant – a person who moves from location to location
milli	One thousandth	Millennium – every thousand years
min/i	small, less	Miniscule – very small
mis/o	bad, badly, wrong, wrongly, to hate	Mistake – an error
miss, mit	send, let go	Remit – to send a payment to someone
mob	move	Mobility – the ability to move
mon/o	one, single, alone	Monocratic – governed by only one person
mot, mov	move	Motor – an engine that makes something move
morph/o	form	Amorphous – shapeless
mort	death	Mortality – death
multi	many, more than one or two	Multifaceted – having many aspects
mut	change	Mutate – to change

narr	tell	Narrative – a story;
nat	born	Innate – natural, instilled at birth
nav	ship	Navigate – to guide/move through water
necr/o	dead, death	Necrology – an obituary
neg	no	Neglect – to give no attention to
neo	new, recent	Neophyte – a beginner
neur/o	nerve	Neurology – the science of the nervous system
nom/in	name	Nominal – existing in name only
non	no, not, without	Nonentity – a person or thing of no importance
not	mark	Notate – to make a note or mark of something
noun, nunc	declare	Renounce – to give up with a formal declaration
nov	new	Novice – a beginner
numer	number	Numerical – indicating a number
ob, op	in the way, against	Obstruct – to be in the way of
oct/a/o	eight	Octogenarian – a person who is in their 80s
ocu	eye	Ocular – relating to the eyes
omni	all	Omnipresent – everywhere
op/t/s	eye, visual condition, sight	Optometrist – an eye doctor
opt	best	Optimist – someone who sees the best in every situation
ortho	straight	Orthopedics – a branch of medicine that deals with the straightening of bones
osteo	bone	Osteoporosis – a degenerative disease of the bones

out	goes beyond, surpasses, exceeds	Outspoken – someone who speaks freely
over	excessive	Overabundant – an excessive amount of something
pale/o	ancient	Paleontology – study of ancient fossils
pan	all, any, everyone	Pandemonium – complete chaos
para	beside, beyond, abnormal, assistant	Paranormal – an event beyond normal perception
para	protection from	Parasol – an umbrella that protects from the sun
pater, patr/i	father	Patriarch – the male head of a household
path	feeling, emotion	Empathetic – the ability to feel the emotions of others
ped/i/e	foot, feet	Pedicure – a cosmetic beautification of the toes and feet
pel	drive, force	Impel – to drive forward
pent/a	five	Pentagon – a figure with 5 angles and 5 sides
pept, peps	digestion	Dyspepsia – abnormal digestion
per	through, throughout	Permeate – to spread throughout
peri	around, enclosing	Perimeter – the border of a two-dimensional figure
phag/e	to eat	Acreophagous – not eating meat
phil/o	love, friend	Philanderer – someone who loves a woman he will not marry
phon/o/e/y	sound	Cacophony – a loud sound
phot/o	light	Photosynthesis – a process that uses the energy of sunlight
phys	nature, medicine, the body	Physical – relating to the body

pneum/o	breathing, lung, air, spirit	Pneumonia – inflammation of the lungs
pod/e	foot	Podiatrist – a foot doctor
poli	city	Megalopolis – a large city
poly	many, more than one	Polymorphous – having many forms
pop	people	Populous – full of people
port	carry	Porter – a person hired to carry luggage
pos	place, put	Posit – to place or to put
post	after, behind	Postmortem – after death
pre	earlier, before, in front of	Prelude – an action or event that comes before
pro	before, in front of, for, forward	Prognosticate – to predict the future
prot/o	primitive, first, chief	Prototype – the original model on which copies are based
pseud/o	wrong, false	Pseudonym – a fake name
psych/o	mind, mental	Psychosis – a mental disorder
pugn/a, pung	to fight	Pugnacious – combative, tending to fight
pul	urge	Repulse – to push (urge) back
purg	clean	Purgatory – a place where souls are purified before entering heaven
put	think	Dispute – to disagree with what someone else thinks
pyr/o	fire, heat	Pyromaniac – a person who likes to start fires
quad/r/ri	four	Quadrilateral – a figure with 4 sides and 4 angles

quart	four	Quatrain – a stanza or poem with 4 lines
quin/t	five, fifth	Quintuplets – a group of 5
radio	radiation, ray	Radioactive – giving off radiation
ram/i	branch	Ramify – to branch out
re	again, back, backward	Return – to come back
reg	guide, rule	Regimen – a guide for living, or a systematic course of action
retro	backward, back	Retrograde – having a backward motion
rhin/o	nose	Rhinoceros – an animal with a big horn on its nose
rid	laugh	Ridicule – to make fun of
rub	red	Rubella – a disease characterized by a red rash
rupt	break, burst	Erupt – to burst forth
san	health	Sanity – mental health
scend	climb, go	Descend – to climb down
sci	know	Conscious – to know what is occurring
scler/o	hard	Multiple sclerosis – a disease characterized by the hardening of the brain and spinal cord tissues
scop/e/y	see, examine, observe	Telescope – an instrument that allows you to see distant objects close up
scrib, script	write, written	Scribe – a person who copies manuscripts
se	apart	Seclusion – the state of being apart from others
sect	cut	Bisect – to cut in half
self	of, for, or by itself	Self-pity – to have pity for oneself
semi	half, partial	Semicircle – half of a circle

sept/i	seven	Septimal – relating to the number 7
serv	save, keep	Reserve – to save for the future
sex	six	Sexagenarian – someone in her 60s
sol	alone	Solitude – the state of being alone
sol	sun	Solstice – when the sun is at its greatest distance from the earth
somn/i	sleep	Insomnia – inability to fall asleep
son	sound	Sonogram – a visual image created by sound waves
soph	wise	Sophisticated – educated, cultured
spec/t, spic	see, look	Spectacles – eyeglasses
sphere	ball	Spherical – having the form of a ball
spir	breathe	Respiration – the act of breathing
sta	stand	Stagnant – standing still
stell	star	Stellar – star performance
struct	build	Instruct – to build someone's knowledge
sub	under, lower than, inferior to	Subterranean – under the surface of the earth
sum	highest	Summit – the highest point
super	higher in quality or quantity	Superlative – superior
sy/m/n/l/s	together, with, same	Symbiosis – a cooperative relationship
tact, tang	touch	Tangible – able to be touched
tax/o	arrangement	Taxonomy – the science of classification
tel/e/o	far, distant, complete	Telekinetic – the ability to control a distant object with one's mind

temp/or	time	Temporary – lasting for a short time
term/ina	end, limit	Exterminate – to get rid of completely
terr/a/i	land, earth	Terrain – the ground
tetra	four	Tetrarch – one of 4 rulers
the/o	god	Polytheism – the belief in more than one god
therm/o	heat	Thermometer – an instrument that measures temperature
tort	twist	Tortuous – made up of twists and turns
tox	poison	Toxin – a poison
tract	pull, drag	Contract – to pull the parts of together
trans	across, beyond, through	Transpose – to change the position of
tri	three, once in every three, third	Triathlon – an athletic marathon with 3 events
ultra	beyond, extreme, more than	Ultramodern – extremely modern
un	not, opposite of, lacking	Unceasing – not stopping
uni	one, single	Unicorn – a mythological creature with one horn
urb	city	Urban – pertaining to the city
vac	empty	Vacuous – empty or lacking in intelligence
ven/t	come	Intervention – to come between
ver/i	truth	Veracity – truthful
verb	word	Verbose – wordy
vers, vert	turn	Revert – to return to

vice	acting in place of, next in rank	Viceroy – someone who acts in the name of his government
vince, vic	conquer	Victor – the winner
vis, vid	see	Visual – able to be seen
viv/i, vit	live, life	Vivacity – liveliness
voc/i	voice, call	Vociferous – crying out loudly
vol/i/u	wish, will	Volition – the act of using one's will
vor, vour	eat	Voracious – eating lots of food
xen/o	foreign	Xenophobic – distrust of foreigners
zo/o	animal life	Zoology – study of animals

Chapter 2
Sentence Completions

Sentence Completions test your reading comprehension and vocabulary prowess.

Vocabulary on the Sentence Completions

ETS uses difficult, and often obscure, vocabulary words in the sentences and in the answer choices. Don't get hung up on a word you don't know; instead concentrate on the other clues in the sentence. Sometimes, however, ETS may only give ONE clue. If the subject of a sentence is described as *sagacious* and you have no idea what sagacious means, you're probably going to have to forfeit that sentence completion point. Likewise, if you understand all the words in the sentence but none of the answer choice words, you're going to have to leave that question blank.

Great SAT word!

ETS also gets creative with vocabulary by testing more obscure definitions of easy words. For example, if the word *champion* is an answer choice, chances are ETS isn't testing the noun definition (winner), but the verb definition (to support).

No matter how many words you learn, there are bound to be a couple of wacky answer choice words you've never seen before. Knowing your roots, prefixes, and suffixes comes in handy and helps on those educated guesses.

> **Gain some easy points on the Sentence Completions to boost your entire Critical Reading score by learning your vocab words!**

Even if vocabulary isn't your thing, you can still work through a significant number of Sentence Completion questions, and work through them correctly.

Sentence Completion Facts

- Sentence Completion questions account for approximately ¼ of your Critical Reading Score.

- Each question contains one or two blanks, and you have to fill the blank(s) in with the best answer choice word(s).

- There are 3 Sentence Completion sections on the SAT: a 5-question section, a 6-question section, and an 8-question section.

- Sentence Completion questions are arranged in order of difficulty.

  - In an 8-question section, #s 1-3 are easy, 4-6 are medium, and 7-8 hard.

  - In a 6-question section, #s 1-2 are easy, 3-4, are medium, and 5-6 are hard.

  - In a 5-question section, # 1 is easy, 2-3 are medium, and 4-5 are hard.

> **Difficult, weird vocabulary words make terrific educated guesses on the medium to hard questions!**

Keep Away from the Answer Choices

Those tempting answers are there to trick you! Most of the answer choice words sound pretty darn good when read back in to the sentence and appear to be logical extensions of the sentence's gist.

Reading the answer choice words back into the sentence not only tempts you to pick the wrong answer, but it is also a waste of time and brainpower. Why read the sentence 5 times, when you can get away with reading it once, max twice? Let's see how ETS likes to trick us by working through the following Sentence Completion problem the WRONG WAY.

Read each of the answer choices back into the sentence. Notice how the majority SOUND right, and take your best guess.

2. Though Mitra is usually ------- and boisterous in social gatherings, at last night's dinner party she spoke and behaved with atypical -------.

   (A) effervescent . . self-confidence
   (B) loquacious . . reticence
   (C) affable . . indignation
   (D) reserved . . languor
   (E) outgoing . . arrogance

The correct answer is (B). *Loquacious* means talkative; the sentence indicates she is *boisterous* (fun and noisy), so talkative is supported within the context of the sentence. *Reticence* means hesitation, or reserve. We know we need a word in the second blank that is opposite to *boisterous* because of the conjunction *though*, which flips the direction of the sentence.

My oh my, all that analyzing for one sentence? Yes!

Instead of plugging in the answer choice words to see how they SOUND…

> **Come up with your own word based on the context of the sentence!**

Keep it in Context

Everything you need to know is in the sentence. Do not bring in any background knowledge or make any assumptions.

> **The SAT does not reward creativity. Stick to the context of the sentence!**

How do you let a cute guy or girl know you like them? You flirt a bit: you make eye contact, smile, give a little wink. You give your crush CLUES that you are interested. ETS does the same. The sentences are full of clues and winks to let you know what the sentence is all about.

I'll be referring to the contextual support in a sentence as **WINKS**.

Let's say the sentence reads: *The exhibit was perfect for ------- enthusiasts.*
What kind of enthusiasts? *Film enthusiasts? Art enthusiasts? Music enthusiasts? History enthusiasts?*
There are no **Winks** in the sentence to let us know what kind of enthusiast we are looking for.

ETS will make the sentence more specific by adding a **Wink**: *The WWII exhibit was perfect for ------- enthusiasts.*

What is our **Wink**? <u>*WWII exhibit.*</u>

What kind of enthusiasts are we looking for now? <u>*History enthusiasts!*</u>

Let's analyze an SAT question.

4. With its considerable distribution, Ms. Magazine
    has maintained ------- only recently challenged by
    topical journals actively seeking feminist readers.

What are our **Winks**? <u>*Considerable distribution*</u> and <u>*only recently challenged by topical journals.*</u>

> **Underline your Winks in the sentence!**

Here's what your test booklet should look like:

4. With its <u>considerable distribution</u>, Ms. Magazine has maintained ------- <u>only recently challenged by topical journals</u> actively seeking feminist readers.

Given our **Winks**, what word or expression could we put in the blank? *<u>Being on top</u>*
<u>a supremacy</u>
<u>the largest readership</u>

Don't worry about coming up with the perfect word or phrase. Just make sure your answer stays as close as possible to the winks. In fact, we could have used our actual **Wink** in the sentence and plugged in *considerable distribution*.

Let's try another:

2. The complex and mesmerizing language in William Faulkner's writing provide a ------- speculation of the subject matter.

What are our **Winks**? *<u>The complex and mesmerizing language</u>*

Underline them!

2. <u>The complex and mesmerizing language</u> in William Faulkner's writing provide a ------- speculation of the subject matter.

What type of word or expression should go in the blank? *<u>Complex and mesmerizing</u>*

Notice how I gave my brain a rest and just used ETS's **Winks**?

Plagiarize ETS's words whenever possible!

Keep Going in the Right Direction

Sentences often contain what I call **COMPASS WORDS**: Words that indicate whether the sentence is traveling in the SAME direction as the **Winks**, or the OPPOSITE direction of the **Winks**.

Here are two simple sentences that demonstrate the power of **Compass Words**.

He was the star quarterback of the football team (and) got a full-ride scholarship to Notre Dame. → *This **Compass Word** lets us know the sentence is continuing in the same direction.*

She wanted to go to prom (but) she didn't have a date. → *This **Compass Word** flips the direction of the sentence.*

Let's analyze an SAT question: <u>Underline the **Winks**</u> and circle the (**Compass Words**.)

1. The artist came to be characterized as -------
    because he sequestered himself in his home,
    avoiding interaction with others.

Here's my marked up version:

This first phrase gives us nothing. What about the artist? We have absolutely no idea! Don't make any assumptions or generalities about artists – Keep within the context of the sentence!

a hermit

1. The artist came to be characterized as -------

    (because) he sequestered himself in his home,

    avoiding interaction with others.

    Compass Word: Same direction
    indicating cause and effect.

I threw in my own word, *hermit*, because he isolated himself at home and avoided other people.

Let's see what happens when the sentence flips direction. Underline your **Winks**, circle your **Compass Words**, and plug your own words in to the blanks. Be sure you write your word(s) down, especially on two-blank sentence completions.

5. After making millions from his invention, Art
    bought a yacht, a ranch, and Rolex watches;
    however, by ------ his ------, he estranged his
    friends.

Here's mine:

After is a **Compass Word** that indicates a shift in time: Flip direction!

5. (After) <u>making millions</u> from his invention, Art

    <u>bought a yacht, a ranch, and Rolex watches</u>;

    showing off   millions

    (however,) by -------- his --------, he <u>estranged his</u>

    <u>friends</u>.

    Compass Word: Flips direction!

The following list of **Compass Words** is by no means comprehensive, but is a great navigational starting point.

SAME DIRECTION	OPPOSITE DIRECTION
And	But
Therefore	Although
Because	Though
Do	However
Due to	Not
Clearly	Usually
Also	In spite of
As a result	Yet
Even	Even though
; (Semicolon)	In contrast
: (Colon)	Despite
As well as	Unlike
Since	In fact
Thus	Instead

Keep Tally with Process of Elimination

Feel free to develop your own tallying system, but here's what I like to use:

Good words get a check (√).
Bad words get a line through them (—).
Words that are just all right get a squiggle (~).
Words that I don't know the meaning of get a question mark (?).

Just because you don't know a word, doesn't mean it's wrong.

> **Never eliminate a (?)! ETS loves hard vocab and it may just be the right answer.**

Let's analyze the answer choices of the first example problem. Notice how I put (?) above the words I don't know.

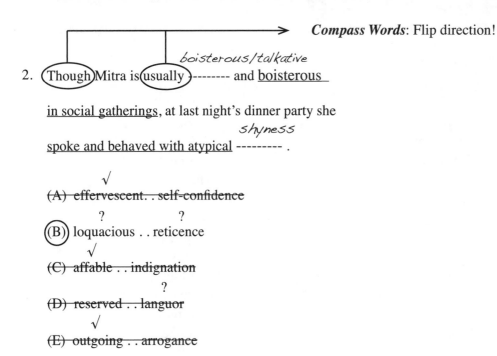

Compass Words: Flip direction!

boisterous/talkative

2. (Though) Mitra is (usually) -------- and <u>boisterous</u>

<u>in social gatherings</u>, at last night's dinner party she

shyness

<u>spoke and behaved with atypical</u> --------- .

√
(A) effervescent. . self-confidence

?   ?
(B) loquacious . . reticence

√
(C) affable . . indignation

?
(D) reserved . . languor

√
(E) outgoing . . arrogance

All we have left is (B) with two question marks. Even without knowing all the vocabulary, you can still get the right answer!

⟶ **Remember: If you can eliminate one answer choice on a Sentence Completion question, be aggressive and take a guess.**

Two-Blank Sentence Completions

I want you to walk through the Two-Blank Sentence Completions a specific way. *After underlining your Winks, circling your Compass Words, and filling in the blanks with your own words, ONLY look at the answer choice words that correspond to the blank you feel most confident about.*

> **Cover up the answer choices with your answer sheet or your hand so you don't accidentally peek at the words and become influenced!**

Let's try it.

Step 1: Read the sentence

6. The successful actress, who remained ------- even after
    scoring parts in major blockbusters, felt certain she
    would be critically ------- .

Step 2: Underline Winks and circle Compass Words

6. The <u>successful</u> actress, who remained ------ (even after)
    →   ***Compass Words***: indicates a shift in time
    <u>scoring parts in major blockbusters</u>, felt certain she   which signals an opposite direction!
    would be <u>critically</u> ------- .

Step 3: Fill in the blanks with your own words

                          fearful
6. The <u>successful</u> actress, who remained ------- even after

    <u>scoring parts in major blockbusters</u>, felt certain she
                       criticized
    would be <u>critically</u> ------- .

Step 4: Walk through the answer choices of the blank you are most confident about. I like my word for blank 2 best because it stays closest to the context of the sentence. Disregard the answer choices in blank 1.

                      √

(A)   . . condemned → Let's put a (√) because *condemned* (blamed) matches *criticized.*

                      √

(B)   . . censured → Put a (√)! Censured means *criticize severely.*

                   ?

(C)   . . lauded → Let's say we don't know what *lauded* means. Mark it with a (?).

                   ?

(D)   . . panned → Let's say we don't know *panned.* Put a (?) above it.

(E)   ~~. . praised~~ → *praised* doesn't mean *criticized.* Eliminate all of (E). It
                               doesn't matter what the first blank is.

We have eliminated (E). Let's take a look at blank 1 answer choices to find a match to *fearful.*

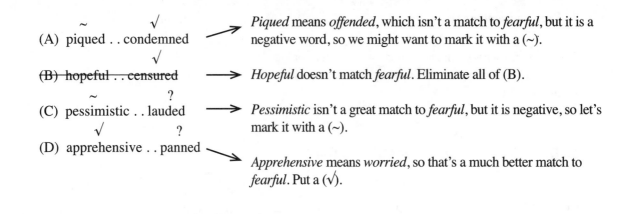

(A) piqued . . condemned — *Piqued* means *offended*, which isn't a match to *fearful*, but it is a negative word, so we might want to mark it with a (~).

(B) hopeful . . censured — *Hopeful* doesn't match *fearful*. Eliminate all of (B).

(C) pessimistic . . lauded — *Pessimistic* isn't a great match to *fearful*, but it is negative, so let's mark it with a (~).

(D) apprehensive . . panned — *Apprehensive* means *worried*, so that's a much better match to *fearful*. Put a (√).

Which answer choice should we pick?

(A) (~) (√)
(B) (~) (?)
(D) (√) (?)

(D) is the winner! AND it's correct!

When analyzing whether to pick a (~) or a (?) just ask: *do I like it enough to go on a second date (~), or would I rather go on a blind date (?)?*

Positive/Negative Hunch

Sometimes it might be a little tricky to fill in the blank with a word or phrase. When words fail you, use your positive/negative hunch.

3.   Although the teacher was alleged to be -------,
     the perfunctory nature of her lesson plans
     indicated she was too ------- .

Find the **Winks** and **Compass Words** in the sentence above before looking at the answer choices.

3.   (Although) the teacher was alleged to be ⁺ -------,

     the perfunctory nature of her lesson plans

     indicated she was too ⁻ ------- .

                    too indicates a degree of something
                    that is TOO MUCH

Even if you don't know what *perfunctory* means, the *too* tells us we need a negative word in blank 2. *Although* signifies a shift in direction, so blank 1 must be positive. Mark the blanks with (+) and (-) signs.

Now we're ready to look at the answer choices. Let's start with the first blank this time, eliminating all negative words.

(A) meticulous . . ⁺

(B) concise . . ⁺

(C) impatient . . ⁻

(D) orderly . . ⁺

(E) stern . . ⁻

Time to look at blank 2 for a negative word.

(A) . . apathetic ⁻

(B) . . structured ⁺

(D) . . precise ⁺

Apathetic is the only negative word. The other two words are pretty neutral. *Structured* and *precise* could be positive or negative depending on the circumstances.

Notice how we worked with the relationship between the blanks. We wanted two words with an opposite relationship: *meticulous* (careful) and *apathetic* (not caring).

Let's take a look at answer choices with a similar relationship.

2. The girl's motivations were ------; once you knew
    her true nature you could detect her ------ lies.

The semi-colon indicates same direction and *lies* is a **Wink** that tells us she is not a very honest person. We know we have a similar relationship and are looking for two negative words.

2. The girl's motivations were ------⁻(;)once you knew

    her true <u>nature</u> you could detect her ------ <u>lies</u>. ⁻

(A) malicious . . deceptive
　　　　‾　　　　‾

(B) ~~elusive . . scrupulous~~
　　‾　　　　　+

(C) ~~ethical . . unctuous~~
　　+　　　　　‾

(D) immoral . . self-righteous
　　‾　　　　　‾

(E) ~~fair . . pure~~
　　+　　　+

We have two possibilities, (A) and (D), and therefore a 50/50 shot of guessing right.

(A) malicious . . deceptive
　‾　　　　　‾

(D) immoral . . self-righteous ⟶ We want a word that means *dishonest*, so *deceptive* is closer in context than *self-righteous*.

An 8-question, 6-question, and 5-question drill follows, along with answers and explanations.

Here's a refresher of the technique:

- *Step 1: Read the sentence*
- *Step 2: Underline Winks and circle Compass Words*
- *Step 3: Fill in the blank(s) with your own word(s) or phrase(s)*
- *Step 4: Go to the answer choices using process of elimination*

⟶ **Remember: Cover up the Answer Choices! No peeking until you've inserted your own word(s) into the blank(s).**

⟶ **Difficult vocab words are great answer choices on medium/hard problems! Don't be afraid to pick those (?)!**

Pacing

I don't want you to time these drills. I want you to carefully and accurately apply the technique. Use the College Board *Official Study Guide* to practice Sentence Completions with time. An 8-question section should take anywhere between 4-7 minutes (you shouldn't exceed 7 minutes). Spend 3-5 minutes on a 6-question drill and 2-4 minutes on a 5-question drill.

⟶ **Don't go too fast! Slow and steady will earn you the most points.**

> *Note: Don't get caught up and frustrated on any one problem. Remember, you get to leave questions blank and should always be moving forward at a steady pace.*

8-Question Drill

1. Years of ------- playing of sports had left him too
   ------ to be able to participate in even milder
   forms of exercise for long periods of time.

   (A) heavy . . agitated
   (B) successful . . flabbergasted
   (C) steadfast . . renowned
   (D) exciting . . weakened
   (E) vigorous . . marred

2. A certain organic compound used to make
   plastic containers is actually a ------- substance,
   a discovery that demonstrates that even the
   most standard products can sometimes ------- .

   (A) artificial . . infect
   (B) chemical . . misfire
   (C) toxic . . vitiate
   (D) purifying . . contaminate
   (E) poisonous . . dominate

3. Because doodling increases memory recall,
   it is sometimes used as a ------- to promote
   concentration in employees.

   (A) hiatus   (B) focus   (C) catalyst
       (D) requirement   (E) edict

4. No longer considered -------, Lamark's theory
   on the inheritance of acquired characteristics
   appears to be ------- now that Darwin's theory
   of natural selection and Mendelian genetics
   have come to the forefront.

   (A) viable . . fallacy
   (B) conjectural . . deviation
   (C) incontrovertible . . certainty
   (D) chimerical . . possibility
   (E) fallacious . . oversight

5. To leave work on time, the CFO ------- his
   remaining duties to his assistant.

   (A) extemporized   (B) renewed
       (C) ameliorated   (D) endorsed
       (E) relinquished

6. The mass production of microprocessors -------
   the burgeoning computer industry by making
   home computers commercially ------- .

   (A) galvanized . . implausible
   (B) cheapened . . inexpensive
   (C) reformed . . excessive
   (D) altered . . unattainable
   (E) energized . . tenable

7. Although mental illness does bring about
   significant psychological changes, it does
   not often modify a person's ------- : a
   staunch twenty-five year old will probably
   still be ------- at thirty.

   (A) physique . . infirmed
   (B) temperament . . strapping
   (C) biology . . comely
   (D) physiology . . robust
   (E) character . . hearty

8. The girl's peers typified her as ------- because
   she had a sentimental, romantic disposition.

   (A) demonstrative   (B) complaisant
       (C) ingenuous   (D) humble
           (E) synergetic

Answers and Explanations

Answer Key:

1. (E)   **5.** (E)
2. (C)   **6.** (E)
3. (C)   **7.** (D)
4. (A)   **8.** (A)

1. Years of -------- playing of sports had left him (too) →   Notice this degree adverb. It is indicating
    extreme   a negative. *Too much of something.*
    hurt
    -------- to be able to participate in even milder

    forms of exercise for long periods of time.

    (A) heavy . . agitated
    (B) successful . . flabbergasted
    (C) steadfast . . renowned
    (D) exciting . . weakened
    (E) vigorous . . marred

I like my second blank best: *hurt*. Let's walk through the answer choices looking only at blank 2, writing synonyms for those words, and eliminating any choices that do not mean *physically hurt*.

<del>(A)</del>   . . <del>agitated</del>   *restless/troubled*

<del>(B)</del>   . . <del>flabbergasted</del> *shocked*

<del>(C)</del>   . . <del>renowned</del>   *famous*
                                        √
(D)   . . weakened   *hurt*
                                        √
(E)   . . marred   *hurt*

We are left with (D) and (E). Let's look at the first blank, write our synonyms, and eliminate the one that doesn't match my word: *extreme*.

                                √
<del>(D) exciting . . weakened</del>   *exciting* (thrilling) does not mean *extreme*
        √   √
(E) vigorous . . marred   *strenuous*

90

2. A certain <u>organic compound</u> used to make

   harmful

   <u>plastic containers</u> is (actually) a -------- substance, → *Compass Word* indicates
   a change in direction.

   a discovery that demonstrates that <u>even the</u>

   harm

   <u>most standard products can sometimes</u> ------- .

   (A) artificial . . infect
   (B) chemical . . misfire
   (C) toxic . . vitiate
   (D) purifying . . contaminate
   (E) poisonous . . dominate

I like my first blank best: *harmful*. Let's walk through the answer choices looking only at blank 1 and eliminating any words that do not match.

~~(A) artificial . .~~   *man-made*

  ~
(B) chemical . .   ⟶   (C) and (E) are better matches, but something *chemical*
  √   may be *harmful*, so we'll leave (B) just in case.
(C) toxic . .

~~(D) purifying . .~~   *decontaminate*
  √
(E) poisonous . .

We are left with (B), (C) and (E). Let's look at blank 2 and eliminate the answer choices that don't match my word: *harm*.

   ~
~~(B) chemical . . misfire~~   *fail*
  √   √
(C) toxic . . vitiate   *hurt*   ⟶   *Remember:* If you don't know the meaning of
  √   a word, put a (?). Question marks make great
~~(E) poisonous . . dominate~~   *control*   answer choices!

                    Compass Word indicates same direction.
                ↗
3. (Because) doodling <u>increases memory recall</u>,

                    memory recall technique

   it is (sometimes) used as a ------- to <u>promote</u>

   <u>concentration</u> in employees.   ⟶   Degree adverb!

   (A) hiatus   (B) focus   (C) catalyst
     (D) requirement   (E) edict

What word matches *memory recall technique?*

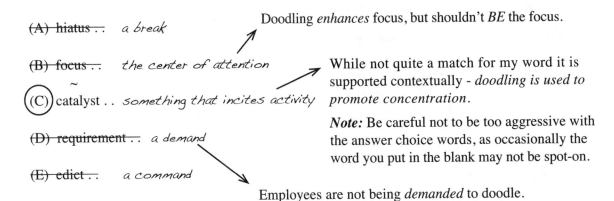

(A) hiatus .. *a break*

Doodling *enhances* focus, but shouldn't *BE* the focus.

(B) focus .. *the center of attention*

(C) catalyst .. *something that incites activity*

While not quite a match for my word it is supported contextually - *doodling is used to promote concentration.*

Note: Be careful not to be too aggressive with the answer choice words, as occasionally the word you put in the blank may not be spot-on.

(D) requirement .. *a demand*

(E) edict .. *a command*

Employees are not being *demanded* to doodle.

Compass Words. Change in direction.

4.
accurate/at the forefront

No longer considered --------, Lamark's theory

on the inheritance of acquired characteristics

wrong

appears to be -------- now that Darwin's theory

Compass Word: Indicates a shift in time.

of natural selection and Mendelian genetics

have come to the forefront.

(A) viable . . fallacy
(B) conjectural . . deviation
(C) incontrovertible . . certainty
(D) chimerical . . possibility
(E) fallacious . . oversight

I want to work with blank 2 first: *wrong.* Let's walk through the answer choices and our synonyms looking only at blank 2.

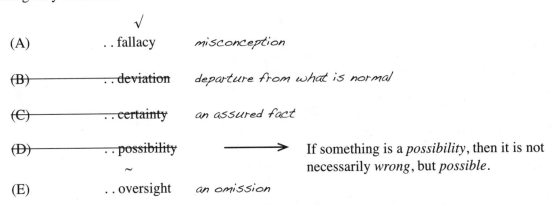

√

(A) . . fallacy *misconception*

(B) . . deviation *departure from what is normal*

(C) . . certainty *an assured fact*

(D) . . possibility If something is a *possibility*, then it is not necessarily *wrong*, but *possible.*

(E) . . oversight *an omission*

Let's leave (E), even though so far (A) seems like the better match.

Left with (A) and (E), let's look at synonyms for blank 1: *accurate*.

(A) viable . . fallacy ~ √ *possible/reasonable*

(E) fallacious . . oversight ~ *false*

5. To leave work on time, the CFO -------- his *abdicated/gave*

   remaining duties to his assistant.

   (A) extemporized   (B) renewed
     (C) ameliorated   (D) endorsed
       (E) relinquished

Let's match my word/phrase: *abdicated/gave*. Write synonyms for the answer choices.

(A) extemporized . . *improvised*

(B) renewed . . *fixed up*
        ?
(C) ameliorated . .

(D) endorsed . . *promoted*
        √
(E) relinquished . . *handed over*

6. The mass production of microprocessors ------- *helped*

   the burgeoning computer industry by making
   burgeoning means *flourishing/growing*

   home computers commercially ------- . *accessible*

   (A) galvanized . . implausible
   (B) cheapened . . inexpensive
   (C) reformed . . excessive
   (D) altered . . unattainable
   (E) energized . . procurable

I feel more confident about blank 1: *helped*. Let's walk through the answer choices and write synonyms for blank 1.

$\sqrt{}$

(A) galvanized . .   *stimulated*   (a good match for *helped*)

(B) cheapened . .   *diminished worth*
$\sqrt{}$

(C) reformed . .   *improved*

(D) altered . .   *changed*
$\sqrt{}$

(E) energized . .   *stimulated*

Let's work our synonyms for blank 2 of answer choices (A), (C), and (E) to find a match for *accessible*.

$\sqrt{}$

(A) galvanized . . implausible   *not likely*
$\sqrt{}$

(C) reformed . . excessive   *too much of something*
$\sqrt{}$ $\sqrt{}$

(E) energized . . tenable   *attainable*

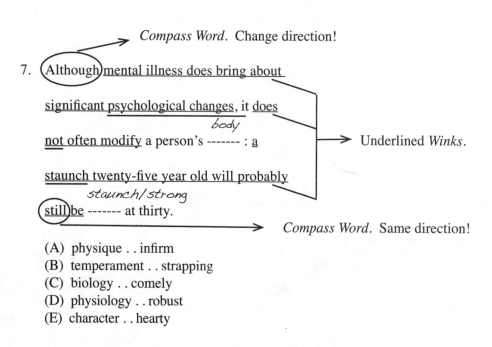

Compass Word. Change direction!

7. Although mental illness does bring about

significant psychological changes, it does

body

not often modify a person's ------- : a   → Underlined *Winks.*

staunch twenty-five year old will probably

staunch/strong

still be ------- at thirty.

Compass Word. Same direction!

(A) physique . . infirm
(B) temperament . . strapping
(C) biology . . comely
(D) physiology . . robust
(E) character . . hearty

Let's look at blank 1 first: *body*, and synonyms for the choices.

√
(A) physique . .   *body*

(B) ~~temperament~~ . .   *personality*
                    √
(C) biology . .   *someone's physical makeup – relates to body*
            √
(D) physiology . .   *anatomy*

(E) ~~character~~ . .   *personality*

Walk-through blank 2 of answer choice (A), (C), and (D) looking for a match to *strong*.

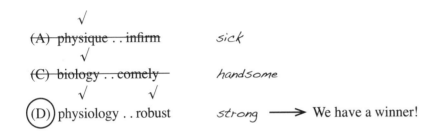

          √
(A) ~~physique . . infirm~~   *sick*
          √
(C) ~~biology . . comely~~   *handsome*
          √   √
(D) physiology . . robust   *strong* ⟶ We have a winner!

emotional/romantic

8. The girl's peers typified her as ------ ⟨because⟩ ⟶ *Compass Word.* Same direction!

   she had a sentimental, romantic disposition.   ⟶ Underlined: *Winks*

   (A) demonstrative   (B) complaisant
     (C) ingenuous   (D) humble
       (E) synergetic

Walk through the answer choices looking for the word that is the closest match to *emotional/romantic*.

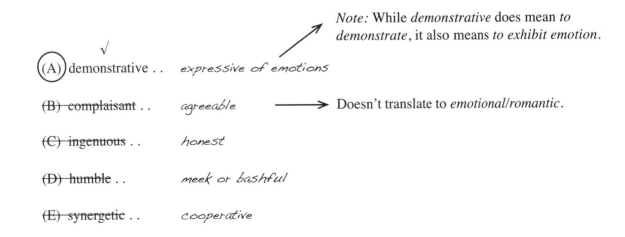

                                    Note: While *demonstrative* does mean *to demonstrate*, it also means *to exhibit emotion*.
          √
(A) demonstrative . .   *expressive of emotions*

(B) ~~complaisant~~ . .   *agreeable*   ⟶ Doesn't translate to *emotional/romantic.*

(C) ~~ingenuous~~ . .   *honest*

(D) ~~humble~~ . .   *meek or bashful*

(E) ~~synergetic~~ . .   *cooperative*

6-Question Drill

1. Unable to determine what had caused the accident, the policeman filed a provisional report stating that the cause was ------- .

   (A) conclusive (B) notable
   (C) decisive (D) indefinite
   (E) integral

2. Not wanting to act -------, Roger ------- the urge to pass his student until he had double checked the test results.

   (A) rashly . . quelled
   (B) hastily . . hastened
   (C) sternly . . obliged
   (D) mistakenly . . recognized
   (E) eagerly . . explained

3. Volcanoes as a rule vary: some may erupt -------, whereas others may have only a short volatile explosion then remain ------- for months or years.

   (A) forcefully . . hazardous
   (B) sporadically . . scarce
   (C) automatically . . erratic
   (D) frequently . . flowing
   (E) perpetually . . latent

4. The Wright brothers did not suddenly learn to fly, but did so over time with numerous breakthroughs equalized by ------- periods.

   (A) perilous (B) anticipated
   (C) stagnant (D) bountiful
   (E) speculative

5. Only after the girl became aware of the clairvoyant's questionable motives could she see the ------- statements made in his seemingly ------- predictions.

   (A) artful . . furtive
   (B) sectarian . . obdurate
   (C) affable . . churlish
   (D) astute . . intuitive
   (E) insidious . . scrupulous

6. Professor Norris disdains intemperance: He lives plainly and donates most of his income, earning a reputation as ------- .

   (A) a miser (B) an abecedarian
   (C) an ascetic (D) a patriarch
   (E) a steward

Answers and Explanations

Answer Key:

1. (D)   4. (C)
2. (A)   5. (E)
3. (E)   6. (C)

1. <u>Unable to determine</u> what had caused the

   <u>accident</u>, the policeman <u>filed a provisional</u>
                          not able to be determined
   <u>report</u> stating that the cause was ------- .

   (A) conclusive   (B) notable
     (C) decisive   (D) indefinite
        (E) integral

Let's walk through the answer choices and write synonyms for them, looking for the best match for *not able to be determined*.

~~(A) conclusive~~   *final*

~~(B) notable~~   *important or famous*

~~(C) decisive~~   *certain*
                    √
(D) indefinite   *uncertain*

~~(E) integral~~   *necessary*

                    too quickly   suppressed/held back
2. Not wanting to act -------, Roger ------- <u>the</u>
                                                        → *Compass Word!*
   <u>urge to pass his student (until) he had double</u>

   <u>checked the test results</u>.

   (A) rashly . . quelled
   (B) hastily . . hastened
   (C) sternly . . obliged
   (D) mistakenly . . recognized
   (E) eagerly . . explained

I feel most confident about my second blank. Walk through the answer choices only looking at blank 2.

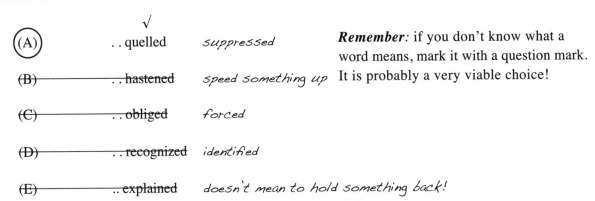

√
(A) .. quelled   *suppressed*   **Remember**: if you don't know what a
                                   word means, mark it with a question mark.
(B) ..hastened   *speed something up*   It is probably a very viable choice!
(C) ..obliged   *forced*
(D) ..recognized *identified*
(E) ..explained   *doesn't mean to hold something back!*

We only have one answer choice left! Let's see if it's a match for *too quickly.*

√   √
(A) rashly .. quelled   *abruptly/hurriedly*

3.
                                         constantly
   <u>Volcanoes</u> as a rule <u>vary</u>: some may erupt -------,   → *Compass Word:* Flips direction!
   (whereas) others may have only a short volatile
                        inactive
   <u>explosion</u> (then) <u>remain</u> ------- for months or   → *Compass Word:* Flips direction!
   years.

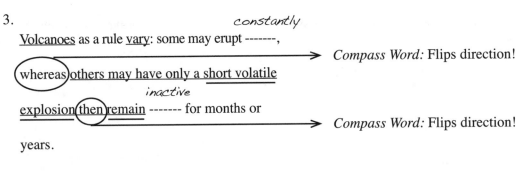

(A) forcefully . . hazardous
(B) sporadically . . scarce
(C) automatically . . erratic
(D) frequently . . flowing
(E) perpetually . . latent

I filled in blank 2 first (*inactive*), so let's work with it.

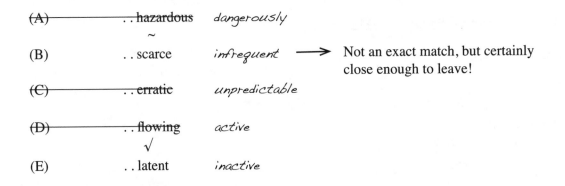

(A) ..hazardous   *dangerously*
          ~
(B) .. scarce   *infrequent* → Not an exact match, but certainly
                                   close enough to leave!
(C) ..erratic   *unpredictable*
(D) ..flowing   *active*
          √
(E) .. latent   *inactive*

Let's work through our leftover answer choices (B) and (E) to find a match to *constantly*.

(B) sporadically .. scarce ~   *every now and then*
     ✓   ✓

(E) perpetually .. latent   *constantly*

4. The Wright brothers <u>did not suddenly learn</u>

<u>to fly,</u> (but) did so <u>over time</u> with <u>numerous</u>   ⟶   *Compass Word:* Flips direction!

going backwards
<u>breakthroughs equalized by</u> ------- periods.

(A) perilous   (B) anticipated
  (C) stagnant   (D) bountiful
    (E) speculative

I couldn't think of the perfect word, but the phrase *going backwards* will do because it is opposite to *breakthroughs*.

(A) perilous   *dangerous*

(B) anticipated   *expected*
     ✓
(C) stagnant   *motionless* ⟶   If something is motionless, there is a lack of progress,
                                   so (C) works!

(D) bountiful   *abundant*

(E) speculative   *hypothetical*

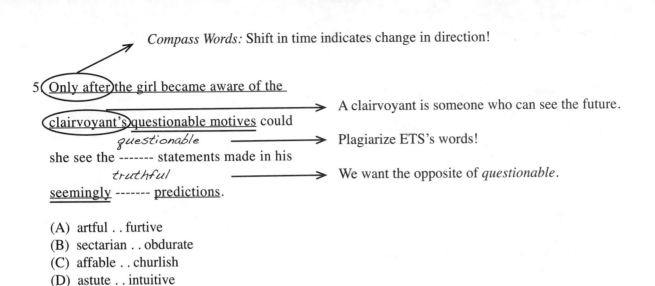

5. Only after the girl became aware of the

clairvoyant's questionable motives could

questionable

she see the ------- statements made in his

truthful

seemingly ------- predictions.

A clairvoyant is someone who can see the future.

Plagiarize ETS's words!

We want the opposite of *questionable.*

(A) artful . . furtive
(B) sectarian . . obdurate
(C) affable . . churlish
(D) astute . . intuitive
(E) insidious . . scrupulous

Let's work through synonyms for blank 1: *questionable.*

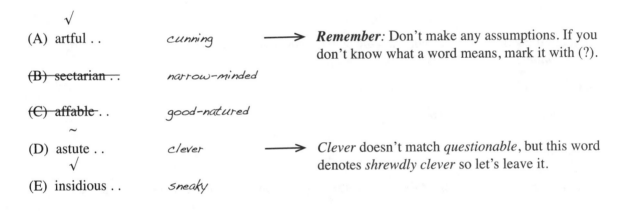

√
(A) artful . .   *cunning*   ⟶   *Remember:* Don't make any assumptions. If you don't know what a word means, mark it with (?).

(B) sectarian . .   *narrow-minded*

(C) affable . .   *good-natured*

~
(D) astute . .   *clever*   ⟶   *Clever* doesn't match *questionable,* but this word denotes *shrewdly clever* so let's leave it.
√
(E) insidious . .   *sneaky*

Let's look at blank 2 (*truthful*) for (A), (D), and (E).

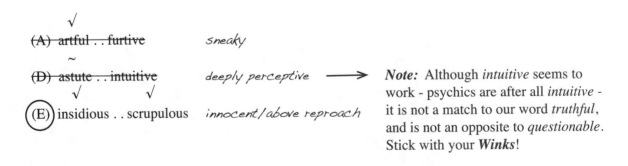

√
(A) artful . . furtive   *sneaky*

~
(D) astute . . intuitive   *deeply perceptive*   ⟶
√   √
(E) insidious . . scrupulous *innocent / above reproach*

Note: Although *intuitive* seems to work - psychics are after all *intuitive* - it is not a match to our word *truthful,* and is not an opposite to *questionable.* Stick with your *Winks*!

Signals same direction.

6. Professor Norris <u>disdains intemperance</u>. He

 <u>lives plainly and donates most of his income</u>,

 someone who lives plainly and donates

 earning a reputation as ------- .

   (A) a miser   (B) an abecedarian
    (C) an ascetic   (D) a patriarch
     (E) a steward

What word best matches our phrase?

   (A) a miser   *cheapskate*

   (B) an abecedarian   *beginner*

          √
   (C) an ascetic   *self-denying*

   (D) a patriarch   *male head*

   (E) a steward   *manager*

5-Question Drill

1. Jeff is ------- in the most trivial and most important matters: he is adaptable and pliable in his opinions.

   (A) adamant   (B) grave   (C) optimistic
   (D) flexible   (E) intractable

2. Nostradamus's ------- proved most astute when he accurately conjectured that King Henry II would die from a jousting accident.

   (A) prescience   (B) genius   (C) madness
   (D) nostalgia   (E) melancholy

3. The senator's speech was both ------- and ------- : though concise, it was informative.

   (A) circumlocutory . . banal
   (B) compendious . . illuminative
   (C) discursive . . enlightening
   (D) brief . . labyrinthine
   (E) inspirational . . specialized

4. Psychologist Susan Apollan asserts that treating patients is an instinctive decision rather than ------- judgment; that is, it was not so much analytical as ------- .

   (A)   a sentimental . . rational
   (B)   a serendipitous . . arbitrary
   (C)   an instinctual . . impetuous
   (D)   a calculated . . visceral
   (E)   a deductive . . premeditative

5. The critic's review, though refined and indirect, was conspicuously ------: it left no uncertainty of her meaning.

   (A) apprehensible   (B) unrestrained
   (C) recidivous   (D) nebulous
   (E) empyrean

Answers and Explanations

Answer Key:

1. (D) 4. (D)
2. (A) 5. (A)
3. (B)

Remember: Plagiarize ETS's words!

adaptable and pliable

1. Jeff is ------- in the most trivial and most important matters: <u>he is adaptable and pliable in his opinions.</u>

   (A) adamant   (B) grave   (C) optimistic
   (D) flexible   (E) intractable

Which answer choice is the closest match to *adaptable and pliable?*

   (A) adamant   *determined/fixed*

   (B) grave   *serious*

   (C) optimistic   *hopeful*

   ✓
   (D) flexible   *pliable*

   (E) intractable   *stubborn*

conjectures/ability to predict

2. Nostradamus's ------- <u>proved most astute</u>

   <u>when he accurately conjectured</u> that King

   Henry II would die from a jousting accident.

   (A) prescience   (B) genius   (C) madness
   (D) nostalgia   (E) melancholy

Note: Even if you don't know what astute or conjecture mean, you do know that *accurate* is a positive word. Knowing that, you can eliminate all the answer choice words that are negative. Focus on what you know!

Let's look for a match to *ability to predict*.

(A) prescience √ *foresight*

(B) ~~genius~~ *highly intelligent*

(C) ~~madness~~ *insanity*

(D) ~~nostalgia~~ *fond memories*

(E) ~~melancholy~~ *depressed*

concise

3. The senator's speech was both ------- and
informative
-------: though concise, it was informative. → Signals a clue is sure to follow!

    (A) circumlocutory . . banal
    (B) compendious . . illuminative
    (C) discursive . . enlightening
    (D) brief . . labyrinthine
    (E) inspirational . . specialized

I feel good about both blanks because I plagiarized ETS's words. Let's work through synonyms for blank 1: *concise*.

(A) ~~circumlocutory~~ *wordy*

(B) compendious √ *shortened/abridged*

(C) ~~discursive~~ *long-winded*

(D) brief √ *concise*

(E) ~~inspirational~~ *enlightening*

With (B) and (D) left, let's match blank 2: *informative*.

(B) compendious . . illuminative √ √ *educational*

(D) ~~brief . . labyrinthine~~ √ *complex*

4. Psychologist Susan Apollan asserts that

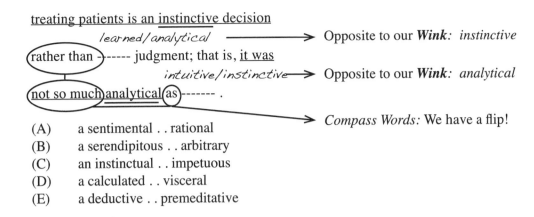

treating patients is an <u>instinctive decision</u>
    learned/analytical ⟶ Opposite to our **Wink**: *instinctive*
rather than - - - - - judgment; that is, <u>it was</u>
     intuitive/instinctive ⟶ Opposite to our **Wink**: *analytical*
not so much <u>analytical</u> as - - - - - - .

         ⟶ *Compass Words:* We have a flip!

 (A) a sentimental . . rational
 (B) a serendipitous . . arbitrary
 (C) an instinctual . . impetuous
 (D) a calculated . . visceral
 (E) a deductive . . premeditative

Let's match blank 2: *intuitive*.

(A)   . . rational *analytical*
     ~

(B)   . . arbitrary *unpredictable* ⟶ Not a great match, but let's leave it.
     ~

(C)   . . impetuous *impulsive* ⟶ Not a great match, but it does mean *acting*
     √   *without thinking*, so let's leave it.

(D)   . . visceral *instinctive*

(E)   . . premeditative *planned*

We have (B), (C), and (D) left. Let's match *learned/analytical*.

     ~
(B) a serendipitous . . arbitrary *random/chance*

     ~
(C) an instinctual . . impetuous *intuitive*

   ~   √
(D) a calculated . . visceral *deliberately planned* ⟶ This word is not a great match to *learned*,
                  but it does match *analytical*, so we have
                  contextual support.

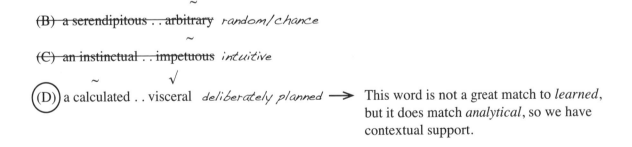

Remember: Your paraphrased words might not be spot-on all the time so be flexible.

Compass Word: Flips direction!

5. The critic's review, (though) refined and

                  certain in meaning

indirect, was conspicuously ------(:)it   Signals a clue is sure to follow!

left no uncertainty of her meaning.

  (A) apprehensible   (B) unrestrained
    (C) recidivous   (D) nebulous
      (E) empyrean

Match the phrase: *certain in meaning*.

          √

(A) apprehensible   *capable of being understood*

(B) unrestrained   *spontaneous/uncontrolled*

(C) recidivous   *uncorrectable*

(D) nebulous   *vague*

(E) empyrean   *heavenly*

Chapter 3
Reading Comprehension Answer Choices

The Reading sections of the SAT tend to be the most frustrating for the majority of students. They are certainly the most frustrating for me. The Math and Grammar sections are black-and-white: $2 + 2 = 4$, and no one can argue differently. The Reading sections, however, are inherently subjective. There is really no "right" answer to Critical Reading questions; there is only the "best" answer (and often that's the best of the worst).

For this reason, Process of Elimination is even more important on the Reading portions of the SAT. Before we delve into technique, let's spend some time analyzing Good versus Bad Critical Reading answer choices.

Answer Choices to Avoid

Extremes

⟶ **Look out for Absolute Words!**

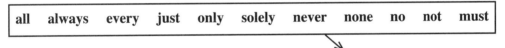

| all | always | every | just | only | solely | never | none | no | not | must |

These words are just too difficult for ETS to justify!

Example: (A) believes that ⟨all⟩ teachers feel as he does during parent/teacher conferences

Extreme!

Had the sentence been written, *"believes that some teachers,"* it would have been a viable option, but *"all"* is much too extreme!

> *Note: When absolute words are qualified, such as **"not the only,"** they become valid answer choice candidates. The addition of the "not" cancels out the extreme, "only."*

⟶ **Avoid Adverbs that Express a Strong Degree!**

| overly | too | undue | excessively | extremely | very | most |

Example: (B)  overly respectful

Extreme!

An acceptable answer choice would be just *"respectful,"* but *"overly respectful"* is too strong and opinionated.

⟶ Be careful on Tone Questions!

Tone questions often contain answer choices that are much too extreme, such as *"righteous indignation"* or *"extreme displeasure."* Even an extreme answer that is positive, such as *"ecstatic joy,"* is considered too strong.

Harsh or Offensive Answers

⟶ Politically Correct Answer Choices Only!

ETS is careful not to offend and is thus very politically correct. Anything that could be deemed offensive to women or minorities will NOT be the correct answer.

Example: (C) to display the 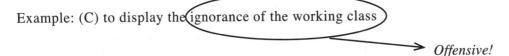 ignorance of the working class

Offensive!

Oh my! If this were the right answer, ETS would have a riot on its hands!

Comparisons

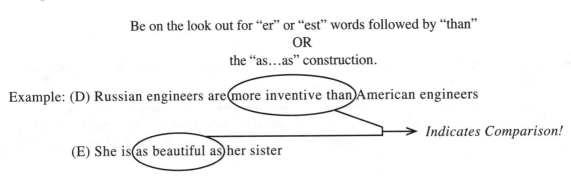

Be on the look out for "er" or "est" words followed by "than"
OR
the "as…as" construction.

Example: (D) Russian engineers are more inventive than American engineers

Indicates Comparison!

(E) She is as beautiful as her sister

Comparisons are inherently offensive, so learn to spot and eliminate quickly!

Exception: (A) her fantasies are *more pleasing than* the truth

Indicates Comparison!

The above example is a comparison, but it is not offending any person, or groups of persons, and could therefore be a legitimate answer.

Word-for-Word Copy

→ **Beware of answers that contain a Literal Repetition of words in the passage!**

Here's what our brains do: *"Oh! I remember reading that! It's right there in paragraph 2!"* Yes, it is, but rest assured, it will not be answering the actual question that ETS is asking.

Let's say in paragraph 3 the passage reads: ***"In art nothing worth doing can be done without genius; in science even a very moderate capacity can contribute to a supreme achievement."***

(For source reference, see endnote [b])

Fast-forward a couple of minutes and we are on question #23, which asks: ***"What parallel does the author draw between art and science?"***

Answer choice (C) reads: "Both artists and scientists of *moderate capacity contribute* significantly to their fields."

Word-for-word copy!

Students get hooked in by phrase *"moderate capacity can contribute,"* which they remember from the passage. If you are on the lookout for word-for-word copies you are more apt to catch that answer choice (C) is actually the OPPOSITE of what is stated in the passage.

> *Note: We are never looking for exact copies of words or phrases in the passage. We are instead looking for soft paraphrases.*

Exception: If you are on a general question, such as a main idea question, a word-for-word copy is allowable. The word-for-word copies in the answer choices could legitimately be part of the main idea, the subject of which will be sprinkled throughout the passage.

⟶ **Sneaking Partial Answers into the answer choices
    is ETS's favorite trick!**

One half of the answer choice (usually the first half) will be spot-on, but then ETS will insert one little word in the second half that throws the entire answer choice off. Surely I won't miss that, you think! Believe it or not, partial answers are the trap answer that students pick the most. Either students don't read carefully enough, or the first half of the answer is so perfect, they disregard the second half, thinking they must have misunderstood the passage.

Let's say the second paragraph of a passage focuses on *an author who worries about how her readers will judge her book.*

A question then asks: ***"the primary purpose of the second paragraph is to show that the author…"***

You answer the question in your own words. That's easy, you think. ***It's to show how the author feels about readers judging her book.***

You look to the answers and see answer choice (B), which reads:
"is insecure about how critics will react to her books."

This answer is good to an extent: the author *is* insecure about someone's reactions to her books, but the someone is her *readers* not the *critics*.

Dissect every word in the answer choices carefully.

Hypotheticals

⟶ **Watch out for an "If…then" Construction!**

Example: *If* Lucy marries Ricky, *then* she will be a television star.

How do we know for sure that Lucy will become a TV star?

Avoid all hypothetical scenarios and predictions! They count as assumptions, and NO assumptions allowed!

Too General or Too Specific

⟶ Not Too General, Not Too Specific, but JUST RIGHT!

Let's say one of the answer choices to a specific question reads: *"to gain the sympathy of critics."* You need to make sure that it is the sympathy of the critics the character or author is trying to gain, rather than the sympathy of, let's say, the readers.

Here's how it works on a more general question:

Let's say the passage is about *a few key influences in Shakespeare's life*. The question asks: *"What's the primary purpose of the passage?"*

The answer choices read:

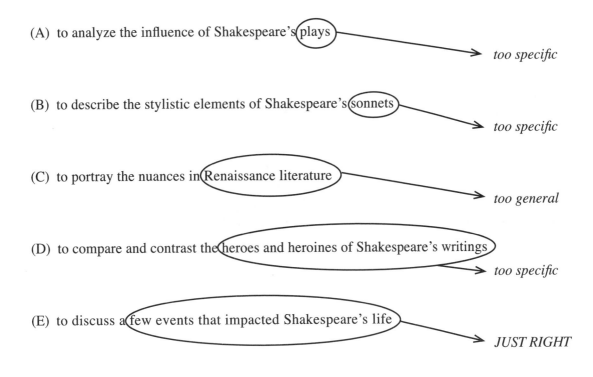

(A) to analyze the influence of Shakespeare's plays → *too specific*

(B) to describe the stylistic elements of Shakespeare's sonnets → *too specific*

(C) to portray the nuances in Renaissance literature → *too general*

(D) to compare and contrast the heroes and heroines of Shakespeare's writings → *too specific*

(E) to discuss a few events that impacted Shakespeare's life → *JUST RIGHT*

Avoid answer choices that make assumptions or draw unsupported conclusions.

Moderate

⟶ **Look for Moderate Words!**

some	may	might	many	can	could	usually	sometimes	often

Example: (A) teachers (may) not fully understand the meaning behind a student's words

Moderate Word

Now that's a nice, safe, moderate answer choice. Also look for middle of the road tone/attitude answers, such as *"mild concern."*

Paraphrases

⟶ **Avoid Word-for-Word Copies and Opt for Soft Paraphrases!**

Take a look at this short excerpt from *The Story of Mankind* by Hendrik Van Loon, Ph.D.:

Without that vague and hard-to-define something which the world calls "personality," there can be no art and the Roman world distrusted that particular sort of personality. The Empire needed efficient soldiers and tradesman. The business of writing poetry or making pictures was left to foreigners.

(For source reference, see endnote c)

A paraphrase might be:

Romans concentrated more on using their inventiveness for practical purposes, rather than for creative endeavors.

Miscellaneous Tips

Ambivalent vs. Indifferent

Ambivalent: Unsure

Indifferent: Don't care

Translation: *Ambivalent* is a valid answer choice. *Indifferent* is not. Why would the author write about something he is indifferent to?

Great SAT Vocab word!
Meaning: *sensible, practical*

Pragmatic and Particular

This little tip is purely for guessing purposes, but the words *pragmatic* and *particular* show up quite often in the correct answer choice. I'm just sayin'…

Nostalgia and Nostalgic

The odds are pretty good that you might run into one of these two words on the SAT. Avoid them! They are traps!

What does *nostalgia* even mean anyway?

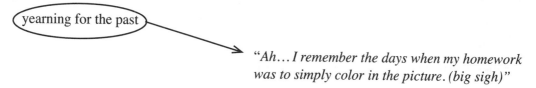

yearning for the past

"Ah…I remember the days when my homework was to simply color in the picture. (big sigh)"

Let's take a look at a Critical Reading section minus the passage, to see how well we can detect good versus bad answer choices. We won't be able to know which answer choice is correct since we don't have a passage to refer to, but we can certainly eliminate a few along the way.

> *Note: Critical Reading sections should never be approached simply based on analyzing the answers without referring back to the passage. This exercise is merely a practice in elimination.*

10. Which statement best summarizes the depiction of the theoretical group of students in lines 10-13 compared to the actual group in line 26?

(A) The first insults the teacher; the second is overly deferential

(B) The first is greedy; the second is magnanimous

(C) The first is uneducated; the second has received academic honors

(D) The first is somewhat invasive; the second is apparently grateful

(E) The first rejects the teacher's approach; the second praises it

Answer choices (B), (D), and (E) are the most attractive, with (C) hanging in there if supported by the passage.

"insults" might be a tad strong, but it could be supported by information in the passage.

"deferential" on its own would be fine, but "overly" makes this answer too extreme!

This could be possibly offensive or even extreme – before you pick it make sure you find support from the passage!

These are great words! (D) is a nice, safe answer choice!

11. Line 15 ("I thought....likewise") implies that the narrator

(A) enjoys the company of her students

(B) is as thrilled about her students' futures as she is about her own

(C) believes that most students feel as she does in regards to low test scores

(D) is insecure about teaching in front of parents and faculty

(E) regards the principal's attitude as odd

Answer choices (A), (C), and (D) seem like the best to me.

The "as…as" construction indicates a comparison. Careful!

Nothing wrong with this answer choice, but be careful – it could be a Partial Answer. Go back to the passage and make sure it is the "parents and faculty" that make her insecure, and not "students."

The meaning behind this answer choice seems a bit "odd." While a person's behavior can be odd, it seems strange to describe an attitude as odd.

12. In line 49 the author assumes that "fairness" would be

   (A) praising the unique accomplishments of a student

   (B) ensuring that a student's performance is evaluated by all the teachers in the school   → Too extreme! Eliminate.

   (C) providing first-rate classrooms to improve student performance

   (D) enhancing the students' experiences with better educational material

   (E) arranging the classroom in a way that promotes increased concentration and focus

Answer choices (A), (C), (D), and (E) all seem feasible, but (B) has to go!

13. "It was a lapse in judgment" (line 51) because the narrator

   (A) had no other avenues of employment to pursue   → The "no" makes this answer way too extreme!"

   (B) allowed pragmatic worries to supersede her concern for the student   → Remember: "Pragmatic" is a good word.

   (C) was unable to appreciate the student's efforts   → Hmm…the logic of this seems a bit off. A teacher couldn't appreciate a student's efforts? We don't have a passage, so we can't check it out, but I'd be a bit wary.

   (D) felt that she had damaged the student's confidence

   (E) did not realize how successful the student would be as an adult

Answer choice (A) has to go, but we can keep all the others.

14. In line 60, the simile describing "recklessness" suggests that judgment can

   (A) bring back painful feelings from childhood
   (B) lose its sting when expressed too often
   (C) arouse feelings of inadequacy in others
   (D) reinforce misleading intentions from peers
   (E) provoke students to make hasty decisions

   I would be leery of answer choice (B), but I see no reason to eliminate any of the other answer choices.

We have an adverb that expresses a strong degree. Careful!

Be sure to test this answer choice with info from the passage. Make sure it is "intentions from peers" and not a different group of people such as "authority figures."

15. The passage serves primarily to

   (A) portray the influence of environment on learning
   (B) defend the methods of an eccentric educator
   (C) stimulate interest in an overlooked profession
   (D) explore the emotional impact of a particular style of teacher/student interaction
   (E) argue against placing undue emphasis on test scores

   Be sure to eliminate (E)!

We like this word!

"undue" makes this answer choice too extreme!

Chapter 4
Reading Comprehension Fundamentals

The Reading Comp on the SAT is difficult because of time and tedium. The passages are often very boring and very confusing. But let's focus on the positive.

#1 – It is an open book test. The answers are RIGHT THERE IN THE PASSAGE. No outside knowledge necessary.

#2 – Everything is pretty darn literal. No need to come up with an in-depth analysis as is necessary in your high school English class. You simply need to approach the passages in a literal frame of mind.

#3 – It is not necessary to answer every single reading question.

#4 – We can tailor reading technique according to your individual needs.

Types of Passages

There are _____ on the SAT:

anthropology, government, history, cultural psychology. These subjects sound interesting be anything but. Social Science passages often orities and women. Keep in mind, that ETS will ple.

up passage, be diligent about differentiating between using, because the author will probably be challenging the means the passage carries three points of view: that of the up, and that of the white male. The answer choices will *be sure you know from which perspective you are answering*

Humanities

Humanities passages focus on philosophy, art, literature, performing arts, culture, and linguistics. They are similar in topic to the Social Science passages, but they tend to be more descriptive and confusing.

ETS often utilizes the memoir as its Humanities passage. ***The memoir will typically be written by a person of color or a woman, and often deals with themes such as assimilation versus tradition.*** Memoirs involve more "story" and read like a work of fiction; I have found that students tend to enjoy memoir passages more so than other nonfiction passages on the SAT.

Fiction

ETS pulls Fiction passages from novels and short stories. Victorian literature, such as the more obscure Jane Austen and Edith Wharton stories, loves to make an appearance. It is important to "read between the lines" on these types of passages, as the majority of the time the characters don't outright say what they are ACTUALLY thinking. ***Irony and satire pop up quite a bit in the Fiction passages, so dig deeper than you would on the nonfiction passages.***

Fiction passages on the SAT deal with human relations, not with intricate plot. Read with the following in mind:

- *Who is in the scene?*
  This also includes the person or situation the characters are discussing. Chances are, the person being discussed will not be physically present.

- *What is their relationship with one another?*
  Are they sisters, friends, business associates, lovers?

- *How do they feel about each other?*
  Is there tension? Animosity? The stirrings of love?

- *What do they want from each other? What is the conflict?*
  Money? Respect? Love?

- *How do they attempt to get what they want from each other?*
  Coercion? Manipulation? Flattery?

- *What is the author's attitude toward the characters?*
  This is, of course, only applicable if the author writes in third person. If the author writes in first person "I," include her as one of the characters.

Science

You don't have to be a science buff to be able to digest a Science passage, which will range in topic from physics to geology. Remember, as with all Reading Comp passages, no outside knowledge is necessary. You don't need to know the definition of little known scientific terms (ETS will either notate the definition with an asterisk and a footnote, or include the definition in the passage). You won't be bogged down with too many facts, as often the Science passages are discussing a controversial topic, such as stem cell research, and the author is weighing his opinion against that of other researchers.

The topic won't, of course, be too controversial (stem cell research might just fall into the too taboo category). The passage could also be discussing a new hypothesis and pitting it against more traditional theories. This means you need to understand the difference between each of the hypotheses presented, and be sure to know which hypothesis (if any) the author supports.

The Italicized Introduction

No matter what Reading Comp technique you choose, you should ALWAYS read the italicized introduction. At the very least the Italicized Intro will tell you what type of passage you are dealing with, and at the very most it will include the main idea of the passage.

Let's break down a couple:

This passage, adapted from a 1996 book, discusses the ability of some soft-bellied mollusks to utilize three different camouflage body patterns in order to avoid detection.

Before even reading the passage we have ascertained quite a bit of information:
  #1 – It's a science passage.
  #2 – The topic is about mollusks that can camouflage in 3 different ways. Not that I recommend skipping a read-through of the passage, but we just may be able to answer one or two questions with that information alone!

This passage has been adapted from a memoir published in 1976. The year is 1962 and the author, then a young girl, has just moved to Stockton, California with her family.

What do we know?
  #1 – It's a memoir.
  #2 – It's written by a woman, and chances are she is a woman of color if the passage is from the 1940s or later. ETS usually follows that pattern.

Passage 1 was adapted from a well-known 1990 study of video games. Passage 2 was adapted from a 2005 analysis of the most popular video games of the 80s and 90s.

What do we know?
  #1 – We are on a compare/contrast section.
  #2 – The topic of each passage is video games, so be on the lookout for similarities and differences.

Technique Overview

I will be teaching three different techniques. If you tend to score in the 500 and below range, I would play around with each of these techniques to see which one you feel the most comfortable with and to analyze which technique is gaining you the most points. If you are a higher scoring student who is looking to maximize your reading comp potential, I would stick with Technique #1. Here are the techniques in a nutshell:

- **Technique #1:** For the student who typically does not have difficulty reading the passage and answering the questions in the allotted time; and for the student whose mind doesn't drift every other sentence to what he is going to eat for lunch. All of our minds wander, especially on boring passages. Please be honest with yourself. If you are capable of reading and staying focused, Technique #1 is the best method to use. If you ABSOLUTELY CANNOT focus due to learning challenges or medical diagnoses, then this technique is probably not your best bet.

- **Technique #2:** For the student who is capable of reading the entire passage but prefers to answer questions as she goes because she gets overwhelmed reading the passage all at once. This technique can cost you a few points, because it weakens comprehension - you might not have the full gist of the passage until you've read through to the last paragraph and by then you've answered most of the questions - but if you have a bit of trouble focusing and do better taking things step by step, Technique #2 might just be the best technique for you.

- **Technique #3:** For the student who has significant focusing problems (you know who you are) and ABSOLUTELY CANNOT read an entire passage. For all other students: This technique is only to be used in dire circumstances: such as you only have 2 minutes left or you are unable to manage the other techniques after having given them a fair shot. Technique #3 will gain many students points, because it makes the reading comp much more manageable, but for medium to higher scoring students, this technique will only cost you.

> **Exception:** Fiction passages must be managed with Technique #1 and ONLY Technique #1. Fiction passages cannot be broken up and must be read in their entirety.

You'll notice that with each of these techniques I do not tell you to look at the questions first. Some SAT instructors swear by that approach; I think it sucks up precious time. In my opinion, it is much more effective to read for the main idea and then read for more detailed specifics later. Don't worry, you'll get to the questions in due time.

The Big Secret:

All of the techniques share the same big secret. The key to raising your Critical Reading score:

⟶ Answer the questions in your own words first.

In fact, EVERYTHING needs to be put in your own words. You need to *summarize the information in the passage* in your own words, *summarize the question* in your own words, *answer the question* in your own words, and *summarize each of the answer choices* in your own words. I will be urging you to write down these summaries as you go, mainly for the purpose of getting used to the technique. Once the technique becomes second nature, feel free to state your summaries in your head if pacing becomes an issue.

Always keep this in mind as we run through each of the techniques!

Here's another tip:

⟶ Every answer should be justified by information in the passage.

If you can't point to a specific part of the passage as proof, then you shouldn't pick the answer. Remember this golden rule!

Each of the following three chapters tackles one of the Reading Comp techniques and features a reading comprehension passage with which to practice that technique. Each chapter works through a different passage, and no two questions are the same.

Once you've decided which technique works best for you, practice that technique with diagnostic tests from the College Board *Official SAT Study Guide*.

Practice, Practice, Practice!

Chapter 5
Technique #1
The Complete Picture

This technique is definitely the preferred method. While you may sacrifice a bit of time reading the passage (depending on your reading aptitude) you won't sacrifice comprehension. Ultimately, reading the entire passage makes answering the questions a speedier and easier process.

Step 1: Read the Italicized Introduction

Be sure to note the type of passage and the topic discussed.

Step 2: Read the First Paragraph

While reading, underline what you think may be important and circle transition words that signify a shift or emphasis in thought:

| therefore | however | yet | still | although | likewise | but |

Note: Underlining and circling keep you reading actively, which helps you maintain focus and keeps that brain awake and alive!

Step 3: Write down the Main Idea of the First Paragraph in your Own Words

I don't want you to write a novel; a brief summary will do.

Examples: *Mother Theresa questioned faith* or *Animals play like humans*

⟶ Steps 2 and 3 should be repeated for each subsequent paragraph

Step 4: Write down the Main Idea of the Entire Passage

Before you go to any of the questions you should have a solid grasp on the main idea. Again, don't write too much, just a brief summary.

Examples: *Theories on the dangers of TV are stupid* or *Technology has endangered human relations*

Trust me: A written down main idea will be handy to refer to when debating between a couple of answer choices.

> Note: If you are having trouble identifying the main idea, first ask: *What is the subject or topic of the passage?* (For example, *cheetahs*.) Then ask: *What does the passage say about this subject?* (For example, *cheetahs are becoming increasingly endangered*.)

⟶ **Remember: Every correct answer is in line with the main idea of the passage!**

Step 5: Read and Restate the First Question

Turn every question into a Jeopardy question to simplify.

Let's say the question reads: ***The discussion of the city ecosystem in lines 23-34 ("In spite of…life") is best characterized as***

Turn it into a Jeopardy question: *What does the author say about the city ecosystem?*

Here's another: ***The author would most likely characterize the views of the "critics" referred to in line 33 as***

Jeopardy question: *What are the critics' views and how does the author feel about these views?*

Step 6: Go Back to the Passage and Dig

It is best to ***re-read 3 to 5 lines above and 3 to 5 lines below*** the given line numbers. If the question were to indicate lines 23-34, you would read from lines 18-39, and if the question were to indicate line 33, you would read from lines 28-38. If the line number you are starting from sits in the middle of a sentence, then of course pick up the beginning of that sentence. And don't stop reading at line 38 if you are in the middle of a sentence; read to line 40, or wherever that sentence ends. Likewise, be sure to pick up the beginning or end of the paragraph if the line number you are reading from sits directly above or below.

Step 7: Answer the Question in Your Own Words

This is the big secret, the key to an improved reading comp score! Before you look at those answer choices, be sure to summarize what you have just read and answer the question in your own words!

Step 8: Go to the Answer Choices

Once you've answered the question in your own words (and perhaps written that answer down so you don't allow the answer choices to sway you) you are ready to look at the answers.

Your job is to match a given answer choice with your paraphrased answer. Eliminate all those answer choices that have nothing to do with your paraphrased answer or that fall into one of the categories of Answer Choices to Avoid.

I see a lot of students answer the question in their own words correctly, only to go to the answer choices and be swayed by an answer that does not match their original interpretation. Don't doubt yourself and be easily influenced by cleverly crafted ETS answers when there is an answer choice waiting that totally matches your paraphrase. Trust yourself. Your comprehension is probably correct. JUST PICK THE ANSWER THAT MATCHES! Not the answer that makes you go, "Well, that sounds good, and maybe I'm off track." *Writing down your paraphrased answer will help you stay true to it.*

Exception: Occasionally, no answer choice will match your paraphrase. When this occurs, don't just pick an answer arbitrarily or take your best guess; go back to the passage and dig deeper. Find a way to justify one of the answers with information from the passage.

⟶ **Remember: Only pick an answer choice if you can point your finger to a specific portion of the passage and say, "My proof is right here!"**

⟶ **Repeat Steps 5-8 for every question!**

> *Note: When dealing with a general question, such as a main idea or tone question, you won't have to re-read anything, but be sure you have answered the question in your own words first!*

Here's a list of steps for your reference:

Step 1: Read the Italicized Intro

Step 2: Read the First Paragraph

Step 3: Write Down the Main Idea of the First Paragraph in your Own Words

⟶ *Steps 2 and 3 should be repeated for every paragraph in the passage*

Step 4: Write Down the Main Idea of the Entire Passage

Step 5: Read and Restate the First Question

Step 6: Go Back to the Passage and Dig

⟶ *No digging required on general questions such as main idea or tone*

Step 7: Answer the Question in Your Own Words

Step 8: Go to the Answer Choices

⟶ *Repeat Steps 5-8 for every question*

Let's look at a passage with step-by-step guidelines that will help you accurately apply Technique #1.

Follow the directions and answer the questions as you go.

Directly following the exercise are my marked-up version of the same passage and my own answers to the given questions.

Don't peek! Walk through the passage on your own first!

In the following passage from a newspaper commentary written in 2009, a historian discusses the writing of academic history.

The writing of academic history seems to be in crisis. Historical monographs - scholarly works on highly specific subjects - pour from the university presses (at
Line   least 1,200 or so a year) and yet have very few readers.
5   Sometimes, sales of academic history books number only in the hundreds; if it weren't for library purchases, their sales might be measured in the dozens. Most people, it seems, are not interested in reading history, at least not the history written by academic historians. Although
10   some blame this situation on the poor teaching of history in the schools, most critics seem to think that the problem lies with the academic historians themselves. They don't know how to write history, at least the kind of history that people want to read. After all, David McCullough,
15   Walter Isaacson, Jon Meacham and other popular historians sell hundreds of thousands of books. If they can do it, why can't the academic historians write better, more readable, more accessible history?
         Historians who sell lots of books have always thought
20   that it was their ability to write well that made them popular. Samuel Eliot Morison, a historian who was that rare bird, an academic who was a bestseller during the middle decades of the 20th century, certainly believed that. Academic historians, he said, "have forgotten that
25   there is an art of writing history." Instead of scintillating stories that move, they write "dull, solid, valuable monographs that nobody reads outside the profession." Barbara Tuchman, who was America's most popular historian in the 1960s and 1970s, likewise believed that
30   academic historians did not know how to write. The reason professors of history have so few readers, she said, is that they have had too many captive audiences -- first with the dissertation supervisors, then with their students in lecture halls. They really do not know how
35   "to capture and hold the interests of an audience." McCullough agrees, though he is too polite to put it so bluntly. History is in trouble, he suggests, because most academic historians have forgotten how to tell a story. "That's what history is," he says, "a story."
40   Alas, if it were only that simple. Academic historians have not forgotten how to tell a story. Instead, most of them have purposefully chosen not to tell stories; that is, they have chosen not to write narrative history. Narrative history is a particular kind of history-writing whose
45   popularity comes from the fact that it resembles a story. It

---

Step 1: Read and assess the Italicized Intro

What type of passage are we dealing with?

Humanities

What else can we gather?   *writin*

Academic History

Step 2: Read the 1st paragraph

Be sure to underline what you think is important as you read!

Step 3: Write down the main idea of the 1st paragraph

No popularity for academic history

Step 2: Read the 2nd paragraph, underlining as you go

Step 3: Write down the main idea of the 2nd paragraph

Don't how to write good and appeal to audience

Step 2: Read the 3rd paragraph, underlining as you go

lays out the events of the past in chronological order, with a beginning, middle and end. Such works usually concentrate on individual personalities and on unique public happenings, the kinds of events that might have
50 made headlines in the past: a biography of George Washington, for example, or the story of the election of 1800. Since politics tends to dominate the headlines, politics has traditionally formed the backbone of narrative history.

55   Instead of writing this kind of narrative history, most academic historians, especially at the beginning of their careers, write what might be described as analytic history, specialized and often narrowly focused monographs usually based on their PhD dissertations. Recent examples
60 include an account of artisan workers in Petersburg, Va., between 1820 and 1865, a study of the Republican Party and the African American vote between 1928 and 1952, and an analysis of the aristocracy in the county of Champagne in France between 1100 and 1300. Such
65 particular studies seek to solve problems in the past that the works of previous historians have exposed; or to resolve discrepancies between different historical accounts; or to fill in gaps that the existing historical literature has missed or ignored. In other words, beginning
70 academic historians usually select their topics by surveying what previous academic historians have said. They then find errors, openings or niches in the historiography that they can correct, fill in or build upon. Their studies, however narrow they may seem, are not insignificant. It
75 is through their specialized studies that they contribute to the collective effort of the profession to expand our knowledge of the past.

        The writing of these sorts of historical monographs grew out of the 19th-century noble dream that history
80 might become an objective science, a science that would resemble if not the natural sciences of physics or chemistry, then at least the social sciences -- economics, sociology, anthropology, psychology -- that were emerging at the same time as professionally written history. These
85 scholars assume that history is a kind of science; that is, that historical knowledge is accumulative and that the steady accretion of specialized books and articles will eventually deepen and broaden our understanding of the past. Although recent critics have mocked this "noble
90 dream," the monographs written over the past century have gradually built one upon another to the point where we now know more, and more accurately, about more aspects of past human behavior than ever before.

(For source reference, see endnote ᵈ)

Step 3: Write down the main idea of the 3rd paragraph

Narrative story

Step 2: Read the 4th paragraph, underlining as you go

Step 3: Write down the main idea of the 4th paragraph

use monographs to narrate history

Step 2: Read the 5th paragraph, underlining as you go

Step 3: Write down the main idea of the 5th paragraph

know more monographs

Step 4: Before looking at the questions, write down the main idea of the entire passage

Historical monographs isn't a book it are verbal are

When you're done, let's see how similar our answers are!

In the following passage from a newspaper commentary written in 2009, a historian discusses the writing of academic history.

Step 1: Read and assess the Italicized Intro

What type of passage are we dealing with?
Social Science / History

What else can we gather?
The author is a historian and he's discussing history writing. He probably has a definite opinion because the passage concerns his profession. I will probably see lots of different opinions in this excerpt, so I need to be careful to differentiate the author's opinion from that of other historians, readers, or critics.

Step 2: Read the 1st paragraph

I have underlined what I think may be important.

Step 3: Write down the main idea of the 1st paragraph

Academic history writing is not selling. Critics blame poor writing skills of historians.

Step 2: Read the 2nd paragraph

Step 3: Write down the main idea of the 2nd paragraph

Some historians think academic historians don't know how to write.

Step 2: Read the 3rd paragraph

The writing of academic history seems to be in crisis. Historical monographs - scholarly works on highly specific subjects - pour from the university presses (at least 1,200 or so a year) and yet have very few readers.

Line 5 Sometimes, sales of academic history books number only in the hundreds; if it weren't for library purchases, their sales might be measured in the dozens. Most people, it seems, are not interested in reading history, at least not the history written by academic historians. Although

10 some blame this situation on the poor teaching of history in the schools, most critics seem to think that the problem lies with the academic historians themselves. They don't know how to write history, at least the kind of history that people want to read. After all, David McCullough,

15 Walter Isaacson, Jon Meacham and other popular historians sell hundreds of thousands of books. If they can do it, why can't the academic historians write better, more readable, more accessible history?

Historians who sell lots of books have always thought

20 that it was their ability to write well that made them popular. Samuel Eliot Morison, a historian who was that rare bird, an academic who was a bestseller during the middle decades of the 20th century, certainly believed that. Academic historians, he said, "have forgotten that

25 there is an art of writing history." Instead of scintillating stories that move, they write "dull, solid, valuable monographs that nobody reads outside the profession." Barbara Tuchman, who was America's most popular historian in the 1960s and 1970s, likewise believed that

30 academic historians did not know how to write. The reason professors of history have so few readers, she said, is that they have had too many captive audiences -- first with the dissertation supervisors, then with their students in lecture halls. They really do not know how

35 "to capture and hold the interests of an audience." McCullough agrees, though he is too polite to put it so bluntly. History is in trouble, he suggests, because most academic historians have forgotten how to tell a story. "That's what history is," he says, "a story."

40 Alas, if it were only that simple. Academic historians have not forgotten how to tell a story. Instead, most of them have purposefully chosen not to tell stories; that is, they have chosen not to write narrative history. Narrative history is a particular kind of history-writing whose

45 popularity comes from the fact that it resembles a story. It

lays out the events of the past in chronological order, with a beginning, middle and end. Such works usually concentrate on individual personalities and on unique public happenings, the kinds of events that might have
50 made headlines in the past: a biography of George Washington, for example, or the story of the election of 1800. Since politics tends to dominate the headlines, politics has traditionally formed the backbone of narrative history.

55 Instead of writing this kind of narrative history, most academic historians, especially at the beginning of their careers, write what might be described as analytic history, specialized and often narrowly focused monographs usually based on their PhD dissertations. Recent examples
60 include an account of artisan workers in Petersburg, Va., between 1820 and 1865, a study of the Republican Party and the African American vote between 1928 and 1952, and an analysis of the aristocracy in the county of Champagne in France between 1100 and 1300. Such
65 particular studies seek to solve problems in the past that the works of previous historians have exposed; or to resolve discrepancies between different historical accounts; or to fill in gaps that the existing historical literature has missed or ignored. In other words, beginning
70 academic historians usually select their topics by surveying what previous academic historians have said. They then find errors, openings or niches in the historiography that they can correct, fill in or build upon. Their studies, however narrow they may seem, are not insignificant. It
75 is through their specialized studies that they contribute to the collective effort of the profession to expand our knowledge of the past.

The writing of these sorts of historical monographs grew out of the 19th-century noble dream that history
80 might become an objective science, a science that would resemble if not the natural sciences of physics or chemistry, then at least the social sciences -- economics, sociology, anthropology, psychology -- that were emerging at the same time as professionally written history. These
85 scholars assume that history is a kind of science; that is, that historical knowledge is accumulative and that the steady accretion of specialized books and articles will eventually deepen and broaden our understanding of the past. Although recent critics have mocked this "noble
90 dream," the monographs written over the past century have gradually built one upon another to the point where we now know more, and more accurately, about more aspects of past human behavior than ever before.

Step 3: Write down the main idea of the 3rd paragraph

Academic historians choose not to write narrative history, which tells a story. This is the author's p.o.v.

Step 2: Read the 4th paragraph

Step 3: Write down the main idea of the 4th paragraph

Academics write analytic history that contributes significantly.

Step 2: Read the 5th paragraph

Step 3: Write down the main idea of the 5th paragraph

Monographs have aided our understanding of history.

Step 4: Before looking at the questions, write down the main idea of the entire passage

Academic history writing has contributed significantly and is purposely different from narrative writing.

Now we are ready to tackle the questions.

14. The passage is primarily concerned with the ⟶ Step 5: Read and restate the 1st question

   (A) significance of academic history writing
   (B) benefits of narrative history writing over those of analytic history writing
   (C) decline of good history writing
   (D) difficulty making money as a historian
   (E) inaccuracies present in the writings of narrative historians

_____

_____

_____

Note: This is a general question so we can skip Step 6. No need to dig!

Step 7: Answer the question in your own words

Just use the main idea you've already written down!

_____

_____

_____

Step 8: Go to the answer choices and match your paraphrased answer

Circle your answer!

15. The question in lines 16-18 is intended to ⟶ Step 5: Read and restate the question

   (A) expose the folly of academic history writers
   (B) provide an explanation for the waning sales of history books
   (C) convey a common criticism of academic history writing
   (D) imply that academic historians are poor writers
   (E) suggest that academic history writers should write narrative fiction

_____

_____

_____

Step 6: Go back to the passage and dig

Re-read from line 9 to the end of the paragraph ("Although some...history").

Step 7: Answer the question in your own words

_____

_____

_____

Step 8: Go to the answer choices and match your paraphrased answer

Circle your answer!

16. The critics mentioned in lines 11 and 89 would most likely characterize the view of Samuel Eliot Morison referred to in lines 24-27 ("have forgotten…profession") as

(A) legitimate
(B) flawed
(C) incomprehensible
(D) biased
(E) inconsiderate

Step 5: Read and restate the question
_____
_____
_____

Step 6: Go back to the passage and dig

Re-read the sentence that contains line 11 and the sentence that contains line 89 to familiarize yourself with the critics' stance. Then re-read from the beginning of the 2nd paragraph to line 30 ("Historians…write").

Step 7: Answer the question in your own words
_____
_____
_____

Step 8: Go to the answer choices and match your paraphrased answer

Circle your answer!

---

17. The principal function of the third paragraph is to

(A) support the author's argument presented in the preceding paragraphs
(B) defend historians who write narrative history
(C) detail the significant contribution of analytic history writing
(D) refute a point of view presented in the preceding paragraphs
(E) criticize the viewpoints presented in the previous paragraphs

Step 5: Read and restate the question
_____
_____
_____

Step 6: Go back to the passage and dig

Note: You probably don't need to do any digging, as you've already summarized the main idea of the 3rd paragraph.

Step 7: Answer the question in your own words

Just use your summary of the 3rd paragraph!
_____
_____
_____

Step 8: Go to the answer choices and match your paraphrased answer

Circle your answer!

18. The statement in lines 40-43 ("Academic... history") functions primarily to

(A) mock a ridiculous claim
(B) bolster a widely held opinion
(C) dismiss a conceivable assumption
(D) summarize a well-known fact
(E) undermine a controversial theory

Step 5: Read and restate the question

_____
_____
_____

Step 6: Go back to the passage and dig

Re-read from the beginning of the paragraph to line 52 ("Alas...of 1800").

Step 7: Answer the question in your own words

_____
_____
_____

Step 8: Go to the answer choices and match your paraphrased answer

Circle your answer!

19. The reference to George Washington (lines 50-51) is used to emphasize

(A) an example of an individual who has been featured too prominently in historical biographies
(B) the need for more academic historians to write biographies about famous political figures and events
(C) the importance of politics as a subject of history writing, both narrative and analytic
(D) the extent to which a public figure has shaped America's history
(E) the type of subject matter that fits into the framework of narrative history writing

Step 5: Read and restate the question

_____
_____
_____

Step 6: Go back to the passage and dig

Note: We've actually just read this bit, so we can probably just skip ahead to Step 7.

Step 7: Answer the question in your own words

_____
_____
_____

Step 8: Go to the answer choices and match your paraphrased answer

Circle your answer!

132

20. The three examples discussed in lines 59-64 ("Recent...1300") serve primarily to

$\longrightarrow$ Step 5: Read and restate the question

_____

_____

_____

(A) undermine the methodology of recent academic historians who provide overly narrowed focused monographs

(B) underscore the goal of academic historians to provide more in depth analyses of previously published studies

(C) compare recent academic history writing to that of previous historians

(D) illustrate the types of subject matter that must be explored in order for academic history writing to thrive

(E) explain why academic history writing is declining in readership and sales

Step 6: Go back to the passage and dig

Re-read from the beginning of the paragraph to line 71 ("instead...said").

Step 7: Answer the question in your own words

_____

_____

_____

Step 8: Go to the answer choices and match your paraphrased answer

Circle your answer!

21. The author primarily makes use of which of the following to convey his point?

$\longrightarrow$ Step 5: Read and restate the question

_____

_____

_____

(A) Quotations from critics

(B) Historical facts

(C) Hypothetical scenarios

(D) Examples of his own academic history writing

(E) Comparisons of narrative and analytic history writing

Step 6: Go back to the passage and dig

Note: We can skip Step 7 (we can't very well answer the question in our own words) and instead go straight to the answer choices so that we know what we are looking for as we dig through the passage.

Step 8: Go to the answer choices. Justify your answer with proof from the passage.

Circle your answer!

22. The author's attitude toward the "noble dream" (lines 89-90) is best described as one of

    (A) ambivalence
    (B) dismay
    (C) curiosity
    (D) approval
    (E) surprise

→ Step 5: Read and restate the question

_____
_____
_____

Step 6: Go back to the passage and dig

Re-read from line 84 to the end of the paragraph ("These scholars...before").

Step 7: Answer the question in your own words

_____
_____
_____

Step 8: Go to the answer choices and match your paraphrased answer

Circle your answer!

23. The author lists all of the following as perceived reasons why academic history writing is in crisis EXCEPT

    (A) lack of readership
    (B) insufficient purchases by libraries
    (C) declining sales
    (D) inadequate teaching methods
    (E) poorly written academic histories

→ Step 5: Read and restate the question

_____
_____
_____

Step 6: Go back to the passage and dig

Note: We can skip Step 7 (we can't very well answer the question in our own words) and instead go straight to the answer choices so that we know what we are looking for as we dig through the passage.

Cross off the answer choices you find support for in the passage! Whatever you are left with is the EXCEPT. Circle the leftover answer choice!

24. In the last sentence of the passage (lines 89-93) the author suggests that the

(A) writings of academic history have been invaluable in ascertaining the conduct of humans in the past

(B) "noble dream" of academic history writers has been rightfully mocked

(C) historical knowledge is a type of science that has been unfairly undervalued

(D) recent academic historians have made greater strides in uncovering historical truths than have previous historians who focused on more generalized topics

(E) writings of academic history have helped to shed light on the psychological motivation of past humans.

→ Step 5: Read and restate the question

_____

_____

_____

Note: We've already read line 84 to the end of the paragraph so probably no need to read it again. Skip ahead to Step 7.

Step 7: Answer the question in your own words

_____

_____

_____

Step 8: Go to the answer choices and match your paraphrased answer

Circle your answer!

Now we're ready to check your answers with mine. Don't just look to see what answer choices I've circled. Walk through the technique again with me, so you can see if your way of thinking and your paraphrased answers are similar to mine.

14. The passage is primarily concerned with the

(A) significance of academic history writing
(B) benefits of narrative history writing over those of analytic history writing
(C) decline of good history writing
(D) difficulty making money as a historian
(E) inaccuracies present in the writings of narrative historians

Answer choice (A) definitely matches my paraphrased answer. Let's disprove the other answer choices.

(B) While the author details the differences between narrative and analytic history writing, nowhere in the passage does he say that narrative history writing is better. **The author is standing up for the benefits of analytic writing (lines 73-77)**, so this answer choice runs **opposite** to the author's main idea.

(C) This answer choice falls within a category of bad answer choices because it could very well *offend* historians. It is also straight up wrong, **as the author quite clearly states that historians know how to write (lines 40-43).**

(D) The first paragraph informs us that sales of academic history writing have declined (lines 5-7), but careful of making an *assumption*. Does the author explicitly state that historians are having trouble paying the bills? Absolutely not! **The author never tells us how this crisis is affecting historians,** and we cannot draw our own conclusions.

(E) **Nowhere in the passage does the author say that narrative historians have their facts mixed up.** This answer choice is not at all supported by information in the passage.

15. The question in lines 16-18 is intended to

(A) expose the folly of academic history writers
(B) provide an explanation for the waning sales of history books
(C) convey a common criticism of academic history writing
(D) imply that academic historians are poor writers
(E) suggest that academic history writers should write narrative fiction

136

Answer choice (C) is a match: *criticism of academic history writing (critics and others think academic historians are poor writers).* Let's de-justify the other answer choices.

(A) It is important to understand that the author's opinion is NOT the opinion of *most critics*. Yes, the question represents the critics' opinions, but we know the author doesn't think academic history writers are foolish, and I don't think the critics would be this harsh in their assessment either. **We can eliminate (A) because it is *offensive* and not very on target.**

(B) Let's be clear: *most critics* believe that the reason people aren't *interested* in reading academic history books is due to the academic historians' poor writing skills (lines 7-14). But the author does not believe there is a modicum of truth to this. Answer choice (B) would indicate that the author is using the critics' explanations as justification for poor sales, which would go against the main idea of the passage. Also consider that the question is not an *explanation* of anything, but a criticism of academic history writers. **The author states the question to point out the critics' oversimplified and ill-reasoned thought process.**

(D) **Although the critics for the most part believe that academic historians are poor writers, the author doesn't,** so categorize this question as *harsh and offensive* and eliminate it.

(E) The author does not allude to narrative fiction until the third paragraph, in which he details his point of view: **academic writers choose not to write narrative fiction because they are setting out to accomplish something different.** The critics don't seem to know or care about the difference between the narrative history and analytic history; they just want the academic historians to write better. This answer choice is definitely off target and not in line with the main idea.

---

16. The critics mentioned in lines 11 and 89 would most likely characterize the view of Samuel Eliot Morison referred to in lines 24-27 ("have forgotten…profession") as

   (A) legitimate
   (B) flawed
   (C) incomprehensible
   (D) biased
   (E) inconsiderate

Step 5: Read and restate the question

Do the critics agree or disagree with S. E. Morison?

Step 6: Go back to the passage and dig

Re-read the sentence that contains line 11 and the sentence that contains line 89 to familiarize yourself with the critics' stance. Then re-read from the beginning of the 2nd paragraph to line 30 ("Historians…write").

Step 7: Answer the question in your own words

Critics' stance: Academic historians don't know how to write. S. E. Morison: Academic historians' writing is boring. They agree!

We know we are looking for an adjective that shows agreement. **Answer (A)** *Legitimate*, **means** *valid*. Let's find out what's wrong with the other answer choices.

(B) *Flawed* means *wrong*, **the opposite of what we're looking for.**

(C) *Incomprehensible* means *unable to be understood*, and the critics' are perfectly able to understand what Morison is talking about. **They agree with him!**

(D) *Biased* means *unfair*. Careful of making an **assumption**. Sure, Morison might be a bit biased in his assessment - he is a best-selling historian – but would the *critics* say he is biased in his assessment? No! Again, they **support his assessment.**

(E) *Inconsiderate* means *selfish*, and **the critics don't think Morison is being selfish.**

17. The principal function of the third paragraph is to

(A) support the author's argument presented in the preceding paragraphs
(B) defend historians who write narrative history
(C) detail the significant contribution of analytic history writing
(D) refute a point of view presented in the preceding paragraphs
(E) criticize the viewpoints presented in the previous paragraphs

Step 5: Read and restate the question

What's the main idea of the 3rd paragraph?

Step 6: Go back to the passage and dig

I've already summarized it!

Step 7: Answer the question in your own words

Academic historians choose not to write narrative history, which tells a story. This is the author's opinion!

At first glance, none of the answer choices pop out as a match for my paraphrased answer. Let's dissect the answers.

(A) *Support the author's argument* – YES! *Presented in the preceding paragraphs* – NO! This answer choice falls into the category of **partial answers. The author's argument is not presented in preceding paragraphs; it is presented in THIS paragraph.**

(B) The author IS defending historians – *academic historians*, NOT *historians who write narrative fiction*. **Writers of narrative history do not need defending in this passage, as they are not the ones who are coming under attack.**

(C) The author does detail the contribution of analytic writing, but in the *final paragraph* NOT in **the 3rd paragraph**, which **makes no mention of analytic writing.**

(D) What is the point of view presented in the preceding paragraphs? *Academic historians DON'T know how to write well*. What is the point of view presented in the 3rd paragraph? *Academic historians DO know how to write well; they just choose not to write narrative history*. **The author is indeed refuting (proving false) the point of view presented in the 1st and 2nd paragraphs.**

(E) While the author addresses the viewpoints presented in the previous paragraphs, **to say that he criticizes them is much too *extreme*. Eliminate extremes!**

18. The statement in lines 40-43 ("Academic... history") functions primarily to

(A) mock a ridiculous claim
(B) bolster a widely held opinion
(C) dismiss a conceivable assumption
(D) summarize a well-known fact
(E) undermine a controversial theory

Step 5: Read and restate the question

What is the author getting at with this statement and why?

Step 6: Go back to the passage and dig

Re-read from the beginning of the paragraph to line 52 ("Alas...of 1800").

Step 7: Answer the question in your own words

This is the author's main idea: Academic historians do indeed know how to write.

This one might be difficult to match right away as well. Let's dissect the answer choices.

(A) We've already established that the critics' point of view isn't too *ridiculous*, and I don't think the author is at all *mocking* the critics. Rather, **he disagrees quite pleasantly**. The word "mock" is too **extreme**.

(B) The author expresses his *opinion* in this statement, but do we know that his opinion is *widely-held?* Remember: we shouldn't make ANY **assumptions**. The word **"widely-held" is not supported by the information in the passage and is arguably too *extreme*.**

(C) *Dismiss* means *reject*. **The statement in lines 40-43 is essentially the author's opinion, which directly contradicts (*rejects*) the view of *most critics* and *historians who sell a lot of books* (line 19).** The critics and other historians believe that academic historians for the most part have forgotten how to write interesting history. Is this assumption at all *conceivable* (believable)? Sure. While a bit offensive, the assumption isn't too far-fetched.

(D) The author is *summarizing HIS OPINION*, but **his opinion is not fact.**

(E) The author may be *undermining the critics' point of view*, but is the critics' point of view a *controversial theory?* No. **It is an OPINION, and we don't even know how controversial that opinion is.**

139

19. The reference to George Washington (lines 50-51) is used to emphasize

(A) an example of an individual who has been featured too prominently in historical biographies
(B) the need for more academic historians to write biographies about famous political figures and events
(C) the importance of politics as a subject of history writing, both narrative and analytic
(D) the extent to which a public figure has shaped America's history
(E) the type of subject matter that fits into the framework of narrative history writing

Step 5: Read and restate the question

Why does the author mention George?

Step 6: Go back to the passage and dig

I've already read this, so I can skip ahead to Step 7.

Step 7: Answer the question in your own words

George is an example of a topic that historians write about in narrative history.

Answer choice (E) is the winner: *the type of subject matter (George) fits into the framework of narrative history (write about in narrative history).* Let's de-justify the answers that don't match my paraphrase.

(A) We have a *partial answer. An example of an individual who has been featured* works, but *too prominently is too extreme.* Notice that "too!"
(B) **George is being used as an example of the type of subject that shows up in narrative history writing,** NOT as a call for more academic historians to write about political figures.
(C) The last sentence of the paragraph reads, *politics has traditionally formed the backbone of narrative history.* **Nowhere does the author state that politics is an IMPORTANT subject; he simply implies that it is a POPULAR one.**
(D) While George has indeed *shaped America's history,* **this answer choice is off-topic and not at all what the author is aiming to convey.**

20. The three examples discussed in lines 59-64 ("Recent...1300") serve primarily to

(A) undermine the methodology of recent academic historians who provide overly narrowed focused monographs
(B) underscore the goal of academic historians to provide more in depth analyses of previously published studies
(C) compare recent academic history writing to that of previous historians
(D) illustrate the types of subject matter that must be explored in order for academic history writing to thrive
(E) explain why academic history writing is declining in readership and sales

Step 5: Read and restate the question

Why does the author use these three examples? What's the point?

Step 6: Go back to the passage and dig

Re-read from the beginning of the paragraph to line 71 ("instead...said").

Step 7: Answer the question in your own words

Examples of the specialized topics academic historians write about. They expand on previous historians' works.

140

Answer choice (B) pretty much matches my paraphrase. *Underscore* might have confused you. *Underscore* means to *highlight or emphasize. To provide more in depth analyses of previously published studies (to expand on previous historians' works).* Let's prove the other answer choices wrong.

(A) *recent academic historians* DO provide *overly narrowed focused monographs,* but **the author is not UNDERMINING the academic historians; his essay is in SUPPORT of them.** We have a *partial answer* on our hands. The word "overly" is also too *extreme*.

(C) While the author does discuss the methodology of *recent academic history writers,* and its relation to the *works of previous historians* (line 66), **nowhere in the passage does the author inform us of the methodology of past historians.** It might be different than that of recent academic historians, but it might also be the same.

(D) These examples **illustrate the types of subject matter that ARE being explored, not those that MUST be explored.** These topics have recently been explored and academic history writing *isn't thriving,* so this answer choice is clearly not supported by information in the passage.

(E) This paragraph is **NOT about why academic history writing readership and sales are declining.** Information regarding sales and readership can be found in the 1st paragraph, not the 4th.

21. The author primarily makes use of which of the following to convey his point?

(A) Quotations from critics
(B) Historical facts
(C) Hypothetical scenarios
(D) Examples of his own academic history writing
(E) Comparisons of narrative and analytic history writing

Step 5: Read and restate the question

What device does the author use A LOT in the passage?

Step 6: Go back to the passage and dig

Note: We can skip Step 7 (we can't very well answer the question in our own words) and instead go straight to the answer choices so that we know what we are looking for as we dig through the passage.

I can find possible justification for two of the answer choices: (A) and (E).

(A) Quotations abound in the 2nd paragraph, but dig deeper. Who exactly is the author quoting? *Samuel Eliot Morison* (a historian), *Barbara Tuchman* (a historian), *David McCullough* (a historian). While these historians may be criticizing academic history writers, some of them ARE academic historians. **The author has clearly differentiated between critics and historians, so (A) is a** *partial answer. Quotations* works, but *from critics* does not.

(E) The author discusses *narrative history writing* and *analytic history writing* in detail, clearly contrasting each. **Three paragraphs of the passage are devoted to such an analysis.** (E) is the most supported answer choice.

Nowhere does the author mention (B) *historical facts* (he mentions historical subjects), (C) *hypothetical scenarios,* or (D) *examples of his own writing*.

22. The author's attitude toward the "noble dream" (lines 89-90) is best described as one of

    (A) ambivalence
    (B) dismay
    (C) curiosity
    (D) approval
    (E) surprise

> **Step 5: Read and restate the question**

What does the author think about the "noble dream"?

> **Step 6: Go back to the passage and dig**

Re-read from line 84 to the end of the paragraph ("these scholars...before").

> **Step 7: Answer the question in your own words**

The "noble dream" is expanding our knowledge of the past and the author thinks this is good.

Answer choice (D) *approval* **matches my paraphrase** (*the author thinks this is good*). Let's refute the other answers.

    (A) *Ambivalence* means *having conflicting feelings.* **The author is clear on how he feels:** *Their studies, however narrow they may seem, are not insignificant* (lines 73-74).
    (B) *Dismay* means *disappointment*, and **the author is not disappointed;** he feels the *noble dream* is worthwhile.
    (C) The author is not *curious*, or *questioning*. **He has formed his opinion.**
    (E) The author is not *surprised*. **He is much too analytical.**

23. The author lists all of the following as perceived reasons why academic history writing is in crisis EXCEPT

    (A) lack of readership
    (B) insufficient purchases by libraries
    (C) declining sales
    (D) inadequate teaching methods
    (E) poorly written academic histories

> **Step 5: Read and restate the question**

What is mentioned as reasons for the crisis? Pay attention to "perceived" – these reasons may not necessarily be true.

> **Step 6: Go back to the passage and dig**

Note: We can skip Step 7 (we can't very well answer the question in our own words) and instead go straight to the answer choices so that we know what we are looking for as we dig through the passage.

Cross off the answer choices you find support for in the passage! Whatever you are left with is the EXCEPT.

(A) **Check out line 4:** *have very few readers.* I can cross out (A) because it can't be my EXCEPT. I have found justification.

(B) I think I've found the EXCEPT. In **lines 6-7** the passage reads, *If it weren't for library purchases, their sales might be measured in the dozens.* **Currently the sales are in the hundreds BECAUSE OF library purchases, which are not indicated as insufficient, but exactly the opposite.**

(C) **Proof for declining sales is in lines 5-6:** *Sometimes sales of academic history books number only in the hundreds.*

(D) **Lines 9-11 read,** *Although some blame this situation on the poor teaching of history in the schools,* which gives us the proof we need for *inadequate teaching methods.*

(E) **In reference to academic historians, lines 12-14 read,** *They don't know how to write history, at least the kind of history that people want to read.* Obviously some people PERCEIVE *academic histories to be poorly written.*

24. In the last sentence of the passage (lines 89-93) the author suggests that the

> Step 5: Read and restate the question

What is the author saying in the last sentence?

(A) writings of academic history have been invaluable in ascertaining the conduct of humans in the past

(B) "noble dream" of academic history writers has been rightfully mocked

(C) historical knowledge is a type of science that has been unfairly undervalued

(D) recent academic historians have made greater strides in uncovering historical truths than have previous historians who focused on more generalized topics

(E) writings of academic history have helped to shed light on the psychological motivation of past humans.

> Step 6: Go back to the passage and dig

No need to read again. I'm skipping directly to Step 7.

> Step 7: Answer the question in your own words

Monographs have aided our understanding of history.

Notice how I just used my summary of the last paragraph!

You might have to dig a bit deeper to justify answer choice (A). The last two lines of the passage state: *we now know more, and more accurately, about more aspects of past human behavior than ever before.* **This statement indicates that the writings have been helpful in understanding how humans behaved (or conducted) themselves in the past.**

Let's prove the other answer choices wrong.

(B) **The author likes the *noble dream*,** remember? He wouldn't agree that it is *rightfully mocked.*

(C) The final paragraph does refer to *history as an objective science,* but **nowhere does the author indicate that historical knowledge has been unfairly undervalued.** *Unfairly* is an adverb that expresses degree and makes this answer choice too ***extreme.***

(D) We have a *comparison* here, and that falls into a Bad Answer Choice category. **There is also no support for this idea in the passage.**

(E) We have a *partial answer.* The first part works: *writings of academic history have helped shed light on.* The second part – *psychological motivations* – is off. **Behavior of past humans is justified;** *psychological makeup* **of past humans is not.**

If you liked this technique, stick with it and apply it to the passages in Chapters 6 and 7. If you aren't so sure or are curious about the other techniques, then work through Chapters 6 and 7 following the techniques described in those chapters.

Chapter 6
Technique #2
Bite-Sized Bits

For those of you who prefer bite-sized bits we have Technique #2 to the rescue. Technique #2 shares many steps in common with Technique #1, but instead of reading the passage in one go, we read and answer questions paragraph-by-paragraph.

Step 1: Read the Italicized Introduction

Be sure to note the type of passage and the topic discussed.

Step 2: Read the First Paragraph

While reading, underline what you think may be important and circle transition words that signify a shift or emphasis in thought.

therefore	however	yet	still	although	likewise	but

Note: Underlining and circling keep you reading actively, which helps you maintain focus and keep that brain awake and alive!

Step 3: Write down the Main Idea of Paragraph 1 in Your Own Words

I don't want you to write a novel; a brief summary will do.

Examples: *Historical figures shouldn't be idolized* or *No one really knows what causes yawning*

Step 4: Read and Restate the First Specific Question that Pertains to Paragraph 1

$\longrightarrow$ **Leave all general questions (main idea, overall tone or mood, etc.) for the very end. Circle them, or write the question #'s after the last question of the passage so you don't forget to go back and answer them!**

Turn the question into a Jeopardy question to simplify.

Let's say the question reads: **Mr. Holloway's comments in lines 2-9 ("A reasonable…offer") indicate that a divorce is suitable when**

Turn it into a Jeopardy question: *What does Mr. Holloway say about divorce?*

Here's another: **The author's attitude toward the "renovation" (line 5) is best described as one of**

Jeopardy question: *What does the author say about the renovation and how does he feel about it?*

Step 5: Go Back to the Paragraph and Dig

Since you are digesting the passage one paragraph at a time you may not even have to go back and re-read, but by all means, feel free to dig. **_Re-read 3-5 lines above and 3-5 lines below_** the cited line numbers. If the question were to indicate lines 2-9, you would read from the beginning of the paragraph to line 12, and if the question were to indicate line 3, you would read from the beginning of the paragraph to line 6. If the line number you are starting from sits in the middle of a sentence, then of course pick up the beginning of that sentence. And don't stop reading at line 6 if you are in the middle of a sentence; read to line 8, or wherever that sentence ends.

Step 6: Answer the Question in Your Own Words

This is the big secret, the key to an improved reading comp score! Before you look at those answer choices, be sure to summarize what you have just read and answer the question in your own words.

Step 7: Go to the Answer Choices

Once you've answered the question in your own words (and perhaps written that answer down so you don't allow the answer choices to sway you) you are ready to look at the answers.

Your job is to match a given answer choice with your stated answer. Get rid of all those answer choices that have nothing to do with your stated answer or that fall into one of the categories of Answer Choices to Avoid.

I see a lot of students answer the question in their own words correctly, only to go to the answer choices and be tricked by an answer that does not match their original interpretation. Don't doubt yourself and be easily influenced by cleverly crafted ETS answers when there is an answer choice waiting that totally matches your paraphrase. Trust yourself. Your comprehension is probably correct. JUST PICK THE ANSWER THAT MATCHES! Not the answer that makes you go, "Well, that sounds good, and maybe I'm off track." **_Writing down your paraphrased answer will help you stay true to it._**

146

Exception: Occasionally, no answer choice will match your paraphrase. When this occurs, don't just pick an answer arbitrarily or take your best guess; go back to the passage and dig deeper. Find a way to justify one of the answers with information from the passage.

⟶ **Remember: Only pick an answer choice if you can point to a specific portion of the passage and say, "My proof is right here!"**

It is an open book test after all!

⟶ **Repeat Steps 4-7 for every specific question pertaining to Paragraph 1**

*Once you have answered all the specific questions about Paragraph 1, you are ready to move on to Paragraph 2. Repeat steps 2-7.

Paragraph 2
Step 2: Read Paragraph 2
Step 3: Write down the Main Idea of Paragraph 2 in Your Own Words
Step 4: Read and Restate the First Specific Question that Pertains to Paragraph 2
Step 5: Go Back to the Paragraph and Dig
Step 6: Answer the Question in Your Own Words
Step 7: Go to the Answer Choices
        Repeat Steps 4-7 for every specific question pertaining to Paragraph 2

⟶ **Repeat Steps 2-7 for every paragraph of the passage**

Step 8: Write Down the Main Idea of the Entire Passage in Your Own Words

We still have all those general questions to answer, remember? Before answering any general questions paraphrase the main idea. Again, don't write too much, just a brief summary.

Examples: *Thoreau mourning destruction of nature in Walden*
          Popularity of a painting has less to do with artistic skill and more to do with politics

> *Note:* If you are having trouble identifying the main idea, first ask: *What is the subject or topic of the passage?* (For example, *audio books.*) Then ask: *What does the passage say about this subject?* (For example, *audio books are distracting when read by the wrong gender.*)

$\longrightarrow$ **Remember: Every correct answer is in line with the main idea of the passage!**

*If you state the main idea, and some of your answers to specific questions don't support that main idea, you may want to recheck those answers. At this point, you will have read the entire passage, which will shed more light on ALL of the questions.

Step 9: Answer All General Questions

Don't forget to go back and answer the general questions you've left blank. Perhaps before you even read the passage jot down a note at the end of the section to jog your memory. Or put a gigantic circle around the general questions so that you just can't miss them. You've already stated the main idea, but if you are dealing with a tone or mood question, be sure to come up with your own answer before skimming through the answer choices. Keep in mind good versus bad answer choices!

Let's work through a passage together using Technique #2.

Here's a list of steps for your reference:

Step 1: Read the Italicized Intro

Step 2: Read the First Paragraph

Step 3: Write down the Main Idea of Paragraph 1 in your Own Words

Step 4: Read and Restate the 1st Specific Question that Pertains to Paragraph 1

Step 5: Go Back to the Paragraph and Dig

Step 6: Answer the Question in Your Own Words

Step 7: Go to the Answer Choices

$\longrightarrow$ *Repeat Steps 4-7 for every specific question pertaining to Paragraph 1*

$\longrightarrow$ *Repeat Steps 2-7 for every paragraph of the passage*

Step 8: Write Down the Main Idea of the Entire Passage in Your Own Words

Step 9: Answer All General Questions

Following is a passage with step-by-step guidelines that will help you accurately apply Technique #2. The passage is divided into paragraphs with applicable questions written to the side. This is, of course, not the way the passage will appear on the SAT; it is formatted for teaching purposes only. Follow the directions and answer the questions as you go. Directly following are my marked-up version of the same passage and my own answers to the given questions.

Don't peek! Walk through the passage on your own first!

The following excerpt is from a 2003 book written by a former Yale professor emeritus of physics.

→ Step 1: Read and assess the Italicized Intro

What type of passage are we dealing with?

_____

What else can we gather?

_____

Galileo (1564-1642) was the first to develop a quantitative approach to the study of motion of everyday objects. In addition to this fundamental work, he
Line constructed one of the first telescopes and used it to study
5 our planetary system. His observation of the moons of Jupiter gave man his first glimpse of a miniature world system that confirmed the concepts put forward previously by Copernicus (1473 -1543).

(For source reference, see endnote ᵉ)

→ Step 2: Read the 1st paragraph

Be sure to underline what you think is important as you read!

Step 3: Write down the main idea of the 1st paragraph in your own words

_____Galileo____works____

_____

Time to look at the questions!

10. The primary purpose of the passage is to

(A) contrast two opposing scientific theories
(B) discuss one scientist's contribution to modern physics
(C) lament the inaccuracy of a compelling theory
(D) criticize the lack of research on the topic of motion
(E) analyze the inherent differences between physics and philosophy

→ *Put a big circle around this general question, or go to the end of the passage (question #18) and write "#10" so you don't forget to come back!*

11. The purpose of the first paragraph (lines 1-8) is to

(A) provide evidence in support of a controversial theory
(B) challenge the findings of a well-known scientist
(C) introduce the contributions of a classical physicist
(D) present a topic of interest to most scientists
(E) compare two scientists' theories on the planetary system

Step 4: Read and restate the 1st specific question that pertains to paragraph 1

_____

_____

Note: Let's skip Step 5 (no need to dig) and jump to Step 6.

Step 6: Answer the question in your own words

_____

_____

Step 7: Go to the answer choices

Circle your answer!

149

12. The question in lines 10-12 ("Is it...or what?") primarily serves to

    (A) imply that Galileo was at first off-course in his method of reasoning

    (B) propel the reader into making his own guess

    (C) suggest that Galileo was asking the wrong question

    (D) posit possible theories Galileo was attempting to test

    (E) contradict Galileo's method of observation

Notice how #12 refers to lines 10-12, which are in the 2nd paragraph.

Stop! Before we go any further we need to repeat Steps 2-7.

Galileo set out to answer the question: what property
10 of motion is related to force? Is it the position of the
moving object or its velocity or its rate of change of
velocity, or what? The answer to this question can only
be obtained from observations; this is a basic feature of
Physics that sets it apart from Philosophy proper.
15 Galileo observed that force influences changes in
velocity (accelerations) of an object and that, in the
absence of external forces (e.g. friction), no force is
needed to keep an object in motion that is traveling in
a straight line with constant speed. This observationally
20 based law is called the *Law of Inertia*.

(For source reference, see endnote [e])

| Step 2: Read the 2nd paragraph |

| Step 3: Write down the main idea of the 2nd paragraph in your own words |

Physics _____

_____

| Step 4: Read and restate the 1st specific question that pertains to paragraph 2 |

_____

_____

| Step 5: Go back to the paragraph and dig |

Re-read from the beginning of the 2nd paragraph to line 14 ("Galileo...proper").

| Step 6: Answer the question in your own words |

_____

_____

| Step 7: Go to the answer choices |

Circle your answer!

Stop! Repeat Steps 2-7 for paragraph 3.

12. The question in lines 10-12 ("Is it...or what?") primarily serves to

    (A) imply that Galileo was at first off course in his method of reasoning

    (B) propel the reader into making his own guess

    (C) suggest that Galileo was asking the wrong question

    (D) posit possible theories Galileo was attempting to test

    (E) contradict Galileo's method of observation

25　　It is, perhaps, difficult for us to appreciate the impact
of Galileo's new ideas concerning motion. The fact that
an object resting on a horizontal surface remains at rest
unless something we call force is applied to change its
state of rest was, of course, well-known before Galileo's
30　time. However, the fact that the object continues to move
after the force ceases to be applied caused considerable
conceptual difficulties to the early Philosophers. The
observation that, in practice, an object comes to rest due
to frictional forces and air resistance was recognized
35　by Galileo to be a side effect and not germane to the
fundamental question of motion. Aristotle, for example,
believed that the true or natural state of motion is one
of rest. It is instructive to consider Aristotle's conjecture
from the viewpoint of the Principle of Relativity: is a
40　natural state of rest consistent with this general Principle?
First, we must consider what is meant by a natural state
of rest; it means that in a particular frame of reference,
the object in question is stationary. Now, according to the
general Principle of Relativity, the laws of motion have
45　the same form in all frames of reference that move with
constant speed in straight lines with respect to each other.
An observer in a reference frame moving with constant
speed in a straight line with respect to the reference
frame in which the object is at rest, would conclude that
50　the natural state of motion of the object is one of constant
speed in a straight line and not one of rest. All inertial
observers, in an infinite number of frames of reference,
would come to the same conclusion. We see, therefore,
that Aristotle's conjecture is not consistent with this
55　fundamental Principle.

(For source reference, see endnote ᵉ)

Motion Galileo Aristotle

Step 3: Write down the main idea of the
3rd paragraph in your own words

*This is a long paragraph, so feel free to
break it down into two chunks with two
main ideas.*

_____

_____

_____

_____

(Galileo
observation
on motions
of
fact

13. The statement in lines 25-26 ("It is… motion") suggests that

(A) contemporary scientists often disregard the foundations laid by classical physicists
(B) the reader, without a sound grasp of physics, cannot understand the principles of the Law of Inertia
(C) the reader has difficulty appreciating Galileo's ideas because they contradict the laws of motion
(D) Galileo's ideas offered explanations to conceptual theories that had befuddled early philosophers
(E) Galileo's ideas are too simple to be duly appreciated

⟶

Step 4: Read and restate the 1st specific question that pertains to paragraph 3

_____

_____

Step 5: Go back to the paragraph and dig

Re-read from the beginning of the 3rd paragraph to line 32 ("It is…philosophers").

Step 6: Answer the question in your own words

_____

_____

Step 7: Go to the answer choices

Circle your answer!

Stop! Repeat Steps 4-7 for #14.

14. In line 35, "germane" most nearly means

(A) advantageous
(B) originated
(C) unnecessary
(D) opposed
(E) connected

⟶

Step 4: Read and restate the next specific question that pertains to paragraph 3

_____

_____

Step 5: Go back to the paragraph and dig

Re-read from line 32 to line 38 ("The observation…rest").

Step 6: Answer the question in your own words

This requires coming up with your own word for "germane."

_____

_____

Step 7: Go to the answer choices

Circle your answer!

Stop! Repeat Steps 4-7 for #15.

15. In order for Aristotle's hypothesis in lines 36-38 ("Aristotle...rest") to be correct, which statement would have to be true of an object in motion?

(A) The object will not remain in motion unless a force acts continually on it

(B) The object will remain in motion if there are no external forces acting upon it

(C) The object moves at a far slower rate the heavier its mass

(D) The object moves at a far faster rate the heavier its mass

(E) Its speed is faster when the object is traveling in a straight line

→ Step 4: Read and restate the question

_____

_____

Step 5: Go back to the paragraph and dig

We've already read 5 lines above twice, so let's just pick up five lines below. Re-read from line 36 to line 43 ("Aristotle...stationary"). Why line 43 and not 41? Because line 41 leaves us in the middle of a sentence!

Step 6: Answer the question in your own words

_____

_____

Step 7: Go to the answer choices

Circle your answer!

Stop! Repeat Steps 4-7 for #16.

16. The author argues that Aristotle's theory on the laws of motion is inaccurate because

(A) an object does not appear at rest from all frames of reference

(B) it does not address the effect of force on an object

(C) force is needed to change the state of an object at rest

(D) an object appears at rest no matter the frame of reference

(E) an object is never truly at rest

→ Step 4: Read and restate the question

_____

_____

Step 5: Go back to the paragraph and dig

Pick up where you left off at line 43 and read to the end of the passage ("Now...Principle").

Step 6: Answer the question in your own words

_____

_____

Step 7: Go to the answer choices

Circle your answer!

Stop! Repeat Steps 4-7 for #17.

17. The author makes use of all of the following EXCEPT

   (A) rhetorical questions
   (B) comparison and contrast
   (C) personal experience
   (D) concrete details
   (E) general statements

Step 4: Read and restate the question

_____

_____

Step 5: Go back to the passage and dig

Note: We can skip Step 6 (we can't very well answer the question in our own words) and instead go straight to the answer choices so we know what we are looking for as we dig through the passage.

Cross off the answer choices you find support for in the passage! Whatever you are left with is the EXCEPT. Circle the leftover answer choice!

Stop! Repeat Steps 4-7 for #18.

18. The last sentence of the passage primarily serves to

   (A) emphasize the author's opinion
   (B) answer a question posed earlier in the passage
   (C) reiterate the fundamentals of a problem
   (D) summarize the author's evidence
   (E) suggest a topic for further research

Step 4: Read and restate the question

_____

_____

Step 5: Go back to the paragraph and dig

We've just read this sentence. You may be able to jump to Step 6.

Step 6: Answer the question in your own words

_____

_____

Step 7: Go to the answer choices

Circle your answer!

Stop! Don't forget to go back to #10.

Remember Step 8 before answering any general questions.

Step 8: State the main idea of the entire passage in your own words

_____

_____

_____

_____

Step 9: Answer all general questions

10. The primary purpose of the passage is to ⟶ Step 4: Read and restate the 1st general question

(A) contrast two opposing scientific theories
(B) discuss one scientist's contribution to modern physics
(C) lament the inaccuracy of a compelling theory
(D) criticize the lack of research on the topic of motion
(E) analyze the inherent differences between physics and philosophy

_____

_____

Nothing to dig for so jump to Step 6.

Step 6: Answer the question in your own words

You already did this in Step 8. Use your main idea!

_____

_____

Step 7: Go to the answer choices

Circle your answer!

You did it! Now we're ready to check your answers with mine.

Don't just look to see what answer choices I've circled. Walk through the technique again with me, so you can see if your way of thinking and your paraphrased answers are similar to mine.

The following excerpt is from a 2003 book written by a former Yale professor emeritus of physics.

Galileo (1564-1642) was the first to develop a quantitative approach to the study of motion of everyday objects. In addition to this fundamental work, he
Line constructed one of the first telescopes and used it to study
5 our planetary system. His observation of the moons of Jupiter gave man his first glimpse of a miniature world system that confirmed the concepts put forward previously by Copernicus (1473 -1543).

10. The primary purpose of the passage is to

(A) contrast two opposing scientific theories
(B) discuss one scientist's contribution to modern physics
(C) lament the inaccuracy of a compelling theory
(D) criticize the lack of research on the topic of motion
(E) analyze the inherent differences between physics and philosophy

11. The purpose of the first paragraph (lines 1-8) is to

(A) provide evidence in support of a controversial theory
(B) challenge the findings of a well-known scientist
(C) introduce the contributions of a classical physicist
(D) present a topic of interest to most scientists
(E) compare two scientists' theories on the planetary system

Step 1: Read and assess the Italicized Intro

What type of passage are we dealing with?

Science.

What else can we gather?

Not much else.

Step 2: Read the 1st paragraph

I have underlined what I think may be important.

Step 3: Write down the main idea of the 1st paragraph in your own words

Galileo made many important findings.

This is a general question so it needs a circle!

I'll skip to question 11 because it's the first specific question.

Step 4: Read and restate the 1st specific question that pertains to paragraph 1

What's the main idea of the 1st paragraph?

Note: No need to dig. Jump to Step 6!

Step 6: Answer the question in your own words

It's the main idea I already wrote down. Galileo made many important findings.

Step 7: Go to the answer choices

156

Answer choice (C) matches my paraphrased answer: *contributions (findings) of a classical physicist (Galileo).* Let's refute the other answer choices just in case.

(A) If you picked (A) perhaps your line of thought was something like, *the concepts put forward previously by Copernicus* (line 8) could be interpreted as a *theory* and Galileo *confirmed* these concepts. I see the justification, **but it is not the ENTIRE PURPOSE of the paragraph**. It's a bit *too specific* for my liking. And while Copernicus's theory was *controversial*, this fact is not stated in the passage, and remember, ETS does not expect you to rely on background "information."

(B) We have a *partial answer*. *Findings of a well-known scientist* works, but *challenge*? **There is no challenging going on.**

(D) How do we know Galileo is *a topic of interest to most scientists?* **For all we know most scientists might be bored to death of that topic.** Answer choice (D) is one *assumption* we DON'T want to make. The *most* is also *extreme*.

(E) Like (A), I would argue that this answer is *too dang specific.* **While the author states that Galileo confirmed Copernicus's ideas, he doesn't make an outright comparison**, and certainly not a detailed enough one to serve as the purpose of the WHOLE paragraph.

12. The question in lines 10-12 ("Is it...or what?") primarily serves to

(A) imply that Galileo was at first off course in his method of reasoning
(B) propel the reader into making his own guess
(C) suggest that Galileo was asking the wrong question
(D) posit possible theories Galileo was attempting to test
(E) contradict Galileo's method of observation

Notice how #12 refers to lines 10-12, which are in the 2nd paragraph.

Stop! Before we go any further we need to repeat Steps 2-7.

Galileo set out to answer the question: what property
10 of motion is related to force? Is it the position of the moving object or its velocity or its rate of change of velocity, or what? The answer to this question can only be obtained from observations; this is a basic feature of Physics that sets it apart from Philosophy proper.
15 Galileo observed that force influences changes in velocity (accelerations) of an object and that, in the absence of external forces (e.g. friction), no force is needed to keep an object in motion that is traveling in a straight line with constant speed. This observationally
20 based law is called the *Law of Inertia.*

Step 2: Read the 2nd paragraph

Step 3: Write down the main idea of the 2nd paragraph in your own words

Galileo observed the Law of Inertia.

12. The question in lines 10-12 ("Is it...or what?") primarily serves to

(A) imply that Galileo was at first off-course in his method of reasoning
(B) propel the reader into making his own guess
(C) suggest that Galileo was asking the wrong question
(D) posit possible theories Galileo was attempting to test
(E) contradict Galileo's method of observation

Answer choice (D) is my best match: *posit possible theories (asking questions)* and *attempting to test (tried to determine)*. Let's analyze the others.

(A The correct answer definitely has something to do with Galileo's *method of reasoning,* **but the author is certainly not implying that Galileo was *off-course* with his reasoning.** After all, Galileo's reasoning led him to the Law of Inertia (lines 19-20).
(B) At first glance, this answer choice looks sneakily legit, and might just be if we didn't have a better answer to choose. **The passage as a whole doesn't seem to be too intimate or interactive.** It is much more factual.
(C) Like (A), **the author doesn't think Galileo was off-base with his thinking.**
(E) Galileo's *method of observation* led him to the Law of Inertia, **so the author SUPPORTS, not contradicts Galileo's method.**

25   It is, perhaps, difficult for us to appreciate the impact
of Galileo's new ideas concerning motion. The fact that
an object resting on a horizontal surface remains at rest
unless something we call force is applied to change its
state of rest was, of course, well-known before Galileo's
30   time. However, the fact that the object continues to move
after the force ceases to be applied caused considerable
conceptual difficulties to the early Philosophers. The
observation that, in practice, an object comes to rest due
to frictional forces and air resistance was recognized
35   by Galileo to be a side effect and not germane to the
fundamental question of motion. Aristotle, for example,
believed that the true or natural state of motion is one
of rest. It is instructive to consider Aristotle's conjecture
from the viewpoint of the Principle of Relativity: is a
40   natural state of rest consistent with this general Principle?
First, we must consider what is meant by a natural state
of rest; it means that in a particular frame of reference,
the object in question is stationary. Now, according to the
general Principle of Relativity, the laws of motion have
45   the same form in all frames of reference that move with
constant speed in straight lines with respect to each other.
An observer in a reference frame moving with constant
speed in a straight line with respect to the reference
frame in which the object is at rest, would conclude that
50   the natural state of motion of the object is one of constant
speed in a straight line and not one of rest. All inertial
observers, in an infinite number of frames of reference,
would come to the same conclusion. We see, therefore,
that Aristotle's conjecture is not consistent with this
55   fundamental Principle.

Step 2: Read the 3rd paragraph

Step 3: Write down the main idea of the 3rd paragraph in your own words

I've broken it down into two chunks.

Idea #1 – Galileo's observation that an object traveling at a constant speed doesn't need force to stay at that speed is a new one.

Idea #2 – Aristotle's belief – the natural state of motion is rest – is wrong.

13. The statement in lines 25-26 ("It is… motion") suggests that

(A) contemporary scientists often disregard the foundations laid by classical physicists
(B) the reader, without a sound grasp of physics, cannot understand the principles of the Law of Inertia
(C) the reader has difficulty appreciating Galileo's ideas because they contradict the laws of motion
(D) Galileo's ideas offered explanations to conceptual theories that had befuddled early philosophers
(E) Galileo's ideas are too simple to be duly appreciated

Step 4: Read and restate the 1st specific question that pertains to paragraph 3

What's the author's point?

Step 5: Go back to the paragraph and dig

Re-read from the beginning of the 3rd paragraph to line 32 ("It is…philosophers").

Step 6: Answer the question in your own words

To us, the idea seems simple, but back then it was huge and hard to envision.

Step 7: Go to the answer choices

Answer choice (D) is a match: *befuddled early philosophers (back then it was hard to envision)*, but let's dissect the others.

(A) Seems a bit *offensive* to contemporary scientists, not to mention this answer choice is not supported by information in the passage. After all, **the author (a *contemporary scientist*) is spending a whole lot of time analyzing the foundations laid by Galileo and Aristotle.**

(B) This answer choice is just plain negative and way too much of an *assumption*. Many of you who don't have *a sound grasp of physics* may still be able to understand Galileo's principles. *DIFFICULT* to understand is not the same thing as *CANNOT* understand.

(C) Again, let's not make a *false assumption* about the reader. **Galileo's ideas DID NOT contradict the laws of motion, rather they set the laws of motion IN MOTION.**

(E) This answer choice is *offensive* to Galileo. **His ideas justified *conceptual difficulties* that had been puzzling to his fellow philosophers.** I don't think we can label those kinds of ideas as *too simple*. We have a degree adverb (*too*) that makes this answer choice too *extreme*.

14. In line 35, "germane" most nearly means

(A) advantageous
(B) originated
(C) unnecessary
(D) opposed
(E) connected

Step 4: Read and restate the next specific question that pertains to paragraph 3

What does "germane" mean?

Step 5: Go back to the paragraph and dig

Re-read from line 32 to line 38 ("The observation...rest").

Step 6: Answer the question in your own words

I came up with my own word for "germane": important

Step 7: Go to the answer choices

Perhaps the word you threw in for *germane* was a better match, but I didn't really see a great match for my word (*important*). I need to scrutinize each answer choice.

(A) *Advantageous* means *beneficial*. **Is ETS trying to say that the side effect is not *beneficial* to the question of motion?** Not so much.
(B) *Originated* means to *come from*. This definitely doesn't match my word: *important*. **Is ETS trying to say that the side effect does not *come from* the question of motion?** Nope.
(C) *Unnecessary* is the **opposite** of *important*. We can eliminate (C).
(D) *Opposed* means *against*. **Is ETS trying to say that the side effect is not *against* the fundamental question?** No, the side effect can't be *opposed* to anything.
(E) *Connected* means *related to*, which could be a match to *important*, meaning *significant to*. **Is ETS trying to say that the side effect is not *related* to the question of motion?** Possibly. (E) is the best of the worst.

*Note: **Germane means relevant.** If we know our vocabulary, no sweat! Germane is considered a tough word, and ETS only tests the primary definition of more difficult words.*

15. In order for Aristotle's hypothesis in lines 36-38 ("Aristotle...rest") to be correct, which statement would have to be true of an object in motion?

(A) The object will not remain in motion unless a force acts continually on it
(B) The object will remain in motion if there are no external forces acting upon it
(C) The object moves at a far slower rate the heavier its mass
(D) The object moves at a far faster rate the heavier its mass
(E) Its speed is faster when the object is traveling in a straight line

---

Step 4: Read and restate the question

What is Aristotle's hypothesis?

Step 5: Go back to the paragraph and dig

Re-read from line 36 to line 43 ("Aristotle... stationary").

Step 6: Answer the question in your own words

The natural state of an object is one of rest.

Step 7: Go to the answer choices

Answer choice (A) falls in line with Aristotle's theory that *the natural state of an object is one of rest* (lines 36-38). Let's paraphrase the scenario in our own, less complicated terms. **If things are naturally stationary, then they need a kick in the butt to get moving** (like me in the morning) **and keep moving** (in order for me to stay in motion I need caffeine in the afternoon). Still not convinced? Let's look at the other answer choices.

(B) **This is opposite to Aristotle's theory and more akin to Galileo's:** *no force is needed to keep an object in motion that is traveling in a straight line with constant speed* (lines 17-19).
(C) This may be true, but it is **not stated in the passage.** *Far slower* is pretty *extreme* terminology.
(D) This information is **not supported by the passage** and the phrase *far faster* is *extreme.*
(E) The passage refers to a straight line in line 19 to summarize Galileo's finding, and again in lines 51 to the end of the passage to refer to the Principle of Relativity, but **nowhere in the passage is there any mention that an object** *travels FASTER in a straight line.*

16. The author argues that Aristotle's theory on the laws of motion is inaccurate because

(A) an object does not appear at rest from all frames of reference
(B) it does not address the effect of force on an object
(C) force is needed to change the state of an object at rest
(D) an object appears at rest no matter the frame of reference
(E) an object is never truly at rest

Answer (A) supports my paraphrased answer. If an object at rest doesn't appear at rest from a moving train, then an object does not appear at rest from ALL frames of reference.

(B) **Aristotle's theory DOES** *address the effect of force on an object.* Aristotle agreed with his contemporaries' viewpoint - in order to make an object at rest move, some kind of force needs to be exerted on it.
(C) **Aristotle agreed with the theory that** *force is needed to change the state of an object at rest,* **but this theory is not** *inaccurate*; Galileo espoused this theory as well (lines 26-30).
(D) **Lines 47-53 prove this conjecture to be false;** an object DOES NOT *appear at rest at every frame of reference*.
(E) *Never* is an *extreme* word. **The passage challenges Aristotle's belief that the true state of motion is rest, but nowhere in the passage does the author indicate that an object is NEVER truly at rest.**

17. The author makes use of all of the following EXCEPT

    (A) rhetorical questions
    (B) comparison and contrast
    (C) personal experience
    (D) concrete details
    (E) general statements

Step 4: Read and restate the question

What literary device does the author NOT use?

Step 5: Go back to the passage and dig

Let's go through the answer choices seeing what we CAN find. Whatever we are left with is our EXCEPT.

    (A) I see **rhetorical questions in lines 9-12 and lines 39-40.** Eliminate (A).
    (B) The author compares **Galileo's theories to Aristotle's notions.**
    (C) **I can't find any use of personal experience.** Let's check the others just to be sure.
    (D) Concrete details mean the opposite of generalities. Basically, does the author give us facts to back up assumptions? Sure. **The whole first paragraph is full of concrete details.**
    (E) **General statements are everywhere.** Look at **lines 25-30.**

18. The last sentence of the passage primarily serves to

    (A) emphasize the author's opinion
    (B) answer a question posed earlier in the passage
    (C) reiterate the fundamentals of a problem
    (D) summarize the author's evidence
    (E) suggest a topic for further research

Step 4: Read and restate the question

What's the author saying in the last sentence and why?

Step 5: Go back to the paragraph and dig

I've just read this sentence, so I'll jump to Step 6.

Step 6: Answer the question in your own words

Aristotle is wrong and I have proven my point.

Based on my paraphrased answer I am left with two possible answer choices: (A) and (B).

    (A) I need to either justify this answer or de-justify it. **Is the author stating an OPINION or a FACT?** Hmmm....**looks like a fact to me.** Aristotle is indeed wrong. Let's see how (B) holds up.
    (B) I need to go back and look for the possible question. Check out lines 38-40: *is a natural state of rest consistent with this general principle?* **He answers this question with the last sentence:** *Aristotle's conjecture is not consistent with this fundamental principle.*

Let's refute the other answer choices in case you got tricked.

(C) What exactly is the *problem* being *reiterated*? **There is no problem!** Did the *word-for-word copy*, *fundamental* (line 55), trick you?

(D) I suppose one could argue **the author's POINT is summarized, but the *evidence* for that point is not at all summarized in the last sentence.**

(E) **Why would *further research* be needed if the author quite conclusively proved his point?** This statement is clearly wrong.

Step 8: State the main idea of the entire passage in your own words

Galileo contributed significantly to our understanding of motion.

Step 9: Answer all general questions

10. The primary purpose of the passage is to

(A) contrast two opposing scientific theories
(B) discuss one scientist's contribution to modern physics
(C) lament the inaccuracy of a compelling theory
(D) criticize the lack of research on the topic of motion
(E) analyze the inherent differences between physics and philosophy

Step 4: Read and restate the 1st general question

What's the main idea of the passage?

Nothing to dig for, so I'll jump to Step 6.

Step 6: Answer the question in your own words

I already answered it! *Galileo contributed significantly to our understanding of motion.*

Answer choice (B) is a definite match to my paraphrased answer. Let's break down the others.

(A) **While Aristotle's and Galileo's theories are contrasted, albeit indirectly, I wouldn't say this is the PRIMARY purpose.** Had I not answered the question in my own words, I might have been more tempted by this answer.

(C) Galileo's theory is *compelling*, **but not *inaccurate*.**

(D) **Nowhere in the passage did the author mention *lack of research*,** or approach a discussion of research at all.

(E) Lines 12-14 give us one example of what differentiates physics and philosophy: *observation*. PRIMARY means main, and **ONE occurrence does not justify this answer as a primary purpose.**

If you liked this technique, stick with it and apply it to the passages in Chapters 5 and 7. If you aren't so sure or are curious about the other techniques, then work through Chapters 5 and 7 following the different techniques they delineate.

Chapter 7
Technique #3
Less is More

Do your Reading Comp scores fall in the 350-500 range? Are the Reading Comp sections excruciating because you just can't manage to read the passage? It reads like a foreign language (maybe it is) and you've never been able to focus on more than one sentence at a time? Technique #3 is for the student who truly has extreme difficulty reading an entire passage. And that's okay! This is also a handy technique to apply if you only have a few minutes to spare and several questions left to answer.

Step 1: Read the Italicized Introduction

Be sure to note the type of passage and the topic discussed.

Step 2: Read and Restate the First Specific Question

> **Leave all general questions (main idea, overall tone or mood, etc.) for the very end. Circle them, or write the question #'s after the last question of the passage so you don't forget to go back and answer them!**

Turn the question into a Jeopardy question to simplify.

Let's say the question reads: *In lines 5-7 ("What...imagination") the author of Passage 1 argues that the fantasy world of video games*

Turn it into a Jeopardy question: *What does the author say about the fantasy world of video games?*

Here's another: *The first paragraph (lines 1-12) suggests that the narrator experienced Italy as*

Jeopardy question: *What was the author's impression of Italy?*
This example refers to the ENTIRE 1st paragraph, so there would be no getting around reading the ENTIRE 1st paragraph.

Step 3: Go to the Passage and Dig

You must read ***3-5 lines above and 3-5 lines below*** the given line numbers. The more you read, the better off you'll be. If the question were to indicate lines 5-7, you would read from the beginning of the paragraph to line 12, and if the question were to indicate the first paragraph as a whole, well then, you would have to read the whole first paragraph. If the line number you are starting from sits in the middle of a sentence, then of course pick up the beginning of that sentence. And don't stop reading at line 12 if you are in the middle of a sentence; read to line 13, or wherever that sentence ends.

Step 4: Answer the Question in Your Own Words

This is the big secret, the key to an improved reading comp score! Before you look at those answer choices, be sure to summarize what you have just read and answer the question in your own words.

Step 5: Go to the Answer Choices

Once you've answered the question in your own words (and perhaps written that answer down so you don't allow the answer choices to sway you) you are ready to look at the answers.

Your job is to match a given answer choice with your paraphrased answer. Get rid of all those answer choices that have nothing to do with your stated answer or that fall into one of the categories of Answer Choices to Avoid.

I see a lot of students answer the question in their own words correctly, only to go to the answer choices and be tricked by an answer that does not match their original interpretation. Don't doubt yourself and be easily influenced by cleverly crafted ETS answers when there is an answer choice waiting that totally matches your paraphrase. Trust yourself. Your comprehension is probably correct. JUST PICK THE ANSWER THAT MATCHES! Not the answer that makes you go, "Well, that sounds good, and maybe I'm off track." ***Writing down your paraphrased answer will help you stay true to it.***

Exception: Occasionally, no answer choice will match your paraphrase. When this occurs, don't just pick an answer arbitrarily or take your best guess; go back to the passage and dig deeper. Find a way to justify one of the answers with information from the passage.

⟶ **Remember: Only pick an answer choice if you can point to a specific portion of the passage and say, "My proof is right here!"**

It is an open book test after all!

⟶ **Repeat Steps 2-5 for every specific question**

Step 6: Write Down the Main Idea of the Entire Passage in Your Own Words

We still have all those general questions to answer, remember? Before answering any general questions, paraphrase the main idea. Again, don't write too much, just a brief summary.

Examples: *The invention of the airplane was aided by imagination*
Venus's atmosphere is determined by its proximity to the sun

> *Note:* If you are having trouble identifying the main idea, first ask: *What is the subject or topic of the passage?* (For example, *basketball*.) Then ask: *What does the passage say about this subject?* (For example, *there is a discrepancy in NBA salaries.*)

$\longrightarrow$ **Remember: Every correct answer is in line with the main idea of the passage!**

*If you state the main idea, and some of your answers to specific questions don't support that main idea, you may want to recheck those answers. At this point, you will have read the majority of the passage, which will shed more light on ALL of the questions.

Step 7: Answer All General Questions

Don't forget to go back and answer the general questions you've left blank. Perhaps before you even read the passage jot down a note at the end of the section to jog your memory. Or put a gigantic circle around the general questions so that you just can't miss them. You've already stated the main idea, but if you are dealing with a tone or mood question, be sure to come up with your own answer before skimming through the answer choices. Keep in mind good versus bad answers!

Let's work through a passage together using Technique #3.

Here's a list of steps for your reference:

Step 1: Read the Italicized Intro

Step 2: Read and Restate the First Specific Question

Step 3: Go to the Given Line #s and Read 5 Lines Above and 5 Lines Below

Step 4: Answer the Question in Your Own Words

Step 5: Go to the Answer Choices

> *Repeat Steps 2-5 for every specific question!*

Step 6: Write Down the Main Idea of the Entire Passage in Your Own Words

Step 7: Answer All General Questions

Below is a passage with step-by-step guidelines that will help you accurately apply Technique #3. The passage is divided into paragraphs with applicable questions written above each paragraph. The questions sit above each paragraph because with Technique #3 you will be looking at the questions first. This is, of course, not the way the passage will appear on the SAT; it is formatted below for teaching purposes only. Follow the directions and answer the questions as you go. Directly following are my marked-up version of the same passage and my own answers to the given questions.

Don't peek! Walk through the passage on your own first!

This passage about the habitat of Himalayan birds is from a book published in 1915. → Step 1: Read and assess the Italicized Intro

What type of passage are we dealing with?

_____

What else can we gather?

_____

13. The author's overall tone in the passage is described as

→ *Notice how the first question is a general question. Circle it, or go to the last question (#24) and write a reminder note!*

Skip to the 1st specific question: #14.

(A) wistful
(B) restrained
(C) self-congratulatory
(D) admiring
(E) critical

14. The author characterizes the Himalayas as a "mountainous country" (lines 3-4) primarily to emphasize the

Step 2: Read and restate the first specific question

_____

_____

(A) belief that the Himalayas should become an autonomous country
(B) truth of the preceding statement
(C) extensive size and varied nature of the mountain range
(D) rocky terrain that makes up the Himalayas
(E) extreme altitudes of the Himalayan mountains

Step 3: Go to the 1st paragraph and dig

Read from the beginning of the 1st paragraph to the end ("Himalayan… plateaux"). That's only 2 sentences!

Step 4: Answer the question in your own words

_____

_____

Step 5: Go to the answer choices

Circle your answer!

Stop! Repeat Steps 2-5 for question #15.

Himalayan birds inhabit what is perhaps the most wonderful tract of country in the world. The Himalayas are not so much a chain of mountains as a mountainous
Line country, some eighty miles broad and several hundred
5 long - a country composed entirely of mountains and valleys with no large plains or broad plateaux.

(For source reference, see endnote ᶠ)

`Geography of Himalayas mountains`

169

15. The author would most likely characterize the views of the "Sanskrit poet" referred to in line 7 as

    (A) thought-provoking
    (B) erroneous
    (C) unintelligible
    (D) inconclusive
    (E) carefully reasoned

       There is a saying of an ancient Sanskrit poet which, being translated into English, runs: "In a hundred ages of the gods I could not tell you of the glories of Himachal."
10 This every writer on things Himalayan contrives to drag into his composition. Some begin with the quotation, while others reserve it for the last, and make it do duty for the epigram which stylists assure us should terminate every essay.

    (For source reference, see endnote f)

> Step 2: Read and restate the question in your own words
>
> _____
>
> _____

> Step 3: Go to the 2nd paragraph and dig

Read from the beginning of the 2nd paragraph to the end ("There is…essay"). Only 3 sentences!

> Step 4: Answer the question in your own words
>
> _____
>
> _____

> Step 5: Go to the answer choices

Circle your answer!

Stop! Repeat Steps 2-5 for question #16.

16. According to the author, those who "quote the Indian sage only to mock him" (lines 15-16) view the Himalayas as

    (A) a desolate, arid, and dry mountain range that is highly overrated
    (B) a mountain range whose altitudes cannot compare to those of other mountain ranges
    (C) a mountain range whose beauty cannot be adequately expressed in words
    (D) a mountain range that pales in comparison to the splendor of other mountainous regions
    (E) a mountain range ill suited for exploration, unlike the Andes and Alps

15   Some there are who quote the Indian sage only to mock him. Such assert that the beauties of the Himalayas have been greatly exaggerated - that, as regards grandeur, their scenery compares unfavourably with that of the Andes, while their beauty is surpassed by that of the
20 Alps. Not having seen the Andes, I am unable to criticise the assertion regarding the grandeur of the Himalayas, but I find it difficult to imagine anything finer than their scenery. As regards beauty, the Himalayas at their best surpass the Alps, because they exhibit far more variety,
25 and present everything on a grander scale.

    (For source reference, see endnote f)

> Step 2: Read and restate the question in your own words
>
> _____
>
> _____

> Step 3: Go to the 3rd paragraph and dig

Read from the beginning of the 3rd paragraph to line 20 ("Some…Alps").

> Step 4: Answer the question in your own words
>
> _____
>
> _____

> Step 5: Go to the answer choices

Circle your answer!

Stop! Repeat Steps 2-5 for question #17.

17. The author compares the Himalayas to Dr. Jekyll and Mr. Hyde (line 26) in order to

(A) point out the dangers of the mountains if traveling through them in May
(B) assert that the mountains are never very beautiful, fair at best
(C) explain how each mountain in the range is unique and ever-changing
(D) call attention to the mountains' tendency to change appearance according to season
(E) advise as to which region of the mountain range is worth visiting

The Himalayas are a kind of Dr. Jekyll and Mr. Hyde. They have two faces—the fair and the plain. In May they are at their worst. Those of the hillsides which are not afforested are brown, arid, and desolate, and the

30 valleys, in addition to being unpleasantly hot, are dry and dusty. The foliage of the trees lacks freshness, and everywhere there is a remarkable absence of water, save in the valleys through which the rivers flow. On the other hand, September is the month in which the Himalayas

35 attain perfection or something approaching it. The eye is refreshed by the bright emerald garment which the hills have newly donned. The foliage is green and luxuriant. Waterfalls, cascades, mighty torrents and rivulets abound. Himachal has been converted into

40 fairyland by the monsoon rains.

(For source reference, see endnote ᶠ)

details of beauty

Step 2: Read and restate the question in your own words

_____

_____

Step 3: Go to the 4th paragraph and dig

Read from the beginning of the 4th paragraph to line 31 ("The Himalayas...dusty").

Typically we do not have to grab the end of the preceding paragraph, unless the subsequent paragraph directly expands on a particular idea. Let's say the opening sentence of the 4th paragraph was, "This idea is nothing new." Um...WHAT idea? We would have to grab the end of the 3rd paragraph to see. In this instance, totally not necessary!

Step 4: Answer the question in your own words

_____

_____

Having trouble? Maybe we didn't read enough. Perhaps we should read down to line 35 ("...approaching it").

Step 5: Go to the answer choices

Circle your answer!

Stop! Repeat Steps 2-5 for question #18.

18. In line 40, the author uses the word "fairyland" to refer to the

(A) beauty of the Himalayas in the fall
(B) monsoon rains that fall heavily in September
(C) foliage of the Himalayas
(D) mystical nature of the Himalayas
(E) flowers that bloom throughout the Himalayas in May

Step 2: Read and restate the question in your own words

_____

_____

Step 3: Go to the 4th paragraph and dig

Notice we are on the same paragraph as question #17. Read from line 35 to the end of the paragraph ("The eye... rains").

The Himalayas are a kind of Dr. Jekyll and Mr. Hyde. They have two faces—the fair and the plain. In May they are at their worst. Those of the hillsides which are not afforested are brown, arid, and desolate, and the
30 valleys, in addition to being unpleasantly hot, are dry and dusty. The foliage of the trees lacks freshness, and everywhere there is a remarkable absence of water, save in the valleys through which the rivers flow. On the other hand, September is the month in which the Himalayas
35 attain perfection or something approaching it. The eye is refreshed by the bright emerald garment which the hills have newly donned. The foliage is green and luxuriant. Waterfalls, cascades, mighty torrents and rivulets abound. Himachal has been converted into
40 fairyland by the monsoon rains.

Step 4: Answer the question in your own words

_____

_____

Step 5: Go to the answer choices

Circle your answer!

Stop! Repeat Steps 2-5 for question #19.

19. In line 54, "promiscuously" most nearly means

    (A) carnally
    (B) chaotically
    (C) immorally
    (D) orderly
    (E) beautifully

→ Step 2: Read and restate the question in your own words

_____

_____

Mountain height

    A remarkable feature of the Himalayas is the abruptness with which they rise from the plains in most places. In some parts there are low foothills; but speaking generally the mountains that rise from the plain attain a

45 height of 4000 or 5000 feet.

    It is difficult for any person who has not passed from the plains of India to the Himalayas to realise fully the vast difference between the two countries and the dramatic suddenness with which the change takes place.

50 The plains are as flat as the proverbial pancake - a dead monotony of cultivated alluvium, square mile upon square mile of wheat, rice, vetch, sugar-cane, and other crops, amidst which mango groves, bamboo clumps, palms, and hamlets are scattered promiscuously. In some

55 places the hills rise sheer from this, in others they are separated from the alluvial plains by belts of country known as the Tarai and Bhabar. The Tarai is low-lying, marshy land covered with tall, feathery grass, beautifully monotonous. This is succeeded by a stretch

60 of gently-rising ground, 10 or 20 miles in breadth, known as the Bhabar—a strip of forest composed mainly of tall evergreen sal trees (Shorea robusta). These trees grow so close together that the forest is difficult to penetrate, especially after the rains, when the undergrowth is

65 dense and rank. Very beautiful is the Bhabar, and very stimulating to the imagination. One writer speaks of it as "a jungle rhapsody, an extravagant, impossible botanical tour de force, intensely modern in its Titanic, incoherent magnificence." It is the home of the elephant, the tiger,

70 the panther, the wild boar, several species of deer, and of many strange and beautiful birds.

    (For source reference, see endnote ⁱ)

Step 3: Go to the 7th paragraph and dig

Notice we get to skip two paragraphs. Read from the beginning of the 7th paragraph to line 57 ("The plains...Bhabar").

Step 4: Answer the question in your own words

_____

_____

Step 5: Go to the answer choices

Circle your answer!

Stop! Repeat Steps 2-5 for question #20.

Different or country

plains and marsh, animals

20. The author's attitude toward the "alluvial plains" (line 56) is best described as one of

➜ Step 2: Read and restate the question in your own words

_____

_____

(A) appreciation
(B) ambivalence
(C) disregard
(D) animosity
(E) nostalgia

A remarkable feature of the Himalayas is the abruptness with which they rise from the plains in most places. In some parts there are low foothills; but speaking generally the mountains that rise from the plain attain a

45 height of 4000 or 5000 feet.

It is difficult for any person who has not passed from the plains of India to the Himalayas to realise fully the vast difference between the two countries and the dramatic suddenness with which the change takes place.

50 The plains are as flat as the proverbial pancake - a dead monotony of cultivated alluvium, square mile upon square mile of wheat, rice, vetch, sugar-cane, and other crops, amidst which mango groves, bamboo clumps, palms, and hamlets are scattered promiscuously. In some

55 places the hills rise sheer from this, in others they are separated from the alluvial plains by belts of country known as the Tarai and Bhabar. The Tarai is low-lying, marshy land covered with tall, feathery grass, beautifully monotonous. This is succeeded by a stretch

60 of gently-rising ground, 10 or 20 miles in breadth, known as the Bhabar—a strip of forest composed mainly of tall evergreen sal trees (Shorea robusta). These trees grow so close together that the forest is difficult to penetrate, especially after the rains, when the undergrowth is

65 dense and rank. Very beautiful is the Bhabar, and very stimulating to the imagination. One writer speaks of it as "a jungle rhapsody, an extravagant, impossible botanical tour de force, intensely modern in its Titanic, incoherent magnificence." It is the home of the elephant, the tiger,

70 the panther, the wild boar, several species of deer, and of many strange and beautiful birds.

Step 3: Go to the 7th paragraph and dig

Notice that the alluvial plains are first mentioned at the beginning of the paragraph. Technique says we should read from the beginning of the paragraph (line 50) to line 61, but nothing is mentioned of the alluvial plains after line 56. The information you need is in line 56 and above. Re-read, keeping the question in mind.

Step 4: Answer the question in your own words

_____

_____

Step 5: Go to the answer choices

Circle your answer!

Stop! Repeat Steps 2-5 for question #21.

174

21. The passage distinguishes between the "belts of country" (line 56) primarily by

(A) contrasting the beauty of one region with the barrenness of another
(B) highlighting each region's most abundant and useful natural resources
(C) recounting the crops planted by farmers in each region
(D) describing the flora and fauna of each region
(E) stimulating the reader's imagination with figurative language

Step 2: Read and restate the question in your own words

_____

_____

Step 3: Go to the 7th paragraph and dig

We need to dig further in the 7th paragraph for this. Read from line 54 (approximately where we left off) to line 62 ("In some... Shorea robusta").

Step 4: Answer the question in your own words

_____

_____

Step 5: Go to the answer choices

Circle your answer!

Stop! Repeat Steps 2-5 for question #22.

A remarkable feature of the Himalayas is the abruptness with which they rise from the plains in most places. In some parts there are low foothills; but speaking generally the mountains that rise from the plain attain a
45 height of 4000 or 5000 feet.

It is difficult for any person who has not passed from the plains of India to the Himalayas to realise fully the vast difference between the two countries and the dramatic suddenness with which the change takes place.
50 The plains are as flat as the proverbial pancake - a dead monotony of cultivated alluvium, square mile upon square mile of wheat, rice, vetch, sugar-cane, and other crops, amidst which mango groves, bamboo clumps, palms, and hamlets are scattered promiscuously. In some
55 places the hills rise sheer from this, in others they are separated from the alluvial plains by belts of country known as the Tarai and Bhabar. The Tarai is low-lying, marshy land covered with tall, feathery grass, beautifully monotonous. This is succeeded by a stretch
60 of gently-rising ground, 10 or 20 miles in breadth, known as the Bhabar—a strip of forest composed mainly of tall evergreen sal trees (Shorea robusta). These trees grow so close together that the forest is difficult to penetrate, especially after the rains, when the undergrowth is
65 dense and rank. Very beautiful is the Bhabar, and very stimulating to the imagination. One writer speaks of it as "a jungle rhapsody, an extravagant, impossible botanical tour de force, intensely modern in its Titanic, incoherent magnificence." It is the home of the elephant, the tiger,
70 the panther, the wild boar, several species of deer, and of many strange and beautiful birds.

22. The author makes use of all of the following EXCEPT

(A) quotations
(B) scientific terminology
(C) metaphor
(D) figurative language
(E) hyperbole

→ *#22 is more of a general question. Let's hold off. Circle it or make a note after #24. Jump to #23.*

23. The writer's description of the Himalayas in lines 67-69 ("a jungle...magnificence") primarily serves to

(A) explain a contradiction
(B) develop a theory
(C) note an impression
(D) recount an anecdote
(E) establish a precedent

Step 2: Read and restate the question in your own words

_____

_____

Step 3: Go to the 7th paragraph and dig

We need to dig further in the 7th paragraph for this one. Read from line 65 to the end of the paragraph ("Very beautiful...birds").

Step 4: Answer question in your own words

_____

_____

Step 5: Go to the answer choices

Circle your answer!

Stop! Repeat Steps 2-5 for question #24.

50 The plains are as flat as the proverbial pancake - a dead monotony of cultivated alluvium, square mile upon square mile of wheat, rice, vetch, sugar-cane, and other crops, amidst which mango groves, bamboo clumps, palms, and hamlets are scattered promiscuously. In some
55 places the hills rise sheer from this, in others they are separated from the alluvial plains by belts of country known as the Tarai and Bhabar. The Tarai is low-lying, marshy land covered with tall, feathery grass, beautifully monotonous. This is succeeded by a stretch
60 of gently-rising ground, 10 or 20 miles in breadth, known as the Bhabar—a strip of forest composed mainly of tall evergreen sal trees (Shorea robusta). These trees grow so close together that the forest is difficult to penetrate, especially after the rains, when the undergrowth is
65 dense and rank. Very beautiful is the Bhabar, and very stimulating to the imagination. One writer speaks of it as "a jungle rhapsody, an extravagant, impossible botanical tour de force, intensely modern in its Titanic, incoherent magnificence." It is the home of the elephant, the tiger,
70 the panther, the wild boar, several species of deer, and of many strange and beautiful birds.

24. Which of the following is NOT an aspect of the Himalayas that the author discusses?

(A) They are home to Himalayan birds
(B) They rise suddenly and to great heights
(C) They are at times waterless and dusty
(D) The foliage is rich and verdant
(E) They have regions that are flat and monotonous

#24 is a general question as well. Before we can answer our general questions we have to summarize our main idea.

Step 6: State the main idea of the entire passage in your own words

_____

_____

Let's go back to our first specific question: #13.

13. The author's overall tone in the passage is described as

(A) wistful
(B) restrained
(C) self-congratulatory
(D) admiring
(E) critical

Step 2: Read and restate the question in your own words

_____

_____

It's a general question so jump to Step 4!

Step 4: Answer question in your own words

_____

_____

Step 5: Go to the answer choices

Circle your answer!

Stop! Repeat Steps 2-5 for question #22.

22. The author makes use of all of the following EXCEPT

(A) quotations
(B) scientific terminology
(C) metaphor
(D) figurative language
(E) hyperbole

→ Step 2: Read and restate the question in your own words

_____

_____

Note: We can skip Step 4 (we can't very well answer the question in our own words) and instead go straight to the answer choices so that we know what we are looking for as we dig through the passage.

Cross off the answer choices you find support for in the passage. Whatever you are left with is the EXCEPT. Circle the leftover answer choice!

Step 5: Go to the answer choices

Circle your answer!

Stop! Repeat Steps 2-5 for question #24.

24. Which of the following is NOT an aspect of the Himalayas that the author discusses?

(A) They are home to Himalayan birds
(B) They rise suddenly and to great heights
(C) They are at times waterless and dusty
(D) The foliage is rich and verdant
(E) They have regions that are flat and monotonous

→ Step 2: Read and restate the question in your own words

_____

_____

Note: We can skip Step 4 and instead go straight to the answer choices so that we know what we are looking for as we dig through the passage.

Cross off the answer choices you find support for in the passage. Whatever you are left with is the NOT. Circle the leftover answer choice!

Step 5: Go to the answer choices

Circle your answer!

Let's take a look at the passage as a whole to see just how much we ended up reading.

⟶ **The underlined portions indicate sections read.**

This passage about the habitat of Himalayan birds is from a book published in 1915.

Himalayan birds inhabit what is perhaps the most wonderful tract of country in the world. The Himalayas are not so much a chain of mountains as a mountainous
Line country, some eighty miles broad and several hundred
5 long - a country composed entirely of mountains and valleys with no large plains or broad plateaux.

There is a saying of an ancient Sanskrit poet which, being translated into English, runs: "In a hundred ages of the gods I could not tell you of the glories of Himachal."
10 This every writer on things Himalayan contrives to drag into his composition. Some begin with the quotation, while others reserve it for the last, and make it do duty for the epigram which stylists assure us should terminate every essay.

15 Some there are who quote the Indian sage only to mock him. Such assert that the beauties of the Himalayas have been greatly exaggerated - that, as regards grandeur, their scenery compares unfavourably with that of the Andes, while their beauty is surpassed by that of the
20 Alps. Not having seen the Andes, I am unable to criticise the assertion regarding the grandeur of the Himalayas, but I find it difficult to imagine anything finer than their scenery. As regards beauty, the Himalayas at their best surpass the Alps, because they exhibit far more variety,
25 and present everything on a grander scale.

The Himalayas are a kind of Dr. Jekyll and Mr. Hyde. They have two faces—the fair and the plain. In May they are at their worst. Those of the hillsides which are not afforested are brown, arid, and desolate, and the
30 valleys, in addition to being unpleasantly hot, are dry and dusty. The foliage of the trees lacks freshness, and everywhere there is a remarkable absence of water, save in the valleys through which the rivers flow. On the other hand, September is the month in which the Himalayas
35 attain perfection or something approaching it. The eye

is refreshed by the bright emerald garment which the hills have newly donned. The foliage is green and luxuriant. Waterfalls, cascades, mighty torrents and rivulets abound. Himachal has been converted into
40 fairyland by the monsoon rains.

A remarkable feature of the Himalayas is the abruptness with which they rise from the plains in most places. In some parts there are low foothills; but speaking generally the mountains that rise from the plain attain a
45 height of 4000 or 5000 feet.

It is difficult for any person who has not passed from the plains of India to the Himalayas to realise fully the vast difference between the two countries and the dramatic suddenness with which the change takes place.
50 The plains are as flat as the proverbial pancake - a dead monotony of cultivated alluvium, square mile upon square mile of wheat, rice, vetch, sugar-cane, and other crops, amidst which mango groves, bamboo clumps, palms, and hamlets are scattered promiscuously. In some
55 places the hills rise sheer from this, in others they are separated from the alluvial plains by belts of country known as the Tarai and Bhabar. The Tarai is low-lying, marshy land covered with tall, feathery grass, beautifully monotonous. This is succeeded by a stretch
60 of gently-rising ground, 10 or 20 miles in breadth, known as the Bhabar—a strip of forest composed mainly of tall evergreen sal trees (Shorea robusta). These trees grow so close together that the forest is difficult to penetrate, especially after the rains, when the undergrowth is
65 dense and rank. Very beautiful is the Bhabar, and very stimulating to the imagination. One writer speaks of it as "a jungle rhapsody, an extravagant, impossible botanical tour de force, intensely modern in its Titanic, incoherent magnificence." It is the home of the elephant, the tiger,
70 the panther, the wild boar, several species of deer, and of many strange and beautiful birds.

Whether from the flat plains or the gently-sloping Bhabar, the mountains rise with startling suddenness.

A pretty good compromise if you ask me!

Now we're ready to check your answers with mine. Don't just look to see what answer choices I've circled. Walk through the technique again with me, so you can see if your way of thinking and your paraphrased answers are similar to mine.

This passage about the habitat of Himalayan birds is from a book published in 1915.

Step 1: Read and assess the Italicized Intro

What type of passage are we dealing with?

Well, it's a nature passage, so science.

What else can we gather?

It's about the place the birds live.

13. The author's overall tone in the passage is described as

(A) wistful
(B) restrained
(C) self-congratulatory
(D) admiring
(E) critical

The first question is a general question, so I circled it!

14. The author characterizes the Himalayas as a "mountainous country" (lines 3-4) primarily to emphasize the

(A) belief that the Himalayas should become an autonomous country
(B) truth of the preceding statement
(C) extensive size and varied nature of the mountain range
(D) rocky terrain that makes up the Himalayas
(E) extreme altitudes of the Himalayan mountains

Step 2: Read and restate the first specific question

Why does the author call the Himalayas a mountainous country?

Step 3: Go to the 1st paragraph and dig

Read from the beginning of the 1st paragraph to the end ("Himalayan…plateaux").

Step 4: Answer the question in your own words

Because it's really huge (like a country) and made up of a lot of mountains and valleys.

Step 5: Go to the answer choices

Himalayan birds inhabit what is perhaps the most wonderful tract of country in the world. The Himalayas are not so much a chain of mountains as a mountainous
Line   country, some eighty miles broad and several hundred
5   long - a country composed entirely of mountains and valleys with no large plains or broad plateaux.

Answer choice (C) matches my paraphrased answer and we have contextual support in lines 4-6:
some eighty miles broad and several hundred long (extensive size)…*composed of mountains and valleys* (varied nature).

Let's refute the other answer choices.

(A) *Autonomous* means *independent*. **This is a science passage, not a social science passage; the author is not espousing political propaganda.**

(B) We have to go back and dig. What is the preceding statement? *Himalayan birds inhabit what is perhaps the most wonderful tract of country in the world.* **The author is not using the phrase "mountainous country" to emphasize that the Himalayas are *wonderful*,** especially when you consider the contextual support surrounding the statement.

(D) *Mountainous* doesn't necessarily mean *rocky*. **There is no contextual support.**

(E) The altitudes of the Himalayas are extreme; the author even mentions just how high in line 45 (*4000 or 5000 feet*), but that's nowhere near the section of the passage the question is referencing; we haven't even read that yet! **Nowhere in the first paragraph does the author mention the height of the mountains.**

---

15. The author would most likely characterize the views of the "Sanskrit poet" referred to in line 7 as

(A) thought-provoking
(B) erroneous
(C) unintelligible
(D) inconclusive
(E) carefully reasoned

> There is a saying of an ancient Sanskrit poet which, being translated into English, runs: "In a hundred ages of the gods I could not tell you of the glories of Himachal."
> 10 This every writer on things Himalayan contrives to drag into his composition. Some begin with the quotation, while others reserve it for the last, and make it do duty for the epigram which stylists assure us should terminate every essay.

Step 2: Read and restate the question in your own words

What are the views of the Sanskrit poet and how does the author feel about these views?

Step 3: Go to the 2nd paragraph and dig

Read from the beginning of the 2nd paragraph to the end ("There is…essay").

Step 4: Answer the question in your own words

The Himalayas are so terrific – even if he had a million years he couldn't tell us of them (possible exaggeration). The author says the Himalayas are the "most wonderful tract of country in the world," so he would agree with the poet.

Step 5: Go to the answer choices

I know I'm looking for a positive word, so that leaves me with answer choices (A) and (E). Let's look at these answers more closely.

(A) *Thought-provoking* means they *inspire thought*. In lines 11-12, the author goes on to say that **many people refer to the poet** (*Some begin with the quotation, while others reserve it for last*), **which seems to indicate that the quote inspires thought.**

(E) *Carefully reasoned* means the poet arrived at this statement through a *logical analytical assessment of the Himalayas*. But, he's a poet! **The poet is using *figurative devices,* such as hyperbole or exaggeration** (*in a hundred ages of the gods*) to share his opinion. I can knock (E) out of the running and confidently pick (A).

Let's go through the others just in case you got tricked.

(B) *Erroneous* means *wrong* and **the author agrees with the poet.**

(C) *Unintelligible* means you *can't make sense of it.* You might have read the quote and thought, "What is that nonsense?" **But just because *you* didn't get it, doesn't mean the *author* didn't get it.**

(D) *Inconclusive* means *uncertain*, or *questionable*. While OTHERS might debate the Sanskrit poet, **the AUTHOR is not questioning the poet's opinion.**

---

16. According to the author, those who "quote the Indian sage only to mock him" (lines 15-16) view the Himalayas as

(A) a desolate, arid, and dry mountain range that is highly overrated

(B) a mountain range whose altitudes cannot compare to those of other mountain ranges

(C) a mountain range whose beauty cannot be adequately expressed in words

(D) a mountain range that pales in comparison to the splendor of other mountainous regions

(E) a mountain range ill suited for exploration, unlike the Andes and Alps

15   Some there are who quote the Indian sage only to mock him. Such assert that the beauties of the Himalayas have been greatly exaggerated - that, as regards grandeur, their scenery compares unfavourably with that of the Andes, while their beauty is surpassed by that of the

20   Alps. Not having seen the Andes, I am unable to criticise the assertion regarding the grandeur of the Himalayas, but I find it difficult to imagine anything finer than their scenery. As regards beauty, the Himalayas at their best surpass the Alps, because they exhibit far more variety,

25   and present everything on a grander scale.

> **Step 2: Read and restate the question in your own words**

> *What do the people who mock the poet think of the Himalayas?*

> **Step 3: Go to the 2nd paragraph and dig**

> ***Read from the beginning of the 3rd paragraph to line 20 ("Some…Alps").***

> **Step 4: Answer the question in your own words**

> *The Himalayas aren't very grand or very beautiful.*

> **Step 5: Go to the answer choices**

Answer choice (D) matches my paraphrased answer. Check it out: *pales in comparison to the splendor* (*not very grand or beautiful*). This answer choice is also contextually supported; the author compares the Himalayas to the Andes (line 19) and the Alps (line 20.) Let's dissect the other answer choices.

(A) *Those who mock him* would consider the Himalayas *highly overrated* (perhaps *highly* is a tad extreme) but is there any support for the description of the Himalayas as *desolate, arid, and dry?* ETS is attempting to trick us with a *word-for-word copy.* Lines 29-31 (which you haven't read yet, as we are dissecting the passage in chunks) read, *arid, and desolate, and the valleys, in addition to being unpleasantly hot, are dry and dusty.* Very tempting! But this statement represents **the author's** perception of the Himalayas in May, not the perception of *those who mock him.*

(B) *Those who mock him* state that their *scenery compares unfavourably* and *their beauty is surpassed.* **No mention is made of *altitude*.**

(C) *Those who mock him* are **DOWNPLAYING the beauty of the Himalayas, not PRAISING it.**

(E) **There is no mention made of *exploration*.**

17. The author compares the Himalayas to Dr. Jekyll and Mr. Hyde (line 26) in order to

(A) point out the dangers of the mountains if traveling through them in May
(B) assert that the mountains are never very beautiful, fair at best
(C) explain how each mountain in the range is unique and ever-changing
(D) call attention to the mountains' tendency to change appearance according to season
(E) advise as to which region of the mountain range is worth visiting

The Himalayas are a kind of Dr. Jekyll and Mr. Hyde. They have two faces—the fair and the plain. In May they are at their worst. Those of the hillsides which are not afforested are brown, arid, and desolate, and the
30 valleys, in addition to being unpleasantly hot, are dry and dusty. The foliage of the trees lacks freshness, and everywhere there is a remarkable absence of water, save in the valleys through which the rivers flow. On the other hand, September is the month in which the Himalayas
35 attain perfection or something approaching it. The eye is refreshed by the bright emerald garment which the hills have newly donned. The foliage is green and luxuriant. Waterfalls, cascades, mighty torrents and rivulets abound. Himachal has been converted into
40 fairyland by the monsoon rains.

> **Step 2: Read and restate the question in your own words**
>
> *Why does the author compare the Himalayas to Dr. Jekyll and Mr. Hyde?*
>
> **Step 3: Go to the 4th paragraph and dig**
>
> ***Read from the beginning of the 4th paragraph to line 31 ("The Himalayas…dusty").***
>
> **Step 4: Answer the question in your own words**
>
> *Because sometimes they are just okay and other times they are tremendously beautiful.*
>
> **Step 5: Go to the answer choices**

None of the answer choices pop out as a definite match to my paraphrased answer. (D) might be a match, but I need to go back to the passage and dig further. **Lines 27-28 mentions the Himalayas in May and lines 34-35 mention how beautiful the Himalayas are in September.** I've found my proof for (D)!

Let's work through the other answer choices.

(A) The author discusses the look of the Himalayas in May, **making no mention of *dangers* or *traveling*.**
(B) *Never* is an *extreme* word. **Eliminate!**
(C) **The author doesn't say that every mountain in the range is different (*unique*) from the others and constantly changing (*ever-changing*).** This answer choice is clearly not supported.
(E) **The passage is not a travel-guide.** The author is not trying to drum up tourism. This answer choice is clearly not supported.

18. In line 40, the author uses the word "fairyland" to refer to the

(A) beauty of the Himalayas in the fall
(B) monsoon rains that fall heavily in September
(C) foliage of the Himalayas
(D) mystical nature of the Himalayas
(E) flowers that bloom throughout the Himalayas in May

The Himalayas are a kind of Dr. Jekyll and Mr. Hyde. They have two faces—the fair and the plain. In May they are at their worst. Those of the hillsides which are not afforested are brown, arid, and desolate, and the

30 valleys, in addition to being unpleasantly hot, are dry and dusty. The foliage of the trees lacks freshness, and everywhere there is a remarkable absence of water, save in the valleys through which the rivers flow. On the other hand, September is the month in which the Himalayas

35 attain perfection or something approaching it. The eye is refreshed by the bright emerald garment which the hills have newly donned. The foliage is green and luxuriant. Waterfalls, cascades, mighty torrents and rivulets abound. Himachal has been converted into

40 fairyland by the monsoon rains.

Based on my paraphrased answer, I am apt to pick (A), but I need to make sure that the rains come in the *fall* and not another season. This answer choice could be a partial answer. I read 6 lines above and see lines 34-35, which assure me that **the rain occurs in fall (*September*).**

Let's de-justify the other answer choices.

(B) Let's look at the construction of the sentence grammatically. Lines 39-40 read: *Himachal has been converted into fairyland by the monsoon rains.* **The monsoon rains aren't the fairyland; they are CREATING the fairyland.**

(C) The *foliage* is definitely discussed, but **the fairyland represents ALL the Himalayas**, not just one aspect of the Himalayas.

(D) *Mystical* means *supernatural*. Out of context, the word *fairyland* sounds mystical, but **analyzing the word based on information in the passage gives us no support for the claim that the Himalayas are mystical.** That would be a total *assumption*, and we want to avoid all assumptions!

(E) The word *flowers* is too specific, and May is the wrong month. **Fairyland describes the Himalayas in *September*, not *May*.**

19. In line 54, "promiscuously" most nearly means

    (A) carnally
    (B) chaotically
    (C) immorally
    (D) orderly
    (E) beautifully

      A remarkable feature of the Himalayas is the abruptness with which they rise from the plains in most places. In some parts there are low foothills; but speaking generally the mountains that rise from the plain attain a
45 height of 4000 or 5000 feet.
      It is difficult for any person who has not passed from the plains of India to the Himalayas to realise fully the vast difference between the two countries and the dramatic suddenness with which the change takes place.
50 The plains are as flat as the proverbial pancake - a dead monotony of cultivated alluvium, square mile upon square mile of wheat, rice, vetch, sugar-cane, and other crops, amidst which mango groves, bamboo clumps, palms, and hamlets are scattered promiscuously. In some
55 places the hills rise sheer from this, in others they are separated from the alluvial plains by belts of country known as the Tarai and Bhabar. The Tarai is low-lying, marshy land covered with tall, feathery grass, beautifully monotonous. This is succeeded by a stretch
60 of gently-rising ground, 10 or 20 miles in breadth, known as the Bhabar - a strip of forest composed mainly of tall evergreen sal trees (Shorea robusta). These trees grow so close together that the forest is difficult to penetrate, especially after the rains, when the undergrowth is
65 dense and rank. Very beautiful is the Bhabar, and very stimulating to the imagination. One writer speaks of it as "a jungle rhapsody, an extravagant, impossible botanical tour de force, intensely modern in its Titanic, incoherent magnificence." It is the home of the elephant, the tiger,
70 the panther, the wild boar, several species of deer, and of many strange and beautiful birds.

Step 2: Read and restate the question in your own words

What does the word "promiscuously" mean?

Step 3: Go to the 7th paragraph and dig

Read from the beginning of the 7th paragraph to line 57 ("The plains… Bhabar").

Step 4: Answer the question in your own words

Haphazardly

Step 5: Go to the answer choices

Chaotically **totally matches my word,** *haphazardly,* so I can confidently pick answer choice (B). Let's walk-thru the others.

    (A) *Carnally* means *of the flesh.* It is the primary definition of promiscuously, but **doesn't work in context.**
    (C) *Immorally* means *corruptly.* **I don't think we can describe nature as corrupt.**
    (D) *Orderly* means *neatly arranged* and is the **opposite of what we are looking for.**
    (E) *Beautifully* is a positive word, and **the author indicates that the plains are scattered in a less than beautiful way.** He uses phrases such as *dead monotony* (line 51).

185

20. The author's attitude toward the "alluvial plains" (line 56) is best described as one of

    (A) appreciation
    (B) ambivalence
    (C) disregard
    (D) animosity
    (E) nostalgia

Step 2: Read and restate the question in your own words

What does the author think of the alluvial plains?

Step 3: Go to the 7th paragraph and dig

Re-read from lines 50 to 57.

Step 4: Answer the question in your own words

He thinks they're boring, flat and disorganized.

Step 5: Go to the answer choices

      A remarkable feature of the Himalayas is the abruptness with which they rise from the plains in most places. In some parts there are low foothills; but speaking generally the mountains that rise from the plain attain a
45 height of 4000 or 5000 feet.
      It is difficult for any person who has not passed from the plains of India to the Himalayas to realise fully the vast difference between the two countries and the dramatic suddenness with which the change takes place.
50 The plains are as flat as the proverbial pancake - a dead monotony of cultivated alluvium, square mile upon square mile of wheat, rice, vetch, sugar-cane, and other crops, amidst which mango groves, bamboo clumps, palms, and hamlets are scattered promiscuously. In some
55 places the hills rise sheer from this, in others they are separated from the alluvial plains by belts of country known as the Tarai and Bhabar. The Tarai is low-lying, marshy land covered with tall, feathery grass, beautifully monotonous. This is succeeded by a stretch
60 of gently-rising ground, 10 or 20 miles in breadth, known as the Bhabar—a strip of forest composed mainly of tall evergreen sal trees (Shorea robusta). These trees grow so close together that the forest is difficult to penetrate, especially after the rains, when the undergrowth is
65 dense and rank. Very beautiful is the Bhabar, and very stimulating to the imagination. One writer speaks of it as "a jungle rhapsody, an extravagant, impossible botanical tour de force, intensely modern in its Titanic, incoherent magnificence." It is the home of the elephant, the tiger,
70 the panther, the wild boar, several species of deer, and of many strange and beautiful birds.

I know the author doesn't really dig the alluvial plains. That would leave me with answer choices (C) and (D). Let's analyze.

    (C) *Disregard* means *disdain* or *disrespect*. **A safe enough answer for "doesn't dig."**
    (D) *Animosity* means *hatred*. **That's way too *extreme*.**

(C) is a much safer pick. Let's dissect the others.

    (A) *Appreciation* means *admiration*, which **contradicts my paraphrased word.**
    (B) *Ambivalence* means *uncertainty*, and **the author has a pretty definite opinion.**
    (E) *Nostalgia* means *reminiscence*, and is a **word to avoid.**

21. The passage distinguishes between the "belts of country" (line 56) primarily by

(A) contrasting the beauty of one region with the barrenness of another
(B) highlighting each region's most abundant and useful natural resources
(C) recounting the crops planted by farmers in each region
(D) describing the flora and fauna of each region
(E) stimulating the reader's imagination with figurative language

Step 2: Read and restate the question in your own words

How does the author differentiate between the belts of country?

Step 3: Go to the 7th paragraph and dig

Read from line 54 (approximately where we left off) to line 62 ("In some...Shorea robusta").

Step 4: Answer the question in your own words

By telling us what type of land they are.

Step 5: Go to the answer choices

A remarkable feature of the Himalayas is the abruptness with which they rise from the plains in most places. In some parts there are low foothills; but speaking generally the mountains that rise from the plain attain a
45 height of 4000 or 5000 feet.

It is difficult for any person who has not passed from the plains of India to the Himalayas to realise fully the vast difference between the two countries and the dramatic suddenness with which the change takes place.
50 The plains are as flat as the proverbial pancake - a dead monotony of cultivated alluvium, square mile upon square mile of wheat, rice, vetch, sugar-cane, and other crops, amidst which mango groves, bamboo clumps, palms, and hamlets are scattered promiscuously. In some
55 places the hills rise sheer from this, in others they are separated from the alluvial plains by belts of country known as the Tarai and Bhabar. The Tarai is low-lying, marshy land covered with tall, feathery grass, beautifully monotonous. This is succeeded by a stretch
60 of gently-rising ground, 10 or 20 miles in breadth, known as the Bhabar—a strip of forest composed mainly of tall evergreen sal trees (Shorea robusta). These trees grow so close together that the forest is difficult to penetrate, especially after the rains, when the undergrowth is
65 dense and rank. Very beautiful is the Bhabar, and very stimulating to the imagination. One writer speaks of it as "a jungle rhapsody, an extravagant, impossible botanical tour de force, intensely modern in its Titanic, incoherent magnificence." It is the home of the elephant, the tiger,
70 the panther, the wild boar, several species of deer, and of many strange and beautiful birds.

Answer choice (D) is the best match for my paraphrased answer. *Flora* and *fauna* refer to plant and wildlife. The flora of Tarai is described as *marshy land covered with tall, feathery grass* (line 58), while the flora of the Bhabar is made up of *tall evergreen trees* (lines 61-62). The author tells us the fauna of the Bhabar consists of *elephant, tiger, panther, wild boar, deer, and exotic birds* (lines 69-71). *Fauna* is easy to miss, as it appears in a section you might not have read (lines 69-71). Remember: Even when using this less-reading-heavy technique, it is helpful to skim the passage for keywords that might aid your overall understanding of the passage.

Let's break down the other answer choices.

- (A) **BOTH of the regions (the Tarai and the Bhabar) are described as** *beautiful.* The region that is described as *bare* is the *alluvial plains* (lines 50-54). These plains are not part of the Himalayas and not one of the belts of country.
- (B) The author describes the flora of the two regions, but **doesn't indicate what** *resources* **we use from these regions.**
- (C) The author does not tell us that *crops are planted* on these belts of country. **This answer choice, like (A) relates more to the alluvial plains** (lines 50-54).
- (E) The author uses the *figurative language* of another writer to describe the Bhabar, but **he doesn't use figurative language to describe the Tarai,** so this answer choice is not the most supported.

22. The author makes use of all of the following EXCEPT ⟶ *#22 is more of a general question. Let's hold off.*

    (A) quotations
    (B) scientific terminology
    (C) metaphor
    (D) figurative language
    (E) hyperbole

23. The writer's description of the Himalayas in lines 67-69 ("a jungle...magnificence") primarily serves to

(A) explain a contradiction
(B) develop a theory
(C) note an impression
(D) recount an anecdote
(E) establish a precedent

Step 2: Read and restate the question in your own words

How does does the writer describe the Himalayas and why does he describe them this way?

Step 3: Go to the 7th paragraph and dig

Read from line 65 to the end of the paragraph ("Very beautiful...birds").

Step 4: Answer the question in your own words

To show how it is wild and exotic.

Step 5: Go to the answer choices

50   The plains are as flat as the proverbial pancake - a dead monotony of cultivated alluvium, square mile upon square mile of wheat, rice, vetch, sugar-cane, and other crops, amidst which mango groves, bamboo clumps, palms, and hamlets are scattered promiscuously. In some
55   places the hills rise sheer from this, in others they are separated from the alluvial plains by belts of country known as the Tarai and Bhabar. The Tarai is low-lying, marshy land covered with tall, feathery grass, beautifully monotonous. This is succeeded by a stretch
60   of gently-rising ground, 10 or 20 miles in breadth, known as the Bhabar—a strip of forest composed mainly of tall evergreen sal trees (Shorea robusta). These trees grow so close together that the forest is difficult to penetrate, especially after the rains, when the undergrowth is
65   dense and rank. Very beautiful is the Bhabar, and very stimulating to the imagination. One writer speaks of it as "a jungle rhapsody, an extravagant, impossible botanical tour de force, intensely modern in its Titanic, incoherent magnificence." It is the home of the elephant, the tiger,
70   the panther, the wild boar, several species of deer, and of many strange and beautiful birds.

The answer choices aren't what I expected, so I will probably have to dissect each of them.

(A) A *contradiction* means an *inconsistency* or *disagreement*. **The writer's description doesn't explain an inconsistency,** it simply expands on the author's point of view that the Bhabar region of the Himalayas is spectacular.

(B) The writer's description expands on the author's point of view of the Bhabar. **Nowhere is a *theory* (a hypothesis) posited.**

(C) An *impression* is *the effect something has on you*, or *the mark something makes on you*. The author indicates, *Very beautiful is the Bhabar, and very stimulating to the imagination* (lines 65-66). **Seems like it made quite an impression on the author.** Phrases such as *a jungle rhapsody* indicate that it seems to have made quite an impression on the writer too.

(D) An *anecdote* is a *story*, and **the writer is not telling a story.**

(E) A *precedent* is an *example* or a *model to be followed in the future*. The writer describes the magnificence of the Bhabar; **he isn't establishing a model to be utilized in the future.**

24. Which of the following is NOT an aspect of the Himalayas that the author discusses?

→ *#24 is a general question as well. Before we can answer our general questions we have to summarize our main idea.*

(A) They are home to Himalayan birds
(B) They rise suddenly and to great heights
(C) They are at times waterless and dusty
(D) The foliage is rich and verdant
(E) They have regions that are flat and monotonous

Step 6: State the main idea of the entire passage in our own words

The Himalayas are beautiful and varied.

Let's go back to our first general question: #13.

13. The author's overall tone in the passage is described as

Step 2: Read and restate the question in your own words

How does the author feel about the topic of the passage (the Himalayas)?

(A) wistful
(B) restrained
(C) self-congratulatory
(D) admiring
(E) critical

It's a general question so jump to Step 4!

Step 4: Answer the question in your own words

He thinks they're awesome.

Step 5: Go to the answer choices

Looking for a positive word leads me to (D). Let's pick apart the others.

(A) *Wistful* means *daydreaming* (lost in thought). **The author is not thinking of times gone by or future if onlys.** *Admiring* is much more supported.
(B) *Restrained* means *reserved, held-back.* **I don't think the author is held back in his appreciation of the Himalayas,** do you?
(C) *Self-congratulatory* would indicate that the author thinks he is the one of the coolest cats around. **We have no idea what the author thinks of himself.** He puts the focus on the Himalayas. Don't make *assumptions*!
(E) *Critical.* No way! **The author LOVES the Himalayas.**

22. The author makes use of all of the following EXCEPT

    (A) quotations
    (B) scientific terminology
    (C) metaphor
    (D) figurative language
    (E) hyperbole

Step 2: Read and restate the question in your own words

What device does the author NOT use?

Step 5: Go to the answer choices

Let's go through the answer choices, eliminating answer choices we find support for in the passage, and then see what we have left.

    (A) **I can find quotations in the 2nd and 7th paragraphs.** Eliminate (A) as it's not our EXCEPT.
    (B) Check out **line 62** *"…evergreen sal trees (Shorea robusta)."* **Sounds pretty scientific to me.** Eliminate (B)!
    (C) **Metaphor is everywhere.** Look at **line 26:** *The Himalayas are a kind of Dr. Jekyll and Mr. Hyde.*
    (D) **Figurative language abounds.** Check out the simile in **line 50:** *The plains are as flat as the proverbial pancake.*
    (E) *Hyperbole* means *exaggeration.* The only example of exaggeration would be in the Sanskrit poet's quote, *in a hundred ages of the gods* (lines 8-9), but even then, **the *author* is not using hyperbole, the *poet* is.**

24. Which of the following is NOT an aspect of the Himalayas that the author discusses?

    (A) They are home to Himalayan birds
    (B) They rise suddenly and to great heights
    (C) They are at times waterless and dusty
    (D) The foliage is rich and verdant
    (E) They have regions that are flat and monotonous

Step 2: Read and restate the question in your own words

What information is NOT in the passage?

Step 5: Go to the answer choices

Cross off the answer choices you find support for in the passage. Whatever you're left with is the NOT. Circle the leftover answer choice!

    (A) **I can justify this answer with the italicized intro and lines 1-2:** *Himalayan birds inhabit what is perhaps the most wonderful tract of country in the world.*
    (B) **Check out paragraph 5** (we didn't read it so you may have missed it) *abruptness with which they rise from the plains* (line 42) and *attain a height of 4000 or 5000 feet* (lines 44-45.) Eliminate (B)!
    (C) **Lines 29-32** indicate the *Himalayas are sometimes waterless* (arid) and *dusty.* Eliminate (C)!
    (D) This answer choice is a great paraphrase of lines 37-38: *the foliage is green and luxuriant.* Eliminate (D)!
    (E) **The regions that are described as *flat and monotonous* are the *alluvial plains* (lines 50-54) NOT the *Himalayas*.** We have found our NOT!

You can use Technique #3 on any passage EXCEPT for Fiction Passages and Short Passages because you will need to read those in their entirety. In the next chapter we deal with another portion of the Reading Comprehension section that tends to throw some students: The Compare/Contrast section.

Chapter 8
The Compare/Contrast Passages

The compare/contrast passages elicit the most groans from students. Too much to read and too much to keep track of! I get it, but there is really no dramatic difference between these passages and other passages on the SAT.

The only distinction is the 4-to-6 Compare/Contrast questions scattered throughout.

The key to success with these passages is all in the approach.

Compare/Contrast passages can be tackled with any of the three techniques. Remember to always read the *italicized introduction* first!

Here are the steps for each technique when dealing with a Compare/Contrast passage:

Technique #1

Step 1: Read Passage 1

Step 2: State the Main Idea of Passage 1

Step 3: Answer the Questions that Pertain to Passage 1

Step 4: Read Passage 2

Step 5: State the Main Idea of Passage 2

Step 6: Answer the Questions that Pertain to Passage 2

Step 7: Answer all Compare/Contrast Questions

Before answering any Compare/Contrast questions, remind yourself of the main idea of each passage.

Technique #2

Step 1: Read Passage 1 Paragraph by Paragraph Answering the Specific Questions as you go

Step 2: State the Main Idea of Passage 1

Step 3: Answer the General Questions that Pertain to Passage 1

Step 4: Read Passage 2 Paragraph by Paragraph Answering the Specific Questions as you go

Step 5: State the Main Idea of Passage 2

Step 6: Answer the General Questions that Pertain to Passage 2

Step 7: Answer all Compare/Contrast Questions

Before answering any Compare/Contrast questions, remind yourself of the main idea of each passage.

Technique #3

Step 1: Answer the Specific Questions that Pertain to Passage 1

Step 2: State the Main Idea of Passage 1

Step 3: Answer the General Questions that Pertain to Passage 1

Step 4: Answer the Specific Questions that Pertain to Passage 2

Step 5: State the Main Idea of Passage 2

Step 6: Answer the General Questions that Pertain to Passage 2

Step 7: Answer the Compare/Contrast Questions

Before answering any Compare/Contrast questions, remind yourself of the main idea of each passage.

---

*No matter what technique you use, the gist is the same: **Read and answer questions about Passage 1, then read and answer questions about Passage 2, and lastly, answer the Compare/Contrast questions.***

Why? The first question is typically a specific question about Passage 1. If you were to read the passages back to back, you would have the information from Passage 2 stuck in your head. Why load your brain with all that information at once, when you can feed it the information it needs bit by bit?

Note: As you read Passage 2 note how it differs and how it conforms to Passage 1.

Compare/Contrast Questions

Compare/Contrast questions are pretty much about the main idea of each passage. So if you know the main idea of each passage and how the authors' viewpoints are similar and different, the correct answer is easy to find.

> *Before answering any Compare/Contrast questions, you must state the main idea of each passage.*

When answering a Compare/Contrast question, be sure to attack it from the perspective of the passage you understand best. You can eliminate answer choices as you go and ultimately save time.

Say the question asks: *Which best characterizes how the subject of communication is treated in these two passages?*

Turn it into a Jeopardy question: *What does the author of Passage 1 say about communication and what does the author of Passage 2 say about communication?*

Summarize the main idea of each passage:
> Passage 1 – *Communication has suffered with advanced technology*
> Passage 2 – *Communication has strengthened with advanced technology*

Let's say we are more comfortable with Passage 1. We only look at the answer choices from Passage 1's perspective. Disregard the second half of each of the following answer choices.

(A) Passage 1 suggests that communication has become less personal, while Passage 2 contends that it has increased globally

> Yes! "become less personal" matches our paraphrase "has suffered." Don't bother reading the rest yet. Jump to (B).

(B) Passage 1 de-emphasizes the effect of email on communication, while Passage 2 emphasizes its effect

> While there might be information in the passage that supports this statement, based on my main idea it doesn't seem logical. If the author of Passage 1 thinks communication has suffered, wouldn't he want to stress the impersonal nature of email? For technique's sake, let's say this statement is not supported by info from the passage and eliminate it.

(C) Passage 1 argues that people no longer communicate face-to-face, while Passage 2 affirms that more people favor in-person communication to email or text

> Yes! "Communication has suffered." Keep it and jump to (D).

(D) Both passages downplay the effect of the Internet on communication

> The Internet is a major technological advancement. If the authors are discussing the effects of technology on communication, chances are the Internet is included in the discussions. Let's eliminate (D).

(E) Neither Passage 1 nor Passage 2 considers the psychological effect of communicating via email and text

> This might be true. I would have to have read the passages to determine.

We have (A), (C), and (E) left, but the only answer choices that really matched my main idea for Passage 1 were (A) and (C), so let's check those from the perspective of Passage 2.

(A) Passage 1 suggests that communication has become less personal, while Passage 2 contends that it has increased globally ⟶ If communication has "increased globally" then communication "has strengthened." We have a match for both Passage 1 and Passage 2.

(C) Passage 1 argues that people no longer communicate face to face, while Passage 2 affirms that more people favor in-person communication to email or text ⟶ If the author of Passage 2 believes that technological advancements have "strengthened communication," then "more people favoring in-person communication" is contrary to his main idea.

⟶ **Common pitfall: Answering the question from the wrong perspective.**

> *Note: ETS likes to flip perspectives in the answer choices, so make sure you know which author's perspective you are considering!*

Following is a Compare/contrast section to work through. I'm not going to be taking you through these two passages step-by-step, as I want you to employ your favorite technique and walk through them yourself. I do, however, provide my marked-up version of the passage (I have used Technique #1), along with detailed explanations of all answer choices so you can check your work and your thought process.

These two passages, written in 1905, address the music of Ludwig van Beethoven.

Passage 1

If Bach is the mathematician of music, as has been asserted, Beethoven is its philosopher. In his work the philosophic spirit comes to the fore. To the genius of the
Line musician is added in Beethoven a wide mental grasp,
5 an altruistic spirit, that seeks to help humanity on the upward path. He addresses the intellect of mankind.

Up to Beethoven's time musicians in general (Bach is always an exception) performed their work without the aid of an intellect for the most part; they worked by
10 intuition. In everything outside their art they were like children. Beethoven was the first one having the independence to think for himself—the first to have ideas on subjects unconnected with his art. He it was who established the dignity of the artist over that of the
15 simply well-born. His entire life was a protest against the pretensions of birth over mind.

As with all valuable things, however, Beethoven's music is not to be enjoyed for nothing. We must on our side contribute something to the enterprise, something
20 more than simply buying a ticket to the performance. We must study his work in the right spirit, and place ourselves in a receptive attitude when listening to it to understand his message. No other composer demands so much of one; no other rewards the student so richly for
25 the effort required. An initiation is necessary; somewhat of the intense mental activity which characterized Beethoven in the composition of his works is required of the student also.

Like Thoreau, Beethoven came on the world's stage
30 "just in the nick of time," and almost immediately had to begin hewing out a path for himself. He was born in the workshop, as was Mozart, and learned music simultaneously with speaking. Stirring times they were in which he first saw the light, and so indeed continued with ever-
35 increasing intensity, like a good drama, until nearly his end. The American Revolution became an accomplished fact during his boyhood. Nearer home, events were fast coming to a focus, which culminated in the French Revolution. The magic words, Liberty, Equality, Fraternity,
40 and the ideas for which they stood, were everywhere in the minds of the people. The age called for enlightenment, spiritual growth.

On reaching manhood, he found a world in transition; he realized that he was on the threshold of a new order of

45 things, and with ready prescience took advantage of such as could be utilized in his art. Through Beethoven the resources of the orchestra were increased, an added range was given the keyboard of the piano, the human voice was given tasks that at the time seemed impossible
50 of achievement. He established the precedent, which Wagner acted on later, of employing the human voice as a tool, an instrument, to be used in the exigencies of his art, as if it were a part of the orchestra.

Beethoven's birthplace, Bonn, no doubt proved a
55 favorable soil for the propagation of the new ideas. The unrest pervading all classes, an outcome of the Revolution, showed itself among the more serious-minded in increased intellectuality, and a reaching after higher things. The beautiful in music had been sufficiently
60 exploited by Mozart and Haydn. Beethoven demonstrated that music has a higher function than that of mere beauty, or the simple act of giving pleasure. The beautiful in literature is not its best part. To the earnest thinker, the seeker after truth, the student who looks for illumination
65 on life's problem, beauty in itself is insufficient. It is the best office of art, of Beethoven's art in particular, that it leads ever onward and upward; that it acts not only on the esthetic and moral sense, but develops the mental faculties as well, enabling the individual to find a purpose
70 and meaning in life.

(For source reference, see endnote [g])

Passage 2

Ludwig van Beethoven (1770-1827) is widely considered to be one of the pre-eminent classical music figures of the Western world. This German musical genius created numerous works that are firmly entrenched in the
75 repertoire. Except for a weakness in composing vocal and operatic music (to which he himself admitted, notwithstanding a few vocal works like the opera "Fidelio" and the song "Adelaide,") Beethoven had complete mastery of the artform.

80 It is difficult to sum up briefly what his musical works represent or symbolize, since taken together they encompass a vast system of thought. Generally, however, those who apprehend his music sense that it reflects their own personal yearnings and sufferings. It egoistically,
85 and always intelligently, "discusses" with its listener his or her feelings in the wake of personal failure and personal triumph, from the lowest depths of despair to the highest heights of happy or triumphant fulfillment. In his music, he represents the feelings felt by those attempting to

196

90 achieve their goals within their societies, whether they
are competing for love, status, money, power, mates and/
or any other things individuals feel naturally inclined to
attempt to acquire.

In a thematic sense, Beethoven does not promote
95 anarchist ideas. The listener cannot, in listening to
Beethoven's music, apprehend ideas which, if applied,
would compromise the welfare of his society. The music
is thus "civically responsible," as is the music of Bach or
Mozart. For Beethoven, the society exists as a bulwark
100 with which the individual must function in harmony, or
at least not function such as to harm or destroy it. And,
should the society marginalize or hurt the individual, as it
often does, the individual must, according to Beethoven,
humbly accept this, never considering the alternative
105 act of attempting to harm or destroy the society in the
wake of his or her personal frustrations. But, thanks
to Beethoven, such an individual is provided with the
means to sooth his or her misery in the wake of feeling
"hurt" at the hands of society. The means is this music
110 and the euphoric pleasure that it can provide to minds
possessing the psycho-intellectual "wiring" needed to
apprehend it.

(For source reference, see endnote [h])

14. Both passages call attention to which aspect
of Beethoven's work?

(A) Its focus on the feelings of the individual
(B) Its influence on other musicians
(C) Its support of the French and American
Revolutions
(D) Its thoughtful and intellectual bent
(E) Its similarities to that of Bach and Mozart

15. It can be inferred that the author of Passage 1
considers Bach to have been

(A) a musician who used intellect in his
compositions
(B) a lesser musician than Beethoven
(C) a musician who composed mainly by
intuition
(D) a musician who lacked the capability to
think for himself
(E) a primary influence on Beethoven's art

16. In lines 10-11, the author of Passage 1
compares musicians to children primarily to
indicate that

(A) musicians studied music at the exclusion
of other topics, and thus had a limited
knowledge of the world
(B) Beethoven's contemporaries depended on
the financial support of their patrons
(C) with the exception of Beethoven,
musicians were immature
(D) musicians reached their prime at an early
age
(E) Beethoven's predecessors depended on
the guidance of others in matters
unrelated to their music

17. The third paragraph of Passage 1 (lines 17-
28) marks a transition from a

(A) consideration of Beethoven's music to a
critique of people's understanding of it
(B) discussion of Beethoven's predecessors
to an analysis of his contemporaries
(C) summation of Beethoven's contributions
to an appeal to listeners to do their due
diligence in examining his work
(D) celebration of Beethoven's strengths to
an exploration of his weaknesses
(E) discussion of the philosophical nature
of Beethoven's work to a challenge to
those who cannot understand it

197

18. In response to the claim made in lines 75-78 of Passage 2 ("Except for...'Adelaide'"), the author of Passage 1 would most likely assert that

(A) Beethoven was only concerned with the human voice as it supported the music itself
(B) the author of Passage 2 is discounting the influence Beethoven had on Wagner
(C) the author of Passage 2 is not taking into account Beethoven's later works
(D) on the contrary, Beethoven took advantage of the changing nature of the world and stretched the capabilities of the human voice with his music
(E) Beethoven was just being modest in his assessment of his work, thus his opinion should not be taken as fact

19. The author of Passage 2 would most likely view the statement in lines 65-70 ("It is... life") of Passage 1 with

(A) guarded approval
(B) utter disapproval
(C) complete agreement
(D) skeptical disagreement
(E) considerable surprise

20. The first paragraph of Passage 2 (lines 71-79) primarily serves to

(A) indicate the supposed weakness of a musical master
(B) introduce the subject of the passage and highlight his major accomplishments
(C) outline the major events in the life of Beethoven
(D) highlight the most notable of Beethoven's compositions
(E) discuss the thematic elements found in Beethoven's symphonies

21. In line 96, "apprehend" most nearly means

(A) conceive
(B) catch
(C) arrest
(D) disregard
(E) refute

22. In line 98, quotation marks are used to

(A) set off a specialized term
(B) imply skepticism about a theory
(C) mock a flawed hypothesis
(D) emphasize the symbolic meaning of a term
(E) highlight a term being used in an unusual manner

23. The author of Passage 1 would most likely attribute the philosophy of Beethoven outlined by the author of Passage 2 in lines 99-106 ("For Beethoven...frustrations") to

(A) the inspiration of the writings of Thoreau
(B) the influence of the historical period in which he lived
(C) Beethoven's dependency on the support of wealthy patrons
(D) Beethoven's appreciation of the beautiful music of Mozart of Haydn
(E) Beethoven's belief in the importance of society over that of the individual

24. Unlike the author of Passage 1, the author of Passage 2 focuses more on

(A) the overarching themes in Beethoven's work
(B) the differences in Beethoven's symphonies and operas
(C) Beethoven's exploration of feelings in his music
(D) how the spirit of the times shaped Beethoven's music
(E) The effect of Beethoven's deafness on his music

25. The authors of both passages agree that to fully understand Beethoven's work the listener must

(A) be a musician himself
(B) learn to play Beethoven's music
(C) listen in the right atmosphere
(D) be in a receptive mood
(E) engage the faculties of his mind deeply

Ready to see how you did? Walk through the section again with me!

These two passages, written in 1905, address the music of <u>Ludwig van Beethoven.</u>

I know I am on a Humanities passage, but that's about it!

Passage 1

If Bach is the mathematician of music, as has been asserted, <u>Beethoven is its philosopher.</u> In his work the philosophic spirit comes to the fore. To the genius of the
Line musician is added in <u>Beethoven a wide mental grasp,</u>
5 an altruistic spirit, that seeks to <u>help humanity on the upward path</u>. He addresses the intellect of mankind.

B. added intellect and philosophy to his music.

Up to Beethoven's time musicians in general (Bach is always an exception) performed their work without the aid of an intellect for the most part; <u>they worked by</u>
10 <u>intuition.</u> In everything outside their art they were like children. <u>Beethoven was the first one having the independence to think for himself</u>—the first to have ideas on subjects unconnected with his art. He it was who established the dignity of the artist over that of the
15 simply well-born. <u>His entire life was a protest against the pretensions of birth over mind.</u>

B. was opinionated and challenged the aristocracy.

As with all valuable things, however, Beethoven's music is not to be enjoyed for nothing. <u>We must on our side contribute something to the enterprise,</u> something
20 more than simply buying a ticket to the performance. We must study his work in the right spirit, and place ourselves in a receptive attitude when listening to it to understand his message. No other composer demands so much of one; no other rewards the student so richly for
25 the effort required. An initiation is necessary; <u>somewhat of the intense mental activity which characterized Beethoven in the composition of his works is required of the student also.</u>

We need to use our intellect when listening to B.'s music.

Like Thoreau, Beethoven came on the world's stage
30 "just in the nick of time," and almost immediately had to begin hewing out a path for himself. He was born in the

workshop, as was Mozart, and learned music simultaneously
with speaking. <u>Stirring times they were</u> in which he first
saw the light, and so indeed continued with ever-

35   increasing intensity, like a good drama, until nearly his
end. The American Revolution became an accomplished
fact during his boyhood. Nearer home, events were fast
coming to a focus, which culminated in the French
Revolution. The magic words, Liberty, Equality, Fraternity,

40   and the ideas for which they stood, were everywhere in
the minds of the people. <u>The age called for enlightenment,
spiritual growth.</u>

On reaching manhood, he <u>found a world in transition;</u>
he realized that he was on the threshold of a new order of

45   things, and with ready prescience took advantage of such
as could be utilized in his art. <u>Through Beethoven the
resources of the orchestra were increased, an added
range was given the keyboard of the piano, the human
voice was given tasks that at the time seemed impossible

50   of achievement.</u> He established the precedent, which
Wagner acted on later, of employing the human voice as
a tool, an instrument, to be used in the exigencies of his
art, as if it were a part of the orchestra.

Beethoven's birthplace, Bonn, no doubt proved a

55   <u>favorable soil for the propagation of the new ideas.</u> The
unrest pervading all classes, an outcome of the Revolution,
showed itself among the more serious-minded in
increased intellectuality, and a reaching after higher
things. The beautiful in music had been sufficiently

60   exploited by Mozart and Haydn. <u>Beethoven demonstrated
that music has a higher function than that of mere beauty,
or the simple act of giving pleasure.</u> The beautiful in
literature is not its best part. To the earnest thinker, the
seeker after truth, the student who looks for illumination

65   on life's problem, <u>beauty in itself is insufficient. It is the
best office of art, of Beethoven's art in particular, that it
leads ever onward and upward;</u> that it acts not only on
the esthetic and moral sense, but develops the mental
faculties as well, <u>enabling the individual to find a purpose

70   and meaning in life.</u>

*B. born into a tumultuous time –
freedom being fought for.*

*He expanded on previous musical
limitations.*

*Music wasn't made just to be pretty, it
was about philosophy and inspiration.*

14. Both passages call attention to which aspect
of Beethoven's work?

(A) Its focus on the feelings of the individual
(B) Its influence on other musicians
(C) Its support of the French and American
Revolutions
(D) Its thoughtful and intellectual bent
(E) Its similarities to that of Bach and Mozart

Main Idea of Passage 1: *B. applied intellect
to his music, which was shaped by the
times in which he lived.*

Question #14 is a Compare/Contrast question,
so I'm going straight to question #15, which
pertains only to Passage 1.

15. It can be inferred that the author of Passage 1 considers Bach to have been

   (A) a musician who used intellect in his compositions

   (B) a lesser musician than Beethoven

   (C) a musician who composed mainly by intuition

   (D) a musician who lacked the capability to think for himself

   (E) a primary influence on Beethoven's art

Question: What does the author say about Bach?

Answer: Bach was smart, like a mathematician.

Answer choice (A) is a great match to my paraphrase: *used intellect (smart).* Check out line 1 *(Bach is the mathematician of music)* and lines 7-10 which assert that with the EXCEPTION of Bach, musicians didn't use their intellect. Let's disprove the others.

   (B) Notice the **comparison** tip-off, *lesser*. This answer choice has no support in the passage, as **the author never states that Beethoven is a BETTER musician than Bach.** The author seems to have the utmost respect for both composers.

   (C) This answer is **opposite** to the information stated in the passage. Check out lines 7-10: *Musicians in general performed their work without the aid of intellect for the most part; they worked by intuition.* **The parentheses in the middle** *(Bach is always an exception)* **indicate that Bach did NOT work so much intuitively as mathematically** (line 1).

   (D) **All those OTHER musicians lacked the capability to think for themselves.** Remember, *(Bach is always an exception).*

   (E) While Bach and Beethoven are compared - Bach is the *mathematician* while Beethoven is the *philosopher* (lines 1-2) - **nowhere does the author state that Bach *influenced* Beethoven.** This answer choice is clearly not supported.

16. In lines 10-11, the author of Passage 1 compares musicians to children primarily to indicate that

   (A) musicians studied music at the exclusion of other topics, and thus had a limited knowledge of the world

   (B) Beethoven's contemporaries depended on the financial support of their patrons

   (C) with the exception of Beethoven, musicians were immature

   (D) musicians reached their prime at an early age

   (E) Beethoven's predecessors depended on the guidance of others in matters unrelated to their music

Question: Why does the author say musicians are like children?

Answer: They didn't think for themselves in matters that didn't involve their music.

Answer choices (A) and (E) are the most similar to my paraphrase. Let's pick both of these apart first.

   (A) Lines 11-13 read: *Beethoven...was the first to have ideas on subjects unconnected to his art*. **We cannot make such a drastic leap and assume that the reason other musicians didn't have ideas on topics unrelated to their music is that they didn't STUDY other subjects.** Perhaps Beethoven's predecessors were well-traveled, and therefore *knowledgeable about the world*. There is no support for such an **assumption**.

   (E) **We know his predecessors did not think** *independently* (lines 11-12), which justifies *depended on the guidance of others* **and we know they did not** *have ideas on subjects unconnected to their art* (lines 12-13), which justifies *in matters unrelated to their music*. We have a winner.

Let's analyze the others.

   (B) Perhaps this is true, but **nowhere in the passage does the author reveal that Beethoven's contemporaries** *depended on the financial support of patrons*.

   (C) We have a *comparison*, and the statement, *musicians were immature* is **offensive**. Out of context, this answer choice looks good, but go back to the passage and dig and we see it has **no contextual support.**

   (D) Where in the passage can we find support for this answer? Nowhere! **It is clearly incorrect.**

17. The third paragraph of Passage 1 (lines 17-28) marks a transition from a

→ *Question: What's the shift in paragraph 3?*

Answer: The focus is now on the listener.

   (A) consideration of Beethoven's music to a critique of people's understanding of it
   (B) discussion of Beethoven's predecessors to an analysis of his contemporaries
   (C) summation of Beethoven's contributions to an appeal to listeners to do their due diligence in examining his work
   (D) celebration of Beethoven's strengths to an exploration of his weaknesses
   (E) discussion of the philosophical nature of Beethoven's work to a challenge to those who cannot understand it

Answer choices (A), (C), and (E) deal with Beethoven's listeners, so let's analyze those first.

   (A) While there is some support for the first half of this answer choice (*consideration of Beethoven's music*) I would argue that the first two paragraphs are more concerned with characterizing Beethoven the man than with characterizing his music. The second half, however, is off-base. **The author never says that people are misinterpreting Beethoven's music; he merely suggests that listening to his music takes mental concentration and aptitude.**

(C) What *contributions* are mentioned in the first two paragraphs? Beethoven added intellect to the *genius of the musician* (lines 3-4), he was the first to *think for himself* (line 12), he *established the dignity of the artist over that of the simply well-born* (lines 14-15). We've found support for the first half. Does the author state that listeners should *do their due diligence in examining his work*? Yes! **It matches my main idea for paragraph 3** (*We need to use our intellect when listening to B.'s music*). Check out the last sentence of the paragraph for more justification (lines 25-28).

(E) We definitely get a dose of Beethoven's *philosophical nature* in the first two paragraphs, but the third paragraph does not **challenge listeners who cannot understand Beethoven's music,** so we have a *partial answer.*

Let's refute the others.

(B) While the first two paragraphs do mention Beethoven's *predecessors*, **the third paragraph is not about his *contemporaries*, it is about his listeners.** We have a *partial answer.*

(D) One can argue that the first two paragraphs do indeed celebrate Beethoven's *strengths*, but **the third paragraph does NOT discuss his *weaknesses*.** We have a *partial answer.*

Questions #18 and #19 are Compare/Contrast questions and #20 is a specific question that pertains only to Passage 2, so it's time for me to read Passage 2.

Passage 2

Ludwig van Beethoven (1770-1827) is widely considered to be one of the pre-eminent classical music figures of the Western world. This German musical genius created numerous works that are firmly entrenched in the
75 repertoire. Except for a weakness in composing vocal and operatic music (to which he himself admitted, notwithstanding a few vocal works like the opera "Fidelio" and the song "Adelaide,") Beethoven had complete mastery of the artform.

80 It is difficult to sum up briefly what his musical works represent or symbolize, since taken together they encompass a vast system of thought. Generally, however, those who apprehend his music sense that it reflects their own personal yearnings and sufferings. It egoistically,
85 and always intelligently, "discusses" with its listener his or her feelings in the wake of personal failure and personal triumph, from the lowest depths of despair to the highest heights of happy or triumphant fulfillment. In his music, he represents the feelings felt by those attempting to
90 achieve their goals within their societies, whether they

This is opposite to Passage 1 (lines 48-50).

B. is one of the best.

B.'s music represents his listeners' emotions.

are competing for love, status, money, power, mates and/
or any other things individuals feel naturally inclined to
attempt to acquire.

95   In a thematic sense, Beethoven does not promote
anarchist ideas. The listener cannot, in listening to
Beethoven's music, apprehend ideas which, if applied,
would compromise the welfare of his society. The music
is thus "civically responsible," as is the music of Bach or
Mozart. For Beethoven, the society exists as a bulwark
100 with which the individual must function in harmony, or
at least not function such as to harm or destroy it. And,
should the society marginalize or hurt the individual, as it
often does, the individual must, according to Beethoven,
humbly accept this, never considering the alternative
105 act of attempting to harm or destroy the society in the
wake of his or her personal frustrations. But, thanks
to Beethoven, such an individual is provided with the
means to sooth his or her misery in the wake of feeling
"hurt" at the hands of society. The means is this music
110 and the euphoric pleasure that it can provide to minds
possessing the psycho-intellectual "wiring" needed to
apprehend it.

B. felt sake of society is more important than sake of individual.

But listen to his music and you'll feel better.

Main Idea of Passage 2: *B.'s music appeals to listeners' emotions, and while intelligent does not rock the boat.*

20. The first paragraph of Passage 2 (lines 71-79) ⟶
primarily serves to

  (A) indicate the supposed weakness of a
       musical master
  (B) introduce the subject of the passage and
       highlight his major accomplishments
  (C) outline the major events in the life of
       Beethoven
  (D) highlight the most notable of
       Beethoven's compositions
  (E) discuss the thematic elements found in
       Beethoven's symphonies

Question: What's the main idea of the first paragraph?

Answer: B. is one of the best.

Answer choice (B) looks like an acceptable paraphrase: *Introduce the subject (Beethoven)* and
highlight his major accomplishments (Beethoven is one of the best). Also check out lines 71-75
for proof from the passage. Let's disprove the others.

    (A) The author does mention one *weakness* in lines 75-76 (*composing vocal and operatic music*),
        but ONE weakness is not the primary purpose of the first paragraph; quite the *opposite*.

(C) The first paragraph *highlights* Beethoven's major musical ACCOMPLISHMENTS; **it does not detail *events* in Beethoven's life.**

(D) What specific *compositions* are noted in the first paragraph? *Adelaide* and *Fidelio* (lines 77-78). Why does the author mention these two works? To provide examples of Beethoven's vocal works that weren't a complete bust. Does the author note Beethoven's 5th or 9th symphonies, arguably his most popular? Nope. **The first paragraph is much more general, and answer (D) is much too specific.**

(E) **Paragraphs 2 and 3 discuss the *thematic elements* of Beethoven's work, paragraph 1 does not.**

---

21. In line 96, "apprehend" most nearly means   ⟶   *Question: What does "apprehend" mean?*

   (A) conceive   *Answer: Come up with.*
   (B) catch
   (C) arrest
   (D) disregard
   (E) refute

Answer choice (A) is a good match to my word: *Conceive* means *the way one perceives* (*comes up with*) *something.* Let's de-justify the others.

(B) Notice how *catch* is the primary definition of *apprehend*, as in "to apprehend a criminal." That's definitely not a match. **Be sure to check for contextual support.**

(C) *Arrest* and *catch* are along the same lines, so eliminate (C)!

(D) *Disregard* means *to ignore.* **This would completely change the meaning of the sentence**, indicating that the listener would not be able to ignore ideas in Beethoven's music that threaten society. But the author argues that anarchist ideas did NOT run through Beethoven's music.

(E) *Refute* means *prove false.* **This meaning would change the intended meaning of the sentence** in much the same manner as answer (D).

---

22. In line 98, quotation marks are used to   ⟶   *Question: What is the author trying to convey with the quotation marks?*

   (A) set off a specialized term
   (B) imply skepticism about a theory   *Answer: I know it describes the way*
   (C) mock a flawed hypothesis   *B. uses music, but can't really come*
   (D) emphasize the symbolic meaning of a   *up with why it's in quotation marks.*
        term
   (E) highlight a term being used in an unusual
        manner

I'm going to have to walk-through the answer choices for this one.

(A) A *specialized term* is a term used by experts to describe specialized knowledge in a specific field. For example, "mechanical solidarity" is a specialized term used in anthropology. It is not a term that the layperson is typically familiar with. **Civically responsible is not a specialized term, but a common term.**

(B) **The author is SUMMING Up his *theory*** (opinion) in lines 99-101 (that Beethoven's music does not promote dissonance), NOT *implying skepticism about that theory.*

(C) Again, the author is stating his *hypothesis* (opinion). **He isn't mocking his own point of view, or pointing out that it's flawed.**

(D) The quotes are definitely *emphasizing*, but how is the term *symbolic*? Can you put in words just what the phrase is symbolizing? **The phrase states the author's opinion quite clearly and literally, and isn't being used as a symbolic representation.**

(E) *Highlight* is along the same lines as *emphasize*, so that works well. *Civically responsible* is a bit out of context. **Usually, *civically responsible* is used in discourses regarding politics, ethics, and social issues, not as a descriptive phrase for music.** So yes, I'd say it's being used in an unusual manner.

I've answered all of my questions that relate to Passage 2. Now, it's time to answer all the Compare/Contrast questions. Let me first re-familiarize myself with the main idea of each passage.

Main Idea of Passage 1: *B. applied intellect to his music, which was shaped by the times in which he lived.*

Main Idea of Passage 2: *B.'s music appeals to listeners' emotions, and while intelligent does not rock the boat.*

14. Both passages call attention to which aspect of Beethoven's work?

→ *Question: What do both passages say about Beethoven's music?*

(A) Its focus on the feelings of the individual
(B) Its influence on other musicians
(C) Its support of the French and American Revolutions
(D) Its thoughtful and intellectual bent
(E) Its similarities to Bach and Mozart

Answer: He added intellect to it.

Note: If you were noting similarities between the passages while reading Passage 2, this answer will be easy to come up with in your own words; if not, you will have to use the answer choices as a guide.

Answer choice (D) matches my paraphrase: *intellectual bent* matches *added intellect*. Let's find the proof in the passage: Passage 1 lines 3-6 and lines 25-27, and Passage 2 line 85 (*always intelligently*) and lines 82 (*encompass a vast system of thought*).

(A) Passage 2 focuses on the listener's *feelings*, but **Passage 1 does not.**

(B) While we can **assume** Beethoven's music has *influenced* other musicians, **neither passage discusses this.**

(C) The author of Passage 1 mentions the *French and American Revolutions* in lines 36-39 to demonstrate how the era in which Beethoven lived influenced his music. **He never tells us what Beethoven thought of these revolutions.** We cannot *assume* he supported them. **The author of Passage 2 makes no mention of either revolution.**

(E) In Passage 1, *Bach* is mentioned in the first paragraph to introduce an aspect of Beethoven's music, and in the second as an exception to Beethoven's predecessors. The two *similarities* drawn are that both composers are smart and independent thinkers. **Lines 59-62 note a DIFFERENCE between the music of Mozart and Beethoven:** Mozart's music was just beautiful; Beethoven's music went beyond. The author of Passage 2 does note a *similarity* between Mozart, Bach, and Beethoven in lines 97-99 when he states that all three composers were *civically responsible*, but we've already disproven this answer choice in our analysis of Passage 1.

18. In response to the claim made in lines 75-78 of Passage 2 ("Except for...'Adelaide'"), the author of Passage 1 would most likely assert that

(A) Beethoven was only concerned with the human voice as it supported the music itself

(B) the author of Passage 2 is discounting the influence Beethoven had on Wagner

(C) the author of Passage 2 is not taking into account Beethoven's later works

(D) on the contrary, Beethoven took advantage of the changing nature of the world and stretched the capabilities of the human voice with his music

(E) Beethoven was just being modest in his assessment of his work, thus his opinion should not be taken as fact

Question: What is the author of Passage 2 saying in these lines?

Answer: B. wasn't very good at composing vocal and operatic music.

Question: What would the author of Passage 1 say about this?

Answer: He'd disagree, saying that Beethoven expanded vocal range in his operas.

Answer choice (D) is a good match to both my paraphrase and the main idea of Passage 1: *stretched the capabilities of the human voice* (*expanded vocal range*) and *took advantage of the changing nature of the world* (*his music was shaped by the time in which he lived*). Let's disprove the others.

(A) *Only* is much *too extreme.* Not to mention, **the passage never states this.**

(B) If you picked this answer, you probably used lines 50-53 as justification. Yes, *Beethoven established a precedent* that Wagner later used (in other words, Beethoven *influenced* Wagner). But is the author of Passage 2 *discounting* this influence? **He doesn't mention it, but that doesn't mean he is ignoring it or hasn't considered it.** We have a bit of an *assumption* on our hands. Answer (D) is still the better choice.

(C) The author of Passage 2 DOES take into account some exceptions (*Adelaide* and *Fidelio*). Do we know if these are later works? **Neither passage says.**

(E) Line 76 states, *to which he himself admitted,* but **we have no idea if Beethoven really did feel that he wasn't very good with operas or vocal music,** or if he is *being modest.* Answer (E) is an *assumption.*

19. The author of Passage 2 would most likely view the statement in lines 65-70 ("It is... life") of Passage 1 with

(A) guarded approval
(B) utter disapproval
(C) complete agreement
(D) skeptical disagreement
(E) considerable surprise

→ *Question: What does the statement say?*

Answer: B.'s music helps people find purpose and meaning in their lives.

Question: What would the author of Passage 2 say about this?

Answer: Yes, it does.

Answer choice (C) matches: *Complete agreement (Yes, it does)*, but it does seem awfully strong. Let's check our justification. In Passage 1, lines 69-70 read: *enabling the individual to find a purpose and meaning in life*. In Passage 2, lines 89-90 read: *he represents feelings felt by those attempting to achieve their goals within their societies*. Also consider lines 107-108 (*an individual is provided with the means to sooth his or her misery*). Both passages agree that Beethoven *seeks to help humanity on the upward path* (lines 5-6).

(A) *Guarded approval* is tempting, but **both authors are enamored with Beethoven, so why would his approval be *guarded*?** We have a *partial answer*.

(B) *Utter* is an adverb expressing degree, rendering this an *extreme* answer, and *disapproval* is **just plain wrong.**

(D) The author is neither *skeptical* nor *disagreeing*. **This answer is clearly not supported.**

(E) *Considerable* is an adverb expressing degree making this answer a tad *extreme*. **The author of Passage 2 would not be *surprised*, as he echoes the sentiments presented in Passage 1.**

23. The author of Passage 1 would most likely attribute the philosophy of Beethoven outlined by the author of Passage 2 in lines 99-106 ("For Beethoven...frustrations") to

(A) the inspiration of the writings of Thoreau
(B) the influence of the historical period in which he lived
(C) Beethoven's dependency on the support of wealthy patrons
(D) Beethoven's appreciation of the beautiful music of Mozart of Haydn
(E) Beethoven's belief in the importance of society over that of the individual

→ *Question: What does the author of Passage 2 say about Beethoven's philosophy?*

Answer: The individual should not put his own needs before those of society.

Question: What would the author of Passage 1 say caused this philosophy?

Answer: Not sure I know exactly, so I'll go back to the main idea of Passage 1 - Beethoven's philosophy was intelligent and shaped by the time in which he lived.

Answer choice (B) matches the main idea of Passage 1: *influence of the historical period* coincides with *shaped by his time.*

(A) *Thoreau* is mentioned in line 29 and compared to Beethoven, but **nowhere does the passage state that Beethoven was** *inspired by Thoreau's writings;* in fact Beethoven died when Thoreau was ten!

(C) **Nowhere in either passage does it state that Beethoven depended on** *wealthy patrons.* Careful not to bring in any outside knowledge. *Wealthy patrons* are not mentioned whatsoever.

(D) We have a *word-for-word copy.* Lines 59-60 read: *The beautiful in music had been sufficiently exploited by Mozart and Haydn.* Our brains naturally go, "Oh! I remember reading something like that!" Don't be fooled. Nowhere does the author say that Beethoven *appreciated* their music. **We have no idea how Beethoven felt about their music.** Avoid *assumptions*!

(E) This answer choice is simply Beethoven's philosophy as analyzed by the author of PASSAGE 2; **it does not account for the opinion of the author of Passage 1.** Don't confuse perspectives.

24. Unlike the author of Passage 1, the author of Passage 2 focuses more on

(A) the overarching themes in Beethoven's work
(B) the differences in Beethoven's symphonies and operas
(C) Beethoven's exploration of feelings in his music
(D) how the spirit of the times shaped Beethoven's music
(E) The effect of Beethoven's deafness on his music

Question: What does the author of Passage 2 focus on that the author of Passage 1 doesn't?

Answer: B.'s music appeals to listeners' emotions, *and while intelligent does not rock the boat. They both talk about B.'s intellect, so that's not the part of the equation I am looking for.*

Let's look at the answer choices from the perspective of the main idea of Passage 2:

Answer choice (C) matches my paraphrased main idea of Passage 2: *exploration of feelings (*music appeals to listeners' emotions*).* Let's refute the other answer choices.

(A) **BOTH passages discuss the** *themes in Beethoven's work,* so eliminate (A).
(B) The author of Passage 2 shares his opinion that Beethoven's one *weakness was composing vocal and operatic music* (lines 75-76), **but the author does not tell us how exactly these compositions are** *different* **from Beethoven's symphonies.**
(D) **This is one of the main focuses of Passage 1, not Passage 2.** Don't confuse perspectives!
(E) *Beethoven's deafness* **is not mentioned in either passage.** Don't pull in background knowledge.

25. The authors of both passages agree that to fully understand Beethoven's work the listener must

> *Question: What do both authors say about B.'s listeners?*
>
> *Answer: They have to listen intelligently.*

   (A) be a musician himself
   (B) learn to play Beethoven's music
   (C) listen in the right atmosphere
   (D) be in a receptive mood
   (E) engage the faculties of his mind deeply

Answer choice (E) matches my paraphrase: *engage the faculties of his mind* (*listen intelligently*). Here's the proof from each passage. Passage 1 reads: *somewhat of the intense mental activity which characterized Beethoven in the composition of his works is required of the student also* (lines 26-28). Passage 2 states: *The means is this music and the euphoric pleasure that it can provide to minds possessing the psycho-intellectual "wiring" needed to apprehend it* (lines 109-112).

   (A) **Nowhere in either passage does it state that in order to understand Beethoven's music the listener must be a *musician*.** That would disqualify the intelligence of millions of Beethoven fans that aren't musicians.

   (B) If this were true, the listener would have to go to an awful lot of trouble in order to understand Beethoven's music. Beethoven's symphonies would have fallen out of favor long ago. **This answer is clearly not supported with information from the passage.**

   (C) While the author of Passage 1 says *we must study his work in the right spirit, and place ourselves in a receptive mood when listening* (lines 21-22), **neither author tells us the best *atmosphere* (or location) in which to listen.** Is it in the car, the library… in bed before we go to sleep? Your guess is as good as mine. This answer choice is clearly not supported.

   (D) Passage 1 does state we must be in a *receptive mood* (line 22), but **the author of Passage 2 never states this.** Remember, you are looking for an opinion that is stated in BOTH passages.

The next chapter explains how to handle a Fiction Passage.

Chapter 9
The Fiction Passage

Found your preferred technique? Great! You'll be able to apply much of what you've already learned to the following fiction passage. You'll still be **stating the main idea, answering the questions in your own words, and justifying your answers with proof from the passage**. The main difference is in the reading.

> *EVERYONE, regardless of preferred technique or score range, MUST READ THE WHOLE FICTION PASSAGE!*

It's a story, with plot, characters, dialogue, literary devices, themes – the whole shebang! You can't get a good, or accurate assessment of a fiction passage without reading it in its entirety.

> *No need to break a fiction passage up paragraph-by-paragraph; read it through in one go, underlining key points.*

Here are the steps:

Step 1: Read the Italicized Introduction

Make note of *when* the passage was written, *where* and *when* the passage is set, and any *plot points* or *characters* mentioned.

Step 2: Read the Passage

Underline as you go to keep your brain actively reading. Notice shifts in mood and language, and the subtle dynamics of the characters' interactions.

Step 3: Write Down the Main Idea of the Entire Passage

Think not only of a synopsis, but also of themes.

Example #1: *Frank is engaged to Lucy, but Reverend Pierce doesn't like her.*
Themes: Not worrying what others think, love conquers all

Example #2: *Hughes owes Berkcoff money, but doesn't have it.*
Themes: Deceit, debt, struggles of friendship

Step 4: Read and Restate the First Question

Remember to turn it into a Jeopardy Question!

Example: Let's say the question reads, ***Richie's statement about Vera in lines 13-26 ("She smiles... ingratitude") primarily serves to***

Jeopardy question: *What does Richie say about Vera? What does this statement indicate about Richie? What does this indicate about Vera?*

→ **Keep in mind, there is always something going on beneath the surface in fiction passages. Be on the lookout for the characters' impressions of others, both those with whom they are interacting, and those they are discussing. Always ask: how does a statement reflect on the person they are talking about, and more important, how does it reflect on them?**

Step 5: Go Back to the Passage and Dig

Re-read 3-5 lines up and 3-5 lines down from the cited line numbers. Nothing new there!

> *Note: No need to go back and dig on many of the general questions.*

Step 6: Answer the Question in Your Own Words

This is the most important step, so don't skip it, no matter how tedious or difficult it may seem.

Step 7: Go to the Answer Choices

Remember, you are looking for a match to your paraphrased answer. Can't find one? Go back to the passage and dig deeper. Justify one of the answers with proof from the passage.

> *Remember to read between the lines, and watch out for irony and satire.*

Repeat Steps 4-7 for every question!

Let's apply these steps to the following fiction passage. My worked-through version of the passage follows. Circle your answers.

This passage, taken from an early nineteenth-century novel, presents two characters – Diantha, a young woman who leaves her family and fiancée in the hope of starting a housecleaning business, and Mrs. Weatherstone, a rich widow who has recently attended a meeting at which Diantha expressed her views on domestic service.

→
> **Step 1: Read and assess the Italicized Intro**
>
> What type of passage are we dealing with?
> _____
>
> What else can we gather?
> _____

There was a knock at her door. "Lady to see you, Miss."

"I cannot see anyone," said Diantha; "you must
Line   excuse me."
  5   "Beg pardon, Miss, but it's not a reporter; it's—." The
landlady stretched her lean neck around the door edge
and whispered hoarsely, "It's young Mrs. Weatherstone!"

> **Step 2: Read the passage in its entirety**
>
> *Underline as you go!*

Diantha rose to her feet, a little bewildered. "I'll be
right down," she said. But a voice broke in from the hall,
 10 "I beg your pardon, Miss Bell, but I took the liberty of
coming up; may I come in?"

She came in, and the landlady perforce went out.
Mrs. Weatherstone held Diantha's hand warmly, and
looked into her eyes. "I was a schoolmate of Ellen
 15 Porne," she told the girl. "We are dear friends still; and
so I feel that I know you better than you think. You have
done beautiful work for Mrs. Porne; now I want you to
do to it for me. I need you."

"Won't you sit down?" said Diantha.
 20   "You, too," said Mrs. Weatherstone. "Now I want you
to come to me—right away. You have done me so much
good already. I was just a New England bred school
teacher myself at first, so we're even that far. Then you
took a step up—and I took a step down."
 25   Diantha was a little slow in understanding the quick
fervor of this new friend; a trifle suspicious, even; being
a cautious soul, and somewhat overstrung, perhaps. Her
visitor, bright-eyed and eager, went on. "I gave up school
teaching and married a fortune. You have given it up to
 30 do a more needed work. I think you are wonderful. Now,
I know this seems queer to you, but I want to tell you
about it. I feel sure you'll understand. At home, Madam
Weatherstone has had everything in charge for years and
years, and I've been too lazy or too weak, or too
 35 indifferent, to do anything. I didn't care, somehow. All
the machinery of living, and no living—no good of it all!

213

Yet there didn't seem to be anything else to do. Now
you have waked me all up—your paper this afternoon—
what Mr. Eltwood said—the way those poor, dull, blind
40 women took it. And yet I was just as dull and blind
myself! Well, I begin to see things now. I can't tell you
all at once what a difference it has made; but I have a
very definite proposition to make to you. Will you come
and be my housekeeper, now—right away—at a hundred
45 dollars a month?"

Diantha opened her eyes wide and looked at the eager
lady as if she suspected her nervous balance.

"The other one got a thousand a year—you are worth
more. Now, don't decline, please. Let me tell you about
50 it. I can see that you have plans ahead, for this business;
but it can't hurt you much to put them off six months,
say. Meantime, you could be practicing. Our place at
Santa Ulrica is almost as big as this one; there are lots of
servants and a great, weary maze of accounts to be kept,
55 and it wouldn't be bad practice for you—now, would it?"

Diantha's troubled eyes lit up. "No—you are right
there," she said. "If I could do it!"

"You'll have to do just that sort of thing when you are
running your business, won't you?" her visitor went on.
60 "And the summer's not a good time to start a thing like
that, is it?"

Diantha meditated. "No, I wasn't going to. I was
going to start somewhere—take a cottage, a dozen girls
or so—and furnish labor by the day to the other cottages."
65 "Well, you might be able to run that on the side," said
Mrs. Weatherstone. "And you could train my girls, get
in new ones if you like; it doesn't seem to me it would
conflict. But to speak to you quite frankly, Miss Bell,
I want you in the house for my own sake. You do me
70 good."

They discussed the matter for some time, Diantha
objecting mainly to the suddenness of it all. "I'm a slow
thinker," she said, "and this is so—so attractive that I'm
suspicious of it. I had the other thing all planned—the
75 girls practically engaged."

"Where were you thinking of going?" asked Mrs.
Weatherstone.

"To Santa Ulrica."

"Exactly! Well, you shall have your cottage and our
80 girls and give them part time. Or—how many have you
arranged with?"

"Only six have made definite engagements yet."

"What kind?"

"Two laundresses, a cook and three second maids; all
85 good ones."

"Excellent! Now, I tell you what to do. I will engage all those girls. I'm making a change at the house, for various reasons. You bring them to me as soon as you like; but you I want at once. I wish you'd come home

90 with me tonight! Why don't you?"

Diantha's scanty baggage was all in sight. She looked around for an excuse. Mrs. Weatherstone stood up laughing.

"Put the new address in the letter," she said,

95 mischievously, "and come along!"

(For source reference, see endnote ⁱ)

Step 3: Write down the main idea of the passage

_____

_____

7. The episode given in the passage is best described as a

Step 4: Read and restate the 1st question

_____

_____

(A) disagreement between an employer and her employee
(B) confrontation between two people whose differences seem irresolvable
(C) setback in an otherwise warm friendship
(D) coercion, in which a higher class individual takes advantage of her position to bully a subservient
(E) negotiation between two people with equal opportunity to gain

This is a general question so we can skip Step 5.

Step 6: Answer the question in your own words

_____

_____

Step 7: Go to the answer choices and match your paraphrased answer.

Circle it!

8. Mrs. Weatherstone responds to Diantha's gesture of hospitality in line 19 by

Step 4: Read and restate the question

_____

_____

(A) immediately putting Diantha on equal footing
(B) taking her place as the authority figure
(C) demanding a more comfortable seat
(D) refusing to sit before Diantha sits first
(E) disregarding Diantha's hospitality and immediately launching into her proposal

Step 5: Go back to the passage and dig

Re-read from lines 13-24 ("Mrs. Weatherstone…step down").

Step 6: Answer the question in your own words

_____

_____

Step 7: Go to the answer choices and match your paraphrased answer.

Circle it!

9. Mrs. Weatherstone's comment in lines 23- 24 ("Then...down") implies that

(A) Mrs. Weatherstone withdrew from social life
(B) Diantha is of a higher social class than Mrs. Weatherstone
(C) Diantha has followed a more honorable path than Mrs. Weatherstone
(D) Diantha was a better school teacher than Mrs. Weatherstone
(E) Mrs. Weatherstone married beneath her social class

→ Step 4: Read and restate the question

_____

_____

Step 5: Go back to the passage and dig

We've just read this. Feel free to re-read lines 20-24, but you may be able to immediately answer this question.

Step 6: Answer the question in your own words

_____

_____

Step 7: Go to the answer choices and match your paraphrased answer.

Circle it!

10. Mrs. Weatherstone uses the expression "the machinery of living" (line 36) to suggest that she has been living life

(A) superficially, without any real involvement
(B) systematically, with a set routine
(C) luxuriously, equipped with the most modern appliances
(D) despondently, unable to go about her daily activities
(E) recklessly, seeking adventures to escape her boredom

→ Step 4: Read and restate the question

_____

_____

Step 5: Go back to the passage and dig

Re-read from lines 30-41 ("Now, I know... myself").

Step 6: Answer the question in your own words

_____

_____

Step 7: Go to the answer choices and match your paraphrased answer.

Circle it!

11. Diantha's reaction to Mrs. Weatherstone's proposal quoted in lines 43-45 indicates that Diantha thinks that this proposal $\longrightarrow$

   (A) stems from an imbalance in Mrs. Weatherstone's mental faculties
   (B) is an insult to her worth and skill
   (C) is a scheme designed to prevent her from developing her business
   (D) is a poor attempt at humor
   (E) is utterly surprising and too good to be true

Step 4: Read and restate the question

_____

_____

Step 5: Go back to the passage and dig

We only need to re-read the proposal and Diantha's reaction that follows - lines 43-47 ("Will you…balance").

Step 6: Answer the question in your own words

_____

_____

Step 7: Go to the answer choices and match your paraphrased answer.

Circle it!

12. In line 54, "weary" most nearly means $\longrightarrow$

   (A) fatigued
   (B) apathetic
   (C) shabby
   (D) burdensome
   (E) complicated

Step 4: Read and restate the question

_____

_____

Step 5: Go back to the passage and dig

For this vocab-in-context question we only need to read the sentence that contains the word "weary" - lines 52-55 ("Our place… would it").

Step 6: Answer the question in your own words

_____

_____

Step 7: Go to the answer choices and match your paraphrased answer.

Circle it!

13. Mrs. Weatherstone asks the question in lines 60-61 ("And the...is it") primarily in order to

(A) raise a pressing matter
(B) note an important point
(C) anticipate a possible objection
(D) criticize a widely accepted practice
(E) belittle a fanciful notion

> Step 4: Read and restate the question
> _____
> _____

> Step 5: Go back to the passage and dig

Re-read lines 58-64 ("You'll have... cottages").

> Step 6: Answer the question in your own words
> _____
> _____

> Step 7: Go to the answer choices and match your paraphrased answer.

Circle it!

---

14. Which interpretation of Mrs. Weatherstone's statement in lines 69-70 ("You do...good") is most fully supported by the rest of the passage?

(A) It indicates that Mrs. Weatherstone is sorely in need of Diantha's housekeeping skills
(B) It reveals that Mrs. Weatherstone credits Diantha for her newfound spirit
(C) It hints at Mrs. Weatherstone's need to be waited on hand and foot
(D) It shows Mrs. Weatherstone's increasing discomfort with having servants
(E) It suggests that Mrs. Weatherstone fears Madam Weatherstone and wants Diantha to protect her

> Step 4: Read and restate the question
> _____
> _____

> Step 5: Go back to the passage and dig

Re-read lines 65-70 ("Well, you...good"). Keep in mind that this question pertains to the WHOLE passage, not just the context around the stated line numbers.

> Step 6: Answer the question in your own words
> _____
> _____

> Step 7: Go to the answer choices and match your paraphrased answer.

Circle it!

218

15. Mrs. Weatherstone deflects Diantha's objections to her proposition primarily with

   (A) force and intimidation
   (B) begging and pathos
   (C) sound reasoning and accommodation
   (D) condescension and threats
   (E) stubbornness and eloquence

→ Step 4: Read and restate the question

_____

_____

Step 5: Go back to the passage and dig

This is more of a general question, as it applies to Mrs. Weatherstone's behavior THROUGHOUT the passage. Rather than answering the question in your own words first, let's look at the answer choices and then go back to the passage to see which is the MOST justified.

Step 7: Go to the answer choices and find justification.

Circle it!

16. Mrs. Weatherstone's remark in lines 94-95 is said in a tone of

   (A) command
   (B) witty irony
   (C) impishness
   (D) curtness
   (E) haste

→ Step 4: Read and restate the question

_____

_____

Step 5: Go back to the passage and dig

Re-read from line 86 to the end of the passage ("Excellent...come along").

Step 6: Answer the question in your own words

_____

_____

Step 7: Go to the answer choices and match your paraphrased answer.

Circle it!

17. Diantha and Mrs. Weatherstone would most likely agree on which point?

(A) Diantha must make more money in order to start her new business

(B) Diantha will not be able to find a higher paying housekeeping job

(C) housekeeping is a better career for a woman than is school teaching

(D) the need for improvements in women's opportunities both inside and outside the home

(E) the hotel Diantha is staying at is not a suitable residence for an unchaperoned young lady

→ Step 4: Read and restate the question

_____

_____

Step 5: Go back to the passage and dig

We have a general question that is hard to answer in our own words. Let's go straight to the answers and justify one of them with proof from the passage.

Step 7: Go to the answer choices and justify with proof from the passage.

Circle it!

Let's see how you did by checking your answers with mine. Don't just look to see what answer choices I've circled. Walk through the technique again to see if your paraphrased answers are similar to mine.

This passage, taken from an early nineteenth-century novel, presents two characters – Diantha, a young woman who leaves her family and fiancée in the hope of starting a housecleaning business, and Mrs. Weatherstone, a rich widow who has recently attended a meeting at which Diantha expressed her views on domestic service.

Step 1: Read and assess the Italicized Intro

What type of passage are we dealing with?
Fiction

What else can we gather?
19th century literature, so I need to read between the lines. 2 characters, one is wealthy and older (Mrs. Weatherstone) than the other (Diantha), who wants to run a housecleaning business. The rich one heard the young one speak at a meeting.

There was a knock at her door. "Lady to see you, Miss."

"I cannot see anyone," said Diantha; "you must
Line excuse me."
5   "Beg pardon, Miss, but it's not a reporter; it's—." The landlady stretched her lean neck around the door edge and whispered hoarsely, "It's young Mrs. Weatherstone!"

Diantha rose to her feet, a little bewildered. "I'll be right down," she said. But a voice broke in from the hall,
10 "I beg your pardon, Miss Bell, but I took the liberty of coming up; may I come in?"

She came in, and the landlady perforce went out. Mrs. Weatherstone held Diantha's hand warmly, and looked into her eyes. "I was a schoolmate of Ellen
15 Porne," she told the girl. "We are dear friends still; and so I feel that I know you better than you think. You have done beautiful work for Mrs. Porne; now I want you to do it for me. I need you."

"Won't you sit down?" said Diantha.
20   "You, too," said Mrs. Weatherstone. "Now I want you to come to me—right away. You have done me so much good already. I was just a New England bred school teacher myself at first, so we're even that far. Then you took a step up—and I took a step down."
25   Diantha was a little slow in understanding the quick fervor of this new friend; a trifle suspicious, even; being a cautious soul, and somewhat overstrung, perhaps. Her visitor, bright-eyed and eager, went on. "I gave up school teaching and married a fortune. You have given it up to
30 do a more needed work. I think you are wonderful. Now, I know this seems queer to you, but I want to tell you about it. I feel sure you'll understand. At home, Madam Weatherstone has had everything in charge for years and years, and I've been too lazy or too weak, or too
35 indifferent, to do anything. I didn't care, somehow. All the machinery of living, and no living—no good of it all!

Step 2: Read the passage in its entirety

I've underlined what I think may be important.

Mrs. W. must be important.

She's come with good will.

Yet there didn't seem to be anything else to do. Now you have waked me all up—your paper this afternoon—what Mr. Eltwood said—the way those poor, dull, blind

40 women took it. And yet I was just as dull and blind myself! Well, I begin to see things now. I can't tell you all at once what a difference it has made; but I have a very definite proposition to make to you. Will you come and be my housekeeper, now—right away—at a hundred

45 dollars a month?"

Diantha opened her eyes wide and looked at the eager lady as if she suspected her nervous balance.

"The other one got a thousand a year—you are worth more. Now, don't decline, please. Let me tell you about

50 it. I can see that you have plans ahead, for this business; but it can't hurt you much to put them off six months, say. Meantime, you could be practicing. Our place at Santa Ulrica is almost as big as this one; there are lots of servants and a great, weary maze of accounts to be kept,

55 and it wouldn't be bad practice for you—now, would it?"

Diantha's troubled eyes lit up. "No—you are right there," she said. "If I could do it!"

"You'll have to do just that sort of thing when you are running your business, won't you?" her visitor went on.

60 "And the summer's not a good time to start a thing like that, is it?"

Diantha meditated. "No, I wasn't going to. I was going to start somewhere—take a cottage, a dozen girls or so—and furnish labor by the day to the other cottages."

65 "Well, you might be able to run that on the side," said Mrs. Weatherstone. "And you could train my girls, get in new ones if you like; it doesn't seem to me it would conflict. But to speak to you quite frankly, Miss Bell, I want you in the house for my own sake. You do me

70 good."

They discussed the matter for some time, Diantha objecting mainly to the suddenness of it all. "I'm a slow thinker," she said, "and this is so—so attractive that I'm suspicious of it. I had the other thing all planned—the

75 girls practically engaged."

"Where were you thinking of going?" asked Mrs. Weatherstone.

"To Santa Ulrica."

"Exactly! Well, you shall have your cottage and our

80 girls and give them part time. Or—how many have you arranged with?"

"Only six have made definite engagements yet."

"What kind?"

"Two laundresses, a cook and three second maids; all

85 good ones."

"Excellent! Now, I tell you what to do. I will engage all those girls. I'm making a change at the house, for various reasons. You bring them to me as soon as you like; but you I want at once. I wish you'd come home

90 with me tonight! Why don't you?"

Diantha's scanty baggage was all in sight. She looked around for an excuse. Mrs. Weatherstone stood up laughing.

"Put the new address in the letter," she said,

95 mischievously, "and come along!"

Step 3: Write down the main idea of the passage

D. has inspired Mrs. W., who wants D. to run her household and in turn Mrs. W. will help D. start her business.

222

7. The episode given in the passage is best described as a

(A) disagreement between an employer and her employee
(B) confrontation between two people whose differences seem irresolvable
(C) setback in an otherwise warm friendship
(D) coercion, in which a higher class individual takes advantage of her position to bully a subservient
(E) negotiation between two people with equal opportunity to gain

Step 4: Read and restate the 1st question

What's going on in the passage. – the bones of it?

I'll skip Step 5, because I'm on a general question.

Step 6: Answer the question in your own words

2 women discussing a mutually beneficial business arrangement

Step 7: Go to the answer choices and match your paraphrased answer.

Answer choice (E) matches my paraphrased answer perfectly: *Negotiation* (*discussion*) *between two people* (*2 women*) *with equal opportunity to gain* (*mutually beneficial business arrangement*). Let's disprove the other answer choices.

(A) While Diantha does raise objections (*disagreement* may be a tad strong), the two women reach an agreement by the end of the passage. **Diantha does not yet work for Mrs. Weatherstone,** so *between an employer and her employee* does not hold true.

(B) *Confrontation* means argument, which is a pretty strong word; **the two women seem to get along quite well**. Mrs. Weatherstone immediately *holds Diantha's hand warmly* (line 13) and praises Diantha throughout. Mrs. Weatherstone is quick to level the playing ground, saying, *I was just a New England bred school teacher so we're even that far* (lines 22-23) and Mrs. Weatherstone does indeed convince Diantha to accept the proposal, so no *irresolvable differences* there; **a solution is found.**

(C) **This is the first time Diantha and Mrs. Weatherstone have met** (Mrs. Weatherstone introduces herself as a schoolmate of Ellen Porne in lines 14-15), and lines 25-26 state that *Diantha was a little slow in understanding the quick fervor of this **new** friend*, disproving the phrase *warm friendship*.

(D) *Coercion* means *bullying*, and **while Mrs. Weatherstone doesn't back down, she isn't at all intimidating or threatening**, on the contrary she is reasonable and generous. She offers Diantha a high salary (lines 44-45) and accommodates Diantha's business (lines 65-70). Mrs. Weatherstone does not view Diantha as her *subservient* (see lines 22-24).

8. Mrs. Weatherstone responds to Diantha's gesture of hospitality in line 19 by

(A) immediately putting Diantha on equal footing
(B) taking her place as the authority figure
(C) demanding a more comfortable seat
(D) refusing to sit before Diantha sits first
(E) disregarding Diantha's hospitality and immediately launching into her proposal

Step 4: Read and restate the question

What does Mrs. W. do and say?

Step 5: Go back to the passage and dig

Re-read from lines 13-24 ("Mrs. Weatherstone...step down").

Step 6: Answer the question in your own words

She asks D. to sit as well, and then tells D. that they have a lot in common.

Step 7: Go to the answer choices and match your paraphrased answer.

Let's dissect the answer choices.

(A) Mrs. Weatherstone asks Diantha to sit too (line 20) **so they are physically on *equal footing*** and then tells Diantha that she used to be a schoolteacher as well. Mrs. Weatherstone even uses the phrase *so we're even that far* (line 23), putting them **intellectually and socially on equal footing**. We have justification for answer (A).

(B) Again, Mrs. Weatherstone states, *so we're even that far*. **She is NOT *expressing her authority*, but speaking to Diantha as an equal.**

(C) *Demanding* **does not describe Mrs. Weatherstone's character as portrayed in the passage.** At no point does she say, "This chair is uncomfortable. Give me another one." Answer choice (C) is clearly wrong.

(D) She says, *You too*, but **there is no indication that she WAITS**, not with words, or with physical actions, about which the author remains silent.

(E) **She doesn't *disregard Diantha's hospitality*; she ACKNOWLEDGES it** with *You too*. **The phrase *immediately launching into her proposal* is also off target**, as Mrs. Weatherstone delivers quite a bit of explication (lines 21-43) before making her proposal.

9. Mrs. Weatherstone's comment in lines 23- 24 ("Then...down") implies that

(A) Mrs. Weatherstone withdrew from social life
(B) Diantha is of a higher social class than Mrs. Weatherstone
(C) Diantha has followed a more honorable path than Mrs. Weatherstone
(D) Diantha was a better school teacher than Mrs. Weatherstone
(E) Mrs. Weatherstone married beneath her social class

Step 4: Read and restate the question

What is Mrs. W. really getting at?

Step 5: Go back to the passage and dig

I've already read this, so I'll jump to Step 6.

Step 6: Answer the question in your own words

You're a better person than I am, or you've made better choices than I have.

Step 7: Go to the answer choices and match your paraphrased answer.

Answer choice (C) matches my paraphrase: *Diantha has followed a more honorable path* (*you've made better choices than I have*). Also notice lines 29-30: *You have given it up to do a more needed work.* Let's analyze the others.

(A) **There is no indication that Mrs. Weatherstone *withdrew from social life*.** Lines 28-29 explain that she gave up teaching and married a rich man, not that she never went out and hid behind closed doors. Answer (A) is clearly wrong.

(B) **This is the opposite of what is stated in the passage.** The italicized intro tells us that Mrs. Weatherstone is a *rich widow* who *married a fortune* (line 29) and Diantha is a schooteacher turned house cleaner.

(D) Notice the *comparison* tip-off "better." **There is no comparison made as to who was the better teacher**, and comparisons are one of our answers to avoid.

(E) **She used to be a schoolteacher (lines 22-23) and then *she married a fortune* (line 29)** clearly disproving this answer choice.

10. Mrs. Weatherstone uses the expression "the machinery of living" (line 36) to suggest that she has been living life

(A) superficially, without any real involvement
(B) systematically, with a set routine
(C) luxuriously, equipped with the most modern appliances
(D) despondently, unable to go about her daily activities
(E) recklessly, seeking adventures to escape her boredom

Step 4: Read and restate the question

What is Mrs. W. saying about her life?

Step 5: Go back to the passage and dig

Re-read from lines 30-41 ("Now, I know... myself").

Step 6: Answer the question in your own words

She's been going about her life on automatic pilot not caring about anything.

Step 7: Go to the answer choices and match your paraphrased answer.

Answer choice (A) is a pretty good match: *Superficially* (*automatic pilot*) and *without any real involvement* (*not caring about anything*). Let's pick apart the other answer choices.

(B) Perhaps you found justification for this answer in lines 32-34 (*At home, Madam Weatherstone has had everything in charge for years and years*) which indicate a certain routine. But this routine is Madame Weatherstone's (Mrs. Weatherstone's mother-in-law) and **while Mrs. Weatherstone doesn't challenge it, there is no indication that she follows it as a** *systematic daily routine.*

(C) If you picked this answer choice, you made an **assumption**. **Mrs. Weatherstone is rich, but that doesn't indicate she necessarily lives** *luxuriously*, and there is no mention of *modern appliances* in the passage.

(D) *Despondently* means *hopelessly*, and while Mrs. Weatherstone indicates she has been living life lackadaisically (unenthusiastically) **she never says she is hopelessly depressed and unable to get out of bed.**

(E) Check out lines 34-35 (*I've been too lazy or too weak, or too indifferent, to do anything*). **She has NOT been living life** *recklessly* **or been** *seeking adventures*.

11. Diantha's reaction to Mrs. Weatherstone's proposal quoted in lines 43-45 indicates that Diantha thinks that this proposal

> | Step 4: Read and restate the question |
> | :--- |
>
> *How does D. react to the proposal?*

(A) stems from an imbalance in Mrs. Weatherstone's mental faculties
(B) is an insult to her worth and skill
(C) is a scheme designed to prevent her from developing her business
(D) is a poor attempt at humor
(E) is utterly surprising and too good to be true

> | Step 5: Go back to the passage and dig |
> | :--- |

We only need to re-read the proposal and Diantha's reaction that follows - lines 43-47 ("Will you...balance").

> | Step 6: Answer the question in your own words |
> | :--- |
>
> *She is shocked and thinks Mrs. W. might be crazy.*

> | Step 7: Go to the answer choices and match your paraphrased answer. |
> | :--- |

Looks like (A) is a match. *An imbalance in Mrs. Weatherstone's mental faculties* matches my paraphrase (*might be crazy*). Let's de-justify the others.

(B) **Mrs.Weatherstone at no point insults Diantha's worth and skill, rather she praises her throughout their conversation.** Check out lines 48-49 (*The other one got a thousand a year—you are worth more*). If anyone doubts Diantha's skill it is Diantha herself, who questions in line 57, *If I could do it!*

(C) **Mrs. Weatherstone wants Diantha to come work for her, but not at the expense of sacrificing the girl's dreams.** Mrs. Weatherstone explains that it will be *good practice* (line 52) and suggests that Diantha use the girls that Mrs. Weatherstone already employs or hire new girls if she'd rather (lines 66-67).

(D) **We know that Mrs. Weatherstone is completely serious in her proposal, and** *suspecting her nervous balance* **(line 47), doesn't mean she is trying (and failing) to make a joke,** but rather that Diantha thinks Mrs. Weatherstone may very well have "lost her marbles."

(E) There is proof for *surprising* – Diantha does *open her eyes wide* – but bear in mind that *utterly* is an **adverb expressing degree** and **is too strong**.

12. In line 54, "weary" most nearly means

(A) fatigued
(B) apathetic
(C) shabby
(D) burdensome
(E) complicated

Step 4: Read and restate the question

What does "weary" mean?

Step 5: Go back to the passage and dig

For this vocab-in-context question we only need to read the sentence that contains the word "weary" - lines 52-55 ("Our place… would it").

Step 6: Answer the question in your own words

Weary: Huge and exhausting

Step 7: Go to the answer choices and match your paraphrased answer.

Let's pick apart the answer choice words to find a match for my paraphrase.

(A) *Fatigued* means *exhausted*. **Weary** modifies *maze of accounts*. **While the maze of accounts can be EXHAUSTING, it cannot be EXHAUSTED.** That would be unintentional personification on the author's part.

(B) *Apathetic* means *uninterested*. **While one can assume** (and we want to avoid *assumptions*) **that the** *maze of accounts* **is UNINTERESTING, they cannot be UNINTERESTED.**

(C) *Shabby* means *tattered* and *worn down*, and refers to physical appearance. **Mrs. Weatherstone is not implying that** *her maze of accounts* **LOOKS run down.**

(D) *Burdensome* means *exhausting* and *laborious*. **We have a match!**

(E) *Complicated* means *complex*. She does refer to her accounts as a *maze* (indicating complexity), but **the secondary definition of** *weary* **means** *tiring*, **not** *complicated*.

13. Mrs. Weatherstone asks the question in lines 60-61 ("And the...is it") primarily in order to

(A) raise a pressing matter
(B) note an important point
(C) anticipate a possible objection
(D) criticize a widely accepted practice
(E) belittle a fanciful notion

Step 4: Read and restate the question

Why does Mrs. W. ask the question?

Step 5: Go back to the passage and dig

Re-read lines 58-64 ("You'll have... cottages").

Step 6: Answer the question in your own words

To point out that Diantha has no reason to object and that she can indeed do it.

Step 7: Go to the answer choices and match your paraphrased answer.

Answer choice (B) seems like a good match: *note an important point* matches my paraphrase (*to point out*). Let's dissect the other answer choices.

(A) The two ladies are DISCUSSING *a pressing matter* (Mrs. Weatherstone wants Diantha to come work for her immediately) but **the question itself does not *raise this matter*; it is merely a continuation of the discussion.**
(C) **The question is NOT an *anticipation* but a RESPONSE to** Diantha's *objection* in line 57 (*If I could do it*).
(D) **She is not being at all *critical*, if anything she is ENCOURAGING Diantha.** And what is the *widely accepted practice?* The business Diantha is thinking of starting? Hmm...no support for that.
(E) **She is not being *belittling* (condescending) and she takes Diantha's idea seriously,** disproving the phrase *fanciful notion,* which means *far-fetched idea.*

14. Which interpretation of Mrs. Weatherstone's statement in lines 69-70 ("You do…good") is most fully supported by the rest of the passage?

(A) It indicates that Mrs. Weatherstone is sorely in need of Diantha's housekeeping skills

(B) It reveals that Mrs. Weatherstone credits Diantha for her newfound spirit

(C) It hints at Mrs. Weatherstone's need to be waited on hand and foot

(D) It shows Mrs. Weatherstone's increasing discomfort with having servants

(E) It suggests that Mrs. Weatherstone fears Madam Weatherstone and wants Diantha to protect her

---

Step 4: Read and restate the question

What is Mrs. W getting at and how is it supported by the rest of her statements and actions in the passage?

Step 5: Go back to the passage and dig

Re-read lines 65-70 ("Well, you…good"), keeping in mind the whole passage.

Step 6: Answer the question in your own words

D. inspires her (part of my main idea).

Step 7: Go to the answer choices and match your paraphrased answer.

Answer choice (B) is a match! *Diantha inspires her*, is a paraphrase of *credits Diantha for her newfound spirit*. Let's analyze the others.

(A) This is a tricky one; after all, Mrs. Weatherstone straight up asks Diantha *will you come and be my housekeeper* (lines 43-44). But notice the wording of the question: *most fully supported by the rest of the passage*. Mrs. Weatherstone indicates throughout the passage that Diantha has *waked me all up* (line 38) and that she needs her in the house *for her own sake* and because she *does her good* (lines 69-70). **Mrs. Weatherstone implies throughout the passage that it is not just Diantha's housekeeping skills, but also her outlook she appreciates.** Remember, on fiction passages dig deeper!

(C) **This answer is contrary to the depiction of Mrs. Weatherstone.** She treats Diantha as an equal throughout and does not conduct herself in a superior manner. Answer (C) is clearly wrong.

(D) This answer is purely *assumption*. We know Mrs. Weatherstone HAS many servants; check out lines 53-55 (*Our place at Santa Ulrica is almost as big as this one; there are lots of servants…*). **We have no idea how she FEELS about having these servants.**

(E) Mrs. Weatherstone mentions Madam Weatherstone in lines 32-33. She merely states that Madam Weatherstone has run the house and she (Mrs. Weatherstone) hasn't cared. **Nowhere does it state that Mrs. Weatherstone is AFRAID of her mother-in-law or needs protection.** Answer (E) is clearly wrong.

15. Mrs. Weatherstone deflects Diantha's objections to her proposition primarily with

    (A) force and intimidation
    (B) begging and pathos
    (C) sound reasoning and accommodation
    (D) condescension and threats
    (E) stubbornness and eloquence

Step 4: Read and restate the question

How does Mrs. W. convince D?

Step 5: Go back to the passage and dig

This is more of a general question, as it applies to Mrs. Weatherstone's behavior THROUGHOUT the passage. Rather than answering the question in your own words first, let's look at the answer choices, and then go back to the passage to see which is the MOST justified.

Step 7: Go to the answer choices and find justification.

Let's walk through the answer choices to see which has the most justification.

    (A) Mrs. Weatherstone is *determined*, **but at no point *forceful* or *intimidating*.**

    (B) Mrs. Weatherstone does not *beg*, she *asks*. "Beg" is much too strong. *Pathos* means *pity* or *compassion*. **Mrs. Weatherstone is quite inspired, and does not try to appeal to Diantha on an emotional level, but on a logical one.**

    (C) **Mrs. Weatherstone uses sound reasoning throughout,** responding to each of Diantha's objections with logical reasons why the situation is beneficial to both of them. She is quite *accommodating*, as she gives Diantha a generous salary and promises to let Diantha train her servants for Diantha's business.

    (D) *Condescension* indicates that Mrs. Weatherstone looks down on Diantha and acts in a superior manner. **She treats Diantha as an EQUAL from the beginning and at no point in the passage does she *threaten* the girl.**

    (E) She is quite determined, and that could possibly be interpreted as *stubbornness*, but she also demonstrates that she is *flexible*. After all, **she compromises and adjusts to Diantha's dreams of starting a housecleaning business.** *Eloquence* means *articulacy*, and Mrs. Weatherstone is very articulate so we have a *partial answer* on our hands.

16. Mrs. Weatherstone's remark in lines 94-95 is said in a tone of

(A) command
(B) witty irony
(C) impishness
(D) curtness
(E) haste

> Step 4: Read and restate the question

What's Mrs. W.'s tone?

> Step 5: Go back to the passage and dig

Re-read from line 86 to the end of the passage ("Excellent...come along").

> Step 6: Answer the question in your own words

Mischievous.

> Step 7: Go to the answer choices and match your paraphrased answer.

Some of the answers contain difficult vocabulary words; let's dissect them.

(A) *Command* means *authority*. While she is technically giving an order (*Put the new address in the letter, and come along!*) **she is doing so** *mischievously* (line 95)**, not like a drill sergeant.**

(B) **Her tone is MISCHIEVOUS not** *witty* **or humorous** (she is quite serious when she says, *come along*) **and there is no** *irony* (sarcasm).

(C) *Impishness* **means** *mischief*, **and is therefore supported.** If you didn't know the meaning of this word, your process of elimination should get you there. Remember, words that you don't know the meaning of tend to make good educated guesses!

(D) *Curtness* means *rudely abrupt*, and **Mrs. Weatherstone is not being** *short*, **but** *kind*.

(E) *Haste* means *speed*, and while Mrs. Weatherstone wants Diantha to work for her *right away* (line 44) **there is more proof for** *mischief* **than** *impatience* **or** *hurry*.

17. Diantha and Mrs. Weatherstone would most likely agree on which point?

(A) Diantha must make more money in order to start her new business
(B) Diantha will not be able to find a higher paying housekeeping job
(C) housekeeping is a better career for a woman than is school teaching
(D) the need for improvements in women's opportunities both inside and outside the home
(E) the hotel Diantha is staying at is not a suitable residence for an unchaperoned young lady

> Step 4: Read and restate the question

What do Mrs. W. and D. have the same opinion about?

> Step 5: Go back to the passage and dig

We have a general question that is hard to answer in our own words. Let's go straight to the answers and justify one of them with proof from the passage.

> Step 7: Go to the answer choices and justify with proof from the passage.

231

Since this question is difficult to answer in our own words, let's justify one of the answer choices.

(A) Diantha may need more *practice* (line 52) but **nowhere in the passage does it indicate that she needs more *money*.**

(B) We know that Mrs. Weatherstone has made a generous offer; it is more than she paid her other housekeeper (lines 48-49) but if you picked this answer you made an ***assumption*. Another employer might offer Diantha even more money for all we know.**

(C) We have a ***comparison*.** Notice the tip-off "better." Mrs. Weatherstone does indicate that housekeeping is *more needed work* (line 30) but ***needed* doesn't mean *better*.** We also don't know Diantha's viewpoint on this matter.

(D) This is a compelling ETS answer, as it is pro-women. Is there support in the passage? **Diantha wants to start a business, and Mrs. Weatherstone supports her in this endeavor,** so yes.

(E) **We know nothing of the hotel Diantha is staying at.** Answer (E) is clearly wrong.

See? The Fiction Passages aren't so bad after all. Just dig deep, read between the lines, understand the relationship between the characters and the motivations of each, and your Critical Reading score will skyrocket.

The only other Reading Comprehension topic left to tackle is presented in Chapter 10: Short Passages.

Chapter 10
Short Passages

You will be given 4 short passages (approximately 100-150 words long) to work through on the SAT. One 25-minute Critical Reading section will feature two short passages followed by approximately 4 to 5 questions. While you may be asked questions that pertain to only one of the passages, the majority of the questions will ask you to compare and contrast the two passages.

The other 25-minute Critical Reading section will present a short passage followed by 2 questions and then another short passage followed by an additional 2 questions. These two passages exist independently on two unrelated topics; therefore, you will not be asked to compare and contrast.

Pretty much the same rules apply with the short passages as with the long:

- *Summarize the main idea*
- *Read and restate the questions*
- *Go back to the passage and dig*
- *Answer the questions in your own words*
- *Use your process of elimination*

The differences are slight:

- *There is no italicized introduction*
- *You must read the whole passage (all 100 words) before looking to the questions*

Let's deal first with the Compare/Contrast Short Passages. Here are the steps:

Step 1: Read Passage 1

Step 2: State the Main Idea of Passage 1

Step 3: Answer Questions about Passage 1

Step 4: Read Passage 2

Step 5: State the Main Idea of Passage 2

Step 6: Answer Questions about Passage 2

Step 7: Answer all Compare/Contrast Questions

Ready to try? Work through the following Compare/Contrast passages on your own paying close attention to the steps, and then work through them again with me for an explanation of the questions and answer choices. When reading the passages be on the lookout for similarities and differences.

Passage 1

Science is an ever-evolving creature that develops at a higher speed than the living things from whom it originated. The evolutionary period from flying lemur, to
Line ape, to human is far greater than the transformation time
5 from gas lamp, to incandescent lamp, to LED lamp. In the past, science has always appeared remote. Although stimulating advances in transportation, industry, and entertainment, never has science impacted our lives as completely as genetic engineering seems poised to do.
10 With the advent of this modern technology, anti-science extremists are trying to block its promising future. Disseminating fear by misinterpreting facts, they endorse their secret agendas on Capital Hill.

Passage 2

Genetics is a branch of scientific study that has
15 intrigued mankind for over 2000 years, but the engineering of deoxyribonucleic acid (DNA) has only recently come to the forefront. We have seen man's tendency to manipulate nature to his resolve through modes of practical genetics such as selective breeding.
20 Scientists now have a more complete discernment of the role genetics plays in living things. It is regrettable that some individuals lobby against further research in the field of genetics when such studies will only aid in advancing humankind. Current research will lead to cures for as yet
25 terminal diseases. Genetic research has also ushered in natural solutions for global and environmental problems, as well as provided treatments for impairments in our bodily systems. Further study is imperative, as genetic engineering is a primary means of advancing our
30 knowledge of medicine into the future.

Step 1: Read Passage 1

Step 2: Summarize the Main Idea

_____

_____

_____

There are no questions that pertain only to Passage 1. Skip Step 3 and jump to Step 4.

Step 4: Read Passage 2

Step 5: Summarize the Main Idea

_____

_____

_____

The first question on the next page is a Compare/Contrast question. There are no questions that pertain only to Passage 2, so we can skip Step 6 and jump to Step 7: Answer all Compare/Contrast questions.

9. Which statement best characterizes the relationship between Passage 1 and Passage 2?

(A) Passage 1 ridicules a group of people that Passage 2 extols.
(B) Passage 1 presents ethical support for an action that Passage 2 also endorses.
(C) Passage 1 discusses a scientific phenomenon that Passage 2 praises.
(D) Passage 1 discusses the scientific foundations of genetic engineering, whereas Passage 2 considers the future of genetic engineering.
(E) Passage 1 describes people's fascination with genetic engineering, whereas Passage 2 explains the process of genetic engineering.

Restate the question

_____

_____

Answer the question in your own words

_____

_____

Match your paraphrase and circle your answer.

10. Unlike Passage 1, Passage 2 focuses primarily on genetic engineering's

(A) historical foundations
(B) staunch opponents
(C) popular appeal
(D) moral repercussions
(E) medical benefits

Restate the question

_____

_____

Answer the question in your own words

_____

_____

Match your paraphrase and circle your answer.

11. The author of Passage 1 would most likely characterize the "individuals" mentioned in line 22 as

(A) antiquated
(B) emotional
(C) deceptive
(D) unethical
(E) uninformed

Restate the question

_____

_____

Answer the question in your own words

_____

_____

Match your paraphrase and circle your answer.

12. The authors of both passages would most likely agree that genetic engineering research is

(A) commendable
(B) immoral
(C) fated
(D) threatening
(E) impractical

Restate the question

_____

_____

Answer the question in your own words

_____

_____

Match your paraphrase and circle your answer.

13. Compared to the tone of Passage 2, the tone of Passage 1 is more

(A) pessimistic
(B) arrogant
(C) critical
(D) aggressive
(E) scholarly

Restate the question

_____

_____

Answer the question in your own words

_____

_____

Match your paraphrase and circle your answer.

Check your answers and thought process with mine.

Passage 1

Science is an ever-evolving creature that develops at a higher speed than the living things from whom it originated. The evolutionary period from flying lemur, to
Line ape, to human is far greater than the transformation time
5 from gas lamp, to incandescent lamp, to LED lamp. In the past, science has always appeared remote. Although stimulating advances in transportation, industry, and entertainment, never has science impacted our lives as completely as genetic engineering seems poised to do.
10 With the advent of this modern technology, anti-science extremists are trying to block its promising future. Disseminating fear by misinterpreting facts, they endorse their secret agendas on Capital Hill.

Step 1: Read Passage 1

Step 2: Summarize the Main Idea

Genetic engineering is an important scientific advancement and extremists are blocking its progress.

Genetics is a branch of scientific study that has
15 intrigued mankind for over 2000 years, but the
engineering of deoxyribonucleic acid (DNA) has only
recently come to the forefront. We have seen man's
tendency to manipulate nature to his resolve through
modes of practical genetics such as selective breeding.
20 Scientists now have a more complete discernment of the
role genetics plays in living things. It is regrettable that
some individuals lobby against further research in the field
of genetics when such studies will only aid in advancing
humankind. Current research will lead to cures for as yet
25 terminal diseases. Genetic research has also ushered in
natural solutions for global and environmental problems,
as well as provided treatments for impairments in our
bodily systems. Further study is imperative, as genetic
engineering is a primary means of advancing our
30 knowledge of medicine into the future.

Step 4: Read Passage 2

Step 5: Summarize the Main Idea

Genetic engineering is beneficial and further research is important for medicine.

9. Which statement best characterizes the relationship between Passage 1 and Passage 2?

(A) Passage 1 ridicules a group of people that Passage 2 extols.

(B) Passage 1 presents ethical support for an action that Passage 2 also endorses.

(C) Passage 1 discusses a scientific phenomenon that Passage 2 praises.

(D) Passage 1 discusses the scientific foundations of genetic engineering, whereas Passage 2 considers the future of genetic engineering.

(E) Passage 1 describes people's fascination with genetic engineering, whereas Passage 2 explains the process of genetic engineering.

Restate the question

How are Passage 1 and Passage 2 related?

Answer the question in your own words

They are similar. They both think genetic engineering is good and shouldn't be stopped.

Remember: Compare/Contrast questions really encompass the authors' main ideas.

I can eliminate (A), (D), and (E) because these answer choices indicate an opposite relationship between the two passages. My paraphrased answer points to a similarity. Let's dissect (B) and (C).

(B) Passage 1 does indeed *present support for an action* – the author is pro-genetic engineering (see line 11: *its promising future*). Passage 2 also *endorses this action*; the author states: *genetic engineering is a primary means of advancing our knowledge of medicine into the future* (lines 28-30). We have a ***partial answer*** though, as there is just one word that throws this answer choice off: *ethical*. ***Ethical* means *moral*, and the author of Passage 1 does not address the MORAL insinuations of genetic engineering,** either as an advocate or an opponent.

(C) **What** *scientific phenomenon* **does Passage 1 discuss?** Genetic engineering. **Does Passage 2** *praise* **genetic engineering?** It sure does: see lines 28-30.

Let's refute the other answer choices for those of you who might have been tempted.

(A) Passage 1 does seem to *ridicule a group of people*: *the anti-science extremists* who are *trying to block its promising future* (lines 10-11). But Passage 2 does not *extol* (praise) these extremists. Check out line 22: *Some individuals* are the same *extremists* (discussed in a more moderate way) that Passage 1 refers to. **And Passage 2 is not in support of the** *some individuals* **mentioned.** We have a *partial answer*.

(D) We have another *partial answer.* Passage 2 does *consider the future of genetic engineering* (see lines 28-30) but Passage 1 does not *discuss the scientific foundations of genetic engineering.* Passage 1 discusses science and scientific advancements in general terms. **The phrase** *scientific foundations* **indicates that the author discusses the scientific BASIS for genetic engineering, which she does not.**

(E) **This answer choice is wrong across the board.** Passage 1 indicates specific reactions to genetic engineering (those of *anti-science extremists*) but does not *describe people's fascination* with the topic; perhaps lines 14-15 in Passage 2, which states that the field of genetics has *intrigued mankind for over 2000 years,* tricked you. Passage 2 does not *explain the process of genetic engineering.* This would suggest that the author explains how genetic engineering works, which he does not.

---

10. Unlike Passage 1, Passage 2 focuses primarily on genetic engineering's

(A) historical foundations
(B) staunch opponents
(C) popular appeal
(D) moral repercussions
(E) medical benefits

Restate the question

What does Passage 2 talk about that Passage 1 doesn't?

Answer the question in your own words

Specific benefits of genetic engineering

Answer choice (E) matches my paraphrase: *medical benefits* (*specific benefits of genetic engineering*). Lines 24-28 detail these benefits.

(A) Although the author of Passage 2 indicates that people have been *intrigued by genetics for over 2000 years* (line 15) and that man has had a *tendency to manipulate nature to his resolve* (lines 17-18), this doesn't really give us a *historical foundation* (basis) for genetic engineering. **Had the author discussed the father of genetics and the discovery of DNA and RNA, then perhaps this answer choice would have more support.** Remember, *primarily* means *mainly*, further disproving (A).

238

(B) **The author of Passage 2 mentions genetic engineering's detractors in lines 22-23, but so does the author of Passage 1.** In fact, the author of Passage 1 focuses more on the *staunch opponents* (lines 10-13) than does the author of Passage 2. Remember, we are looking for something that Passage 2 does that Passage 1 does not.

(C) *Popular appeal* means it has received the approval of the majority, and while *genetics might have intrigued mankind for 2000 years,* **there are still some people who steadfastly oppose genetic engineering.** This answer is clearly incorrect.

(D) **Both of the passages support genetic engineering, and never deal with any** *moral repercussions* (ethical ramifications). Had one or both of the passages been opposed to genetic engineering, then the authors would very likely have broached the topic of ethics.

---

11. The author of Passage 1 would most likely characterize the "individuals" mentioned in line 22 as

(A) antiquated
(B) emotional
(C) deceptive
(D) unethical
(E) uninformed

> Restate the question
>
> *Who are the individuals and what would the author of Passage 1 say about them?*

> Answer the question in your own words
>
> *The individuals are those who are trying to stop genetic research and the author of Passage 1 would say that they are twisting the facts for their own aims.*

Answer choice (C) is a good match for my paraphrase: *deceptive (twisting the facts).* Check out lines 12-13 (*misinterpreting facts* and *they endorse their secret agendas*). Let's disprove the others.

(A) *Antiquated* means *out of date.* **Genetic engineering is a** *modern technology* **(line 10) and so is clearly not obsolete.**

(B) *Emotional* means…well, *emotional.* **Nowhere does Passage 1 say that people are throwing temper-tantrums, crying, or overly ecstatic.** This answer choice is clearly not supported.

(D) *Unethical* means *bad,* or *immoral.* This answer choice does have some support, after all they *endorse their own agendas,* but it is a tad **too strong based on the contextual support in the passage.** Answer choice (C) is still the better option.

(E) *Uninformed* means *uneducated.* **The author of Passage 1 would say that** *extremists* **know the facts and are therefore informed, but are choosing to** *misinterpret* **(or twist) these facts.**

12. The authors of both passages would most likely agree that genetic engineering research is

(A) commendable
(B) immoral
(C) fated
(D) threatening
(E) impractical

Restate the question

What do both passages say about genetic engineering research?

Answer the question in your own words

It's a good thing.

Answer choice (A) is a match for my paraphrase: *Commendable* means *praiseworthy*, which matches (*it's a good thing*). Let's de-justify the others.

(B) *Immoral* means *wrong*, but **both authors believe genetic engineering research is BENEFICIAL and shouldn't be stopped.**

(C) *Fated* means *inevitable*. There are *some individuals lobbying against further research in the field of genetics* (lines 22-23), which indicates that **research is threatened, not a certain outcome.**

(D) *Threatening* means *intimidating*. **Genetic engineering research is THREATENED by the** *extremists* **who wish to stop studies, but the research is not** *threatening*.

(E) *Impractical* means not practical or *unrealistic*. **Genetic engineering is a** *new technology* **that offers practical benefits to future medicine.**

13. Compared to the tone of Passage 2, the tone of Passage 1 is more

(A) pessimistic
(B) arrogant
(C) critical
(D) aggressive
(E) scholarly

Restate the question

What's the tone of Passage 1?

Answer the question in your own words

Opinionated.

Let's pick apart the answer choices one-by-one.

(A) *Pessimistic* means *negative*. While the author of Passage 1 distrusts the *anti-science extremists*, she is not negative throughout the passage. **The author is optimistic about genetic engineering.**

(B) *Arrogant* means *conceited* or *superior*. While the author of Passage 1 disagrees with the *anti-science extremists*, **she never puts on the air that she is better than them.**

(C) *Critical* means *not approving*. **The topic of the passage is genetic engineering, of which the author of Passage 1 greatly approves.**

(D) *Aggressive* means *assertive*, which is the **best match for my paraphrased answer** (*opinionated*). The author of Passage 1 refers to opponents as *anti-science extremists* and accuses them of *disseminating fear by misinterpreting facts* and *endorsing secret agendas*. (lines 10-13). The tone of Passage 2 is softer. *Extremists* are referred to as *some individuals* (line 22), and no mention is made of spreading fear or misinterpretation.

(E) *Scholarly* means *academic*. **While the authors of both passages seem educated (and one no more so than the other), neither one of them writes in an academic manner.** The language and wording of scholarly writing is more specialized and formal, and insights are more grounded in research.

Let's try a short passage section that is not a Compare/Contrast.

Here are the steps:

Step 1: Read Passage 1

Step 2: State the Main Idea of Passage 1

Step 3: Answer Questions about Passage 1

Step 4: Read Passage 2

Step 5: State the Main Idea of Passage 2

Step 6: Answer Questions about Passage 2

Passage 1

Because the soul is progressive, it never quite repeats itself, but in every act attempts the production of a new and fairer whole. Thus in our fine arts, not imitation
Line but creation is the aim. In landscapes the painter should
5 give the suggestion of a fairer creation than we know. The details, the prose of nature he should omit and give us only the spirit and splendor. He will give the gloom of gloom and the sunshine of sunshine. In a portrait he must inscribe the character and not the features, and must
10 esteem the man who sits to him as himself only an imperfect picture or likeness of the aspiring original within.

(For source reference, see endnote [a])

9. The reference to "prose of nature" in line 6 serves to suggest that

(A) effective art is more of a realistic rendition than an imaginative interpretation
(B) art dictates to the artist the best means of its portrayal
(C) effective art requires identifying with the viewers' viewpoints
(D) artists need to create not pragmatically, but poetically
(E) nature is such that its spirit is more important than its composition

Step 1: Read Passage 1

Step 2: Summarize the Main Idea

_____

_____

_____

Step 3: Answer questions about Passage 1

Restate the question

_____

_____

Answer the question in your own words

_____

_____

_____

Match your paraphrase and circle your answer.

10. The last sentence of the passage suggests that the author feels a portrait should

   (A) portray the subject as he is, rather than as he would like to be depicted
   (B) reveal both the imperfections and virtues of its subject
   (C) capture the essence of its subject at the expense of less-than-perfect details
   (D) enhance its subject's merits and downplay its flaws
   (E) represent the theoretical qualities of the subject, minimizing the specific features

> Restate the question

_____

_____

> Answer the question in your own words

_____

_____

Match your paraphrase and circle your answer.

Passage 2

The first point to which attention should be called is that the comic does not exist outside the pale of what is
15 strictly HUMAN. You may laugh at an animal, but only because you have detected in it some human attitude or expression. You may laugh at a hat, but what you are making fun of, in this case, is not the piece of felt or straw, but the shape that men have given it - the human
20 caprice whose mould it has assumed. Several have defined man as "an animal which laughs." They might equally well have defined him as an animal which is laughed at; for if any other animal, or some lifeless object, produces the same effect, it is always because of
25 some resemblance to man, of the stamp he gives it or the use he puts it to.

      (For source reference, see endnote j)

> Step 4: Read Passage 2

> Step 5: Summarize the Main Idea

_____

_____

_____

> Step 6: Answer questions about Passage 2

11. The primary purpose of the passage is to

   (A) suggest that laughter is inherently connected to our humanity
   (B) indicate that that which is not human does not provoke laughter
   (C) encourage people to explore the humor in their humanity
   (D) argue that laughter should not be squandered on inanimate objects
   (E) propose that comedy is most effective when poking fun at human foibles

> Restate the question

_____

_____

> Answer the question in your own words

_____

_____

Match your paraphrase and circle your answer.

12. The author refers to the quote "an animal which laughs" (line 21) to make the point that man

    (A) is of the same nature as animals
    (B) laughs at the characteristics that resemble his nature
    (C) is defined by his ability to laugh
    (D) laughs as a way to express his humanity
    (E) is innately comedic and prone to laughter

> Restate the question
> _____
> _____

> Answer the question in your own words
> _____
> _____

Match your paraphrase and circle your answer.

Let's see how you did!

Passage 1

    Because the soul is progressive, it never quite repeats itself, but in every act attempts the production of a new and fairer whole. Thus in our fine arts, not imitation
Line but creation is the aim. In landscapes the painter should
5 give the suggestion of a fairer creation than we know. The details, the prose of nature he should omit and give us only the spirit and splendor. He will give the gloom of gloom and the sunshine of sunshine. In a portrait he must inscribe the character and not the features, and must
10 esteem the man who sits to him as himself only an imperfect picture or likeness of the aspiring original within.

An artist should not imitate but create and capture the spirit of the whole subject instead of worrying about details or features.

9. The reference to "prose of nature" in line 6 serves to suggest that

    (A) effective art is more of a realistic rendition than an imaginative interpretation
    (B) art dictates to the artist the best means of its portrayal
    (C) effective art requires identifying with the viewers' viewpoints
    (D) artists need to create not pragmatically, but poetically
    (E) nature is such that its spirit is more important than its composition

> Restate the question

What does the author mean by "prose of nature"?

> Answer the question in your own words

The details and realism can be left out – just capture the essence!

243

My paraphrase could match answer choices (D) or (E). Let's dissect those first.

(D) *Pragmatically* means *sensibly* and *logically*. The author stresses that the artist should *omit the details* and give us the *spirit* of the subject (lines 6-7), but does that translate to the artist should not create sensibly or logically? **Pragmatic is a great word, but is a leap from the context of the passage.**

(E) The author believes that the artist should sacrifice *details* for *spirit*, so the first half of the answer choice (*nature is such that its spirit is more important*) works well. *Composition* means the *structure* or *makeup* of something. **The *spirit* (essence) is indeed more important than the *features* (the details, or individual parts) of the subject.**

Let's disprove the other answer choices.

(A) This answer choice is *opposite* to the author's main idea. **The author thinks effective art is *imaginative interpretation* NOT a *realistic rendition*.** Check out lines 3-4.

(B) Let's make a paraphrase of this answer choice: **The subject communicates to the artist how it wants to be painted.** This idea is not stated directly or indirectly in the passage. This answer choice sounds tempting, but is not supported.

(C) The passage is not about what people looking at the painting think about the painting. **Viewers are never even mentioned in the passage.** There is clearly no support for (C).

---

10. The last sentence of the passage suggests that the author feels a portrait should

(A) portray the subject as he is, rather than as he would like to be depicted
(B) reveal both the imperfections and virtues of its subject
(C) capture the essence of its subject at the expense of less than perfect details
(D) enhance its subject's merits and downplay its flaws
(E) represent the theoretical qualities of the subject, minimizing the specific features

> **Restate the question**
>
> *What does the author say in the last sentence?*
>
> **Answer the question in your own words**
>
> *A portrait must show the character of the man and represent the unique soul inside rather than the features outside.*

Answer choice (C) matches my paraphrase: *Capture the inner essence (represent the unique soul inside) and at the expense of less than perfect details (show the character rather than the features outside).*

(A) **The first phrase, *portray the subject as he is,* contradicts lines 2-4** (*attempts the production of a new and fairer whole* and *not imitation, but creation is the aim*). The second phrase, *rather than as he would like to be depicted,* is not supported in the passage. **The subject's desire as to how the painting should look is never addressed.**

(B) **The author states that art should NOT be *imitation*** (line 3). *Imitation* would account for both *imperfections* and *virtues*. The author is arguing for *creation*, or *the production of a new and fairer whole* (lines 2-3).

(D) While the author does want the artist to enhance the *aspiring original within* (lines 11-12), which would include *merits*, **nowhere in the passage does the author suggest that *flaws* should be *downplayed*** (lessened).

(E) The phrase, *minimizing the specific features,* does have some support in the passage. The author states, *in a portrait he must inscribe the character and not the features* (lines 8-9) and tells us that *details should be omitted* in line 6. Keep in mind, though, that *minimizing* can also indicate *softening the features*, which the author does not state. The first phrase, however, completely destroys this answer choice. **Nowhere in the passage does the author say that a portrait should *represent the theoretical qualities of the subject* (*theoretical* means *not practical*, or *speculative*).** Had this passage been about Picasso or other abstract artists, we might have read such a statement in the passage.

Passage 2

The first point to which attention should be called is that the comic does not exist outside the pale of what is
15 strictly HUMAN. You may laugh at an animal, but only because you have detected in it some human attitude or expression. You may laugh at a hat, but what you are making fun of, in this case, is not the piece of felt or straw, but the shape that men have given it,--the human
20 caprice whose mould it has assumed. Several have defined man as "an animal which laughs." They might equally well have defined him as an animal which is laughed at; for if any other animal, or some lifeless object, produces the same effect, it is always because of
25 some resemblance to man, of the stamp he gives it or the use he puts it to.

Things that are funny always have an element of " human" in them.

11. The primary purpose of the passage is to

(A) suggest that laughter is inherently connected to our humanity
(B) indicate that that which is not human does not provoke laughter
(C) encourage people to explore the humor in their humanity
(D) argue that laughter should not be squandered on inanimate objects
(E) propose that comedy is most effective when poking fun at human foibles

Restate the question

What's the main idea?

Answer the question in your own words

I've already stated it: Things that are funny always have an element of " human" in them.

Answer choice (A) matches my paraphrase: *laughter is inherently* (naturally) *connected to our humanity* (things that are funny always have an element of human in them). Let's dissect the others.

(B) This answer choice sounds tempting, but if you dissect the words, we discover it is not supported by information in the passage. *Not human* means *not human*: animals, plants, hats, etc. **The author tells us that we laugh at animals and hats because of the human characteristics they possess (lines 15-17), so we are obviously laughing at that which is NOT human.**

(C) **The author tells us that our *humanity is humorous*, but he is not persuading us to *explore this humanity*.** He is simply espousing his theory on humor.

(D) *Squandered* means *wasted*. **The author is not saying that it is a waste to laugh at a hat.** This answer choice has no support in the passage.

(E) This answer choice might have lured you in. *Human foibles* is a great paraphrase of *the human caprice* (lines 19-20). But contextually, this answer choice is not supported. **In lines 17-20 the author is saying that we laugh at a hat because the shape of it has human elements, not that comedy is funniest when human quirks are ridiculed.**

12. The author refers to the quote "an animal which laughs" (line 21) to make the point that man

Restate the question

What's the author saying about man?

(A) is of the same nature as animals
(B) laughs at the characteristics that resemble his nature
(C) is defined by his ability to laugh
(D) laughs as a way to express his humanity
(E) is innately comedic and prone to laughter

Answer the question in your own words

When a man laughs he is laughing at himself.

Answer choice (B) matches my paraphrase: *laughs at the characteristics* (when a man laughs) and *that resemble his nature* (he is laughing at himself). Let's refute the others.

(A) Lines 15-17 say that we laugh at an animal because we detect a human characteristic. **The author is not saying that humans and animals are made of the *same nature*, which would indicate that man and animals are intrinsically the same.**

(C) This is a tough one, and perhaps the answer choice you chose if you did not read the context surrounding this statement. *Several have defined man as "an animal which laughs",* **but the AUTHOR would argue that man is defined as *an animal which is laughed at* (lines 22-23).** Always know whose perspective you are looking for!

(D) This answer choice creates a cause and effect relationship that is not supported by the passage. **Man laughs AT his humanity, not as a way to *EXPRESS* his humanity.**

(E) *Innately* means *naturally* or *something you are born with*. **Humans may have been born with the inclination to laugh, but nowhere in the passage does the author state this idea.**

That's it for the Reading Comprehension portion of the SAT!

It's all about asking the right questions, picking apart the passage, questions, and answer choices, restating in your own words all that confusing information, and staying true to the information in the passage: NO ASSUMPTIONS ALLOWED! Hopefully by now you have my thought process stuck in your head so that you can work through eliminating the bad answer choices and choosing the best answer choices.

Chapter 11
Conclusion

Applying the Critical Reading Techniques is tedious at first, but the more you practice, the more second nature they become. Soon you will be breezing through the Reading at a comfortable pace, confidently picking more correct answers than ever! In my experience, writing down your paraphrased answers and main idea summaries doesn't take too long – remember, you are jotting quick notes, not writing an essay. If you feel, however, that writing your summaries is eating up valuable time, then state your answers in your head; just be sure not to forget them amid all those tempting answer choices! Remember those bad answer choices to avoid and increase your odds on educated guesses. And don't forget to cover those answer choices and fill in the blank with your own word on Sentence Completion questions. Keep learning that vocab!

Get a copy of the College Board Official SAT Study Guide and work through the practice tests. Do not worry about time until you have comfortably mastered technique. Time will take care of itself the more familiar you become with actual SAT passages and questions. Add time constraints to the mix only after you have noticed a score improvement and are feeling more confident. When correcting the Reading questions missed, be sure to go back to the passage to find justification for what ETS claims is the "best" answer. You will find yourself thinking like ETS soon enough. Once you realize your way of thinking isn't in line with ETS's, don't fight for your rationale, rather ask: *What makes MY answer wrong and ETS's answer JUSTIFIED and SUPPORTED?* The justification is in the passage!

Be confident and calm on test day so that your head remains clear. Take a couple of number 2 pencils, and water and a snack to refuel during the break. If you find yourself confused and/or stressed, remember that you can always skip (and come back to) harder problems. Don't be afraid to leave those confusing questions blank. In general, take a deep breath, believe in yourself, and remember the definitions and strategies I have taught you. Good luck!

Endnotes

a   Essay, First Series, XII Art - Ralph Waldo Emerson - *Authorama: Public Doman Books*
http://www.authorama.com/essays-first-series-24.html

b   Mysticism and Logic and Other Essays by Bertrand Russell. II. The Place of Science in a Liberal Education -
Wikisource: the Free Library http://en.wikisource.org/wiki/Mysticism_and_Logic_and_Other_Essays/Chapter_02

c   The Story of Mankind - Hendrik Van Loon, Ph.D. - *Authorama: Public Doman Books*
http://www.authorama.com/story-of-mankind-62.html

d   In Defense of Academic History Writing - Gordon Wood. Used by permission.

e   The Age of Einstein - Frank W. K. Firk - *phsicsforfree.com* http://www.physicsforfree.com/ageofeinstein.html

f   Birds of the Indian Hill - Douglass Dewar - *Project Gutenberg*
http://www.gutenberg.org/files/23755/23755-h/23755-h.htm

g   Beethoven - George Alexander Fischer - *Project Gutenberg*
http://www.gutenberg.org/files/15141/15141-h/15141-h.htm

h   The Man and the Artist, as Revealed in his Own Words - Ludwig van Beethoven, Edited by Friedrich Kerst and
Henry Edward Krehbie - *Project Gutenberg* http://www.gutenberg.org/files/3528/3528-h/3528-h.htm

i   What Diantha Did - Charlotte Perkins Gilman - *Project Gutenberg*
http://www.gutenberg.org/files/3016/3016-h/3016-h.htm

j   Laughter, An Essay on the Meaning of Comic - Henry Bergson - *Authorama: Public Doman Books*
http://www.authorama.com/laughter-2.html